JONATHAN C. SMITH

ROOSEVELT UNIVERSITY

Understanding Stress and Coping

MACMILLAN PUBLISHING COMPANY

NEW YORK

Maxwell Macmillan Canada

TORONTO

Editor: Christine Cardone
Production Supervisor: Betsy Keefer
Production Manager: Linda Greenberg
Text Designer: Robert Freese
Cover Designer: Publication Services
Photo Researcher: Eloise Marion
Illustrations: Vantage Art

This book was set in 10/12 Baskerville by V & M Graphics and was
printed and bound by Book Press. The cover
was printed by New England Book Components, Inc.

Macmillan Publishing Company
866 Third Avenue, New York, New York 10022

Macmillan Publishing Company is part of
the Maxwell Communication Group of Companies.

Maxwell Macmillan Canada, Inc.
1200 Eglinton Avenue East
Suite 200
Don Mills, Ontario M3C 3N1

LIBRARY OF CONGRESS CATALOGING-IN-PUBLICATION DATA

Smith, Jonathan C.
  Understanding stress and coping / Jonathan C. Smith.
    p.   cm.
  Includes bibliographical references and indexes.
    ISBN 0-02-412940-2
    1. Stress (Psychology) 2. Stress (Physiology) 3. Stress
  management. 4. Medicine, Psychosomatic. I. Title.
  BF575.S75S58   1993
  155.9'042—dc20   92-3689
                                                        CIP

Printing: 2 3 4 5 6 7   Year: 3 4 5 6 7 8 9

To Colonel Margarethe Cammermeyer

Preface

This book is about the latest scientific thinking and research regarding stress and coping. My goal is to provide essential background information for anyone who desires to be "stress literate" in an important, expanding, and often confusing field. In Part I, I survey the basics of stress. This includes work on life events, social support, stress arousal, clinical psychodynamic theories of defense, cognitive-behavioral theories of stressful thinking, and finally, the guiding perspective of this text: the transactional approach to understanding stress and coping.

Part II explores more deeply the topic that has perhaps received the greatest attention among stress researchers: stress, health, and illness. I examine personality traits and behavior patterns associated with health and illness. I then focus on specific stress-related physiological processes associated with major categories of illness. Finally, I consider various risk behaviors and their link to stress, health, and illness. Specifically, I examine personality, health, and stress; stress and specific illnesses; and stress and life-style risk behaviors.

In Part III, I look more closely at specific stress-related topics, including crises, catastrophes, and disasters; life span and the family; work; and the environment and society.

Finally, although this book is not about how to cope with or teach others to manage stress, I conclude in Part IV with a brief overview of the major forms of relaxation and active coping techniques now used in stress management. The objective of this section is not to teach techniques, but to provide an overview of what techniques are available. More broadly, this part can be viewed as an exploration of clinicians' answer to the question, "What is coping?"

This book is for anyone interested in the exciting new study of stress. It is of particular interest to college students in the health professions, including psychology, counseling, nursing, social work, personnel administration, medicine, and psychiatry. Those in business and education will find important information on stress and performance. Students will discover new tools for understanding problems of living. In sum, since all of our lives are affected by stress, this book is for everyone.

Acknowledgments

I would like to thank the following reviewers for their helpful suggestions and comments:

    Robert A. Caldwell, Michigan State University
    James F. Calhoun, University of Georgia
    JoAnn M. Eickhoff, University of Nebraska at Omaha
    Paul W. Horn, Indiana State University
    Darrel Lang, Emporia State University
    Steve Nagy, University of Alabama
    Joseph C. Speisman, Boston University

I would also like to thank my editor, Christine Cardone, and the Macmillan staff for all their help and encouragement.

J.C.S.

Brief Contents

Detailed Contents

PART I

Stress Basics

The study of stress has come of age. In Part I we consider how definitions of stress have evolved through the decades. First, stress was
defined in terms of external stimuli, such as crises and catastrophies,
and later, life events. More recently, life events researchers have
argued that events that are undesirable, unpredictable, uncontrollable,
large, and clustered together are most stressful, and that the impact of
events can be buffered by social supports and networks.

A slightly different approach has focused on the stress arousal
response. Here, the nervous system and the endocrine glandular system awaken and energize the body for vigorous emergency activity.
More recent cognitive models have examined various psychological
factors that can contribute to stress—these include defense mechanisms
and traits, irrational beliefs, and various forms of negative thinking.

The contemporary, transactional approach to stress emphasizes the
interrelationship among all variables—stimuli, arousal, cognitions, and
coping. It views stress not so much as a single event but as an ongoing
story complete with central and peripheral characters and interweaving plots.

CHAPTER 1

The Study of Stress

The study of stress has come of age. First a topic popular in magazines and newspapers, then a chapter in psychology textbooks, stress has emerged as a field of study in its own right. The reasons are clear.

An enormous body of theory and research points to the costs of stress on health, productivity, and well-being. Up to 80 percent of all illnesses may well be stress-related. Stress is an important component of heart disease, cancer, respiratory disorders, ulcers, alcoholism, accidents and drug abuse—indeed, all leading causes of death in the West. Stress can reduce productivity, creativity, and the ability to enjoy oneself. Stress has been estimated to cost industry up to $150 billion each year. And stress management works; a good program can save five dollars for each dollar spent. Given the importance of stress, it is clearly a discipline ready for a textbook.

The Need for Stress Literacy

There are hundreds of self-help and other popular books on stress. This book is different. It is a serious textbook designed to cover the entire terrain of an important and growing field. Our goal is to contribute to the *stress literacy* of those seriously interested in discovering how their lives are affected by the pressures and demands of living.

The Problem of Understanding Stress

It is easy to see the importance of stress literacy by using a few examples. Chris is a college student who keeps a diary of each day's events. On one page he describes a particularly stressful experience:

> I don't know why I did so poorly on the midterm. I studied hard. I reviewed with my friends. Maybe my poor performance had something to do with the fact that I was married two months ago, moved away from home, and got a new job.

3

James, a registered nurse, discusses a problem he faced:

> I was assigned to draw blood from Julia, the patient in Room 3B. Julia was a young woman, about twenty-six, and she looked tired. She talked about the "terrible traffic jam" she was in while coming to the hospital. For some reason, I had a particularly hard time obtaining the blood sample. Her veins were constricted, and she was very tense.

Susan is a social worker. Part of her job is to obtain case histories of older clients receiving Medicare. She encounters this problem:

> My client, Berniece, just can't remember important facts about her family. Where is her sister living now? When was the last time she visited the doctor? Berniece is not suffering from any brain disorder; this was determined last month at the hospital. However, her two grandchildren have temporarily moved in with her, and she tends to take things seriously. She complains that she just doesn't know how to deal with "those crazy kids."

Each of these examples is a potential stress problem. Each illustrates the importance of stress literacy. Is Chris's problem caused by the stressful impact of several major life events, or does the fact that the events were positive and occurred months ago reduce this possibility? Is it possible that Julia's hassles on the highway made it harder for James to draw blood? If so, what would be the best way for him to deal with this problem? And is Berniece's loss of memory just one of the nuisances of life, or is it related to her stressful home environment? Is it the increased work responsi-

This New York City rush hour traffic jam illustrates one of the many types of stress people are confronted with today.   (*Photo by David M. Grossman,* Photo Researchers, Inc.)

bility caused by her visiting grandchildren or her tendency to worry that is causing stress for Berniece? How does one go about answering such questions?

It is often tempting to look to simple platitudes for the answers. Indeed, popular culture provides volumes of conflicting bits of stress wisdom. Here are just a few examples that you may have heard:

"Worrying about a problem only makes it worse."

"You can't solve problems by avoiding them. Face your problems and think them through. A little pain won't hurt you."

"If you have experienced a major crisis, having a positive attitude will help you stay healthy."

"Experiencing a major crisis, regardless of your state of mind, causes wear and tear, and leads to illness."

"Relaxation is best for helping you deal with stress."

"Relaxation is best for helping you recover from stress."

"To deal with problems, you need to immerse yourself in them."

"To deal with problems, put them aside. Answers will come on their own."

"Stress helps you grow."

"Stress interferes with growth."

Having a lot of friends will help you cope with stress."

"Having one good friend will help you cope with stress."

"It is good to get 'stressed up' before playing sports."

"It is good to relax before playing sports."

"Belief in God reduces stress."

"Belief in God creates stress."

"All approaches to relaxation work equally well. Just find the approach you like."

"Different approaches to relaxation have different effects. Find the approach that does what you need."

"People are more creative under pressure."

"People are less creative under pressure."

"Stress hormones enhance your body's resistance to disease."

"Stress hormones impair your body's resistance to disease."

With so many conflicting opinions being offered in our popular culture, how do we know which ones are correct? Which advice columnist or tabloid stress expert has the right answers?

Stress Literacy and the Five Questions

Stress literacy begins with a useful definition of stress. Stress can occur at the physical, psychological, and social levels. Physical (or systemic) stress arises when certain demands tax or exceed the adaptive resources of the body, thus contributing to physical wear and tear, lowered resistance, and so on. Illness, heat, cold, war, and worry can all be physically stressful. Psychological stress "is a particular relationship between the person and the environment that is appraised by the person as taxing or exceeding his or her resources and endangering his or her well-being" (Lazarus & Folkman, 1984, p.19). Finally, social stress occurs when demands tax the functioning and stability of society or a social group. For example, divorce threatens the coherence of a family, discrimination threatens the viability of a minority subculture, and war threatens the integrity of a country. In the most general terms, stress is a global area of study that includes physical, psychological, and social variables.

The focus of this book, which is also the one taken by most stress experts, is physical and psychological stress. Indeed, we shall see that it is hard to consider one without the other. In Part I we concentrate on several key dimensions of stress, beginning with external stimulus demands that range from wartime catastrophes to major life events and everyday hassles. It is important to understand such antecedents as contributors to stress as well as warning signals of potential stress problems. We then discuss stress arousal, or the physiological changes associated with stress that often contribute to stress-related illness. We move to a consideration of stress cognitions, which are thoughts and perceptions that modify our experience of stress. We examine how coping involves actively dealing with stressful situations or minimizing their costs. Finally, in the remainder of this book, we consider the consequences of stress in terms of its short- and long-term costs and payoffs.

Together, these five areas of concern can be summarized as five questions that can be used to determine if someone is under stress:

1. Is the person encountering stressful stimuli in the form of environmental demands and events?
2. Is the person experiencing stress arousal?
3. Is the person thinking or perceiving the world in a way that increases stress?
4. Does the person have and use coping resources to manage stress?
5. What are the costs and payoffs of any of these areas of concern?

Perhaps the most serious mistake made by people who are thinking about stress is asking one-dimensional questions. A student may think his stress is caused only by excessive homework (stimulus); a patient may see her stress as a backache problem and nothing else (arousal). Indeed, many health professionals make the same mistake. A beginning counselor may attempt to help a tense client by using an arousal-reducing relaxation technique without considering other strategies. The author of a popular self-help book may focus only on altering "negative thinking." A stress workshop may target only assertive coping skills.

The most important goal of stress literacy, and of this book, is to provide a comprehensive and effective framework for thinking about the many dimensions of stress. As you become a "stress-literate" student, you will have a powerful set of tools for helping both others *and* yourself.

The Beginnings

It is appropriate we begin our exploration of stress with a look at history. Interestingly, early stress researchers often thought in one-dimensional terms. Although this research did make some important discoveries, its simplistic focus eventually led to problems. Indeed, the history of stress research is largely a story of overcoming one-dimensional thinking.

The word *stress* can be traced to the Latin words *strictus*, which means "tight," or "narrow,"and *stringere*, which means "to tighten." These root words refer to the internal feelings of constriction many feel under stress. However, early usage of the term *stress* referred not so much to internal events as to the stressful world of external situations (Cox, 1978). In the fourteenth century, *stress* meant hardship, straits, adversity, or affliction (Lazarus & Folkman, 1984). In the early nineteenth century, *load* was defined as an external force, *strain* as the degree of deformation caused by the force on an object, and *stress* as the ratio of internal force created by the load to the area over which the force acted (Hinkle, 1977). Thus, a heavy truck on a bridge might result in stress of hundreds of pounds per square foot. Similarly, in the late nineteenth century, stress referred to those pressures on the body that contribute to illness.

In the 1930s, the physiologists Walter Cannon and Hans Selye added an important new emphasis to our understanding of stress. Cannon (1939) suggested the term *homeostasis* to describe "the coordinated physiologic processes which maintain most of the steady states in the organism" (p. 333). It is through homeostasis that the body, or the *milieu interieur* (Bernard, 1879), maintains constant temperature, blood pH, and plasma levels of sugar, protein, and the like in the face of changing environmental conditions. Stress is a disturbance of homeostasis caused by outside pressures and demands.

One of Cannon's major contributions is the definition of the stress *fight-or-flight* reaction. Through the sympathetic nervous system and a hormonal discharge from the adrenal glands, a constellation of automatic changes prepare the body for vigorous emergency action. For thousands of years, the fight-or-flight reaction has enabled animals and humans to cope with the attacks and threats of a hostile world. It is this reaction that gives the football player the burst of energy needed just before he makes a touchdown, and helps the mail carrier escape from a sudden attack from the family dog. However, Cannon proposed that the continuous activation of the fight-or-flight reaction through contemporary pressures and worries can be destructive. Physical illness could result from "the persistent derangement of bodily functions . . . due to persistence of the stimuli which evoke the reactions" (Cannon, 1929, p.261). In spite of this contribution, Cannon (1935) left somewhat confused the issue of whether the term *stress* should refer to stimulus conditions or to the response of the organism to those conditions.

Selye (1936, 1956) somewhat clarified our understanding of stress by using the term to refer to an orchestrated set of bodily defenses against environmental demands that he called *stressors*. Thus, a stressor is analogous to the earlier notion of *load* and the bodily response to stress is analogous to *strain*. Selye emphasized that stress is a *nonspecific result of any demand upon the body.* Regardless of the stressor, organisms display the three-stage *general adaptation syndrome:* the alarm reaction (physiological resources are mobilized in a wholesale fashion), the resistance stage (only those resources needed for adaptation continue to be mobilized), and the exhaustion stage (with the depletion of resources, reserves are mobilized once again in a wholesale fashion). The general adaptation syndrome not only disrupts homeostasis but contributes to biological wear and tear, diseases of adaptation, and eventually death (topics we shall consider in later chapters).

There were several other trends in early stress research. Notably, human-factors research focused on the impact of work load and unusual environmental conditions on attention, vigilance (as in signal detection), and performance deterioration (Appley & Trumbull, 1986). The emphasis was again environmental and borrowed from engineering the notion of stress-producing strain. However, this line of research had little impact on stress theory and research in general.

Crises and Catastrophes

During and after World War II, stress research continued to focus on reaction to clearly identified stimuli. Much of this work was based on the thinking of Cannon and Selye. At first, the emphasis was on war-related events, for example, soldiers' reactions to varying levels of combat (Grinker & Spiegal, 1945; Star, 1949; Swank, 1949). Here, the problem appeared to reach serious proportions, since more soldiers were disabled by the stress of combat exhaustion than by any other cause. In addition, researchers examined the symptoms associated with the manipulation of military prisoners (Biderman & Zimmer, 1961), the civilian response to air raids (Freud & Burlingham, 1943; Janis, 1951), and the experience of concentration camp imprisonment (Bettleheim, 1960; Cohen, 1953; Eitinger, 1964).

After the war, researchers continued to examine the impact on health and performance of natural and man-made stressors as well as a wide range of laboratory stress stimuli (shock, cold, crowding, noise, etc.). The subject of major studies often reflected the events of the time. Researchers examined disasters (Barton, 1969; Lifton, 1968; Lindemann, 1944; Tyhurst, 1951), relocation of residents following slum clearance (Fried, 1963), brainwashing and isolation (Solomon et al., 1961), manned space flights (Ruff & Korchin, 1964), bereavement (Lindemann, 1944), graduate examinations (Mechanic, 1962), and President Kennedy's assassination (Sheatsley & Feldman, 1964).

It is easy to see that early work on stress proceeded in a somewhat haphazard fashion. A large number of studies generated volumes of findings but no firm body of knowledge. For several reasons, stress had yet to emerge as a distinct discipline. No unifying perspective had emerged to tie the various studies together. All too often, researchers examined events in isolation from each other. Even the term *stress* had not earned a place as a unifying idea. Stress research proceeded in many separate guises, including anxiety, conflict, frustration, emotional disturbance, trauma, alienation, and anomie (Lazarus & Folkman, 1984). It was not until the 1960s that a major series of studies signaled the beginning of contemporary, comprehensive approaches to stress.

The Life Events Approach

As researchers began to look for general principles to explain the potentially destructive impact of catastrophic events, their attention turned to less dramatic everyday changes. A physician, Adolph Meyer (Lief, 1948), was one of the first to consider the importance of daily life events systematically. Meyer noted stressful events in his patients' lives through "life charts" and made the important observation that illnesses tended to cluster at those times when major events occurred.

Another physician, Harold Wolff, also carefully noted the life circumstances and emotional states surrounding patients' illnesses (Wolff, Wolf, & Hare, 1950). He then went one step further and examined the effects of rapid social changes in central India. Here he found an apparent paradox. As a result of these changes, a number of Indians were upwardly mobile, increasingly affluent, well nourished, and educated. In addition, their living conditions were far healthier than those of others living in surrounding villages and ghettos, who tended to be underfed and uneducated, and to live in unhygienic conditions. The paradox was that the wealthier Indians were more prone to a wide range of illnesses, including diarrhea, colitis, and asthma. Wolff concluded they were stressed by having to adjust to a new social climate. It was *change* that had caused them stress and contributed to what Selye termed "diseases of adaptation" (Wolff, 1968).

With the war and postwar research on severe stressors, and the work of Meyer and Wolff, the stage was set for one of the most important studies in stress research. Drawing on the life-chart work of Wolff, Holmes and Rahe (1967) examined the life charts of more than five thousand patients and identified life events that appeared to cluster at the time of disease onset. They constructed a list of forty-three events representing nine categories: personal, family, community, social, religious, economic, occupational, residential, and vocational life. The events were indicative of significant changes in life that require adaptive or coping behavior. Drawing on the thinking of Cannon, Holmes and Rahe wanted events that represent a change in the "homeostatic," or steady, state of the individual. Their interest was not on psychological meaning, emotion, or social desirability. As we shall see, this intent was, to say the least, naive.

Holmes and Rahe gave their list to 394 students and asked them to rate each event for the intensity and length of time necessary to accommodate the event regardless of its desirability. Marriage was arbitrarily given the value of 500. The other events were to be given ratings in relationship to marriage. The final "life-change unit" scores for each event were then divided by ten, so that the score for marriage became 50. This final list formed the Social Readjustment Rating Scale (SRRS [see Table 1.1]) and the similar Schedule of Recent Experience (SRE) (Rahe, Meyer, Smith, Kjaer, & Holmes, 1964). An individual is given the SRRS and asked to indicate which of the events listed have occurred over a designated period (from six months to two years). The sum of the weights for the checked items is the life-change score for a subject. The SRRS is by far the most widely used, and perhaps the most criticized, stress test ever devised. Indeed, for over a decade research on stress was primarily research on *life events.*

Early life events research involved retrospective designs. Typically, subjects would be asked to recall which life events and which health problems they had experienced during a certain period of time. For example, Holmes and Masuda (1974) mailed the SRE to eighty-eight resident physicians at the University of Washington. In addition, these subjects were asked to list all of their major health changes of the last ten years. Results indicated that those who had a life-change score of 300 or more for a one-year period were nearly twice as likely to experience an illness in the following two years than subjects who had a life-change score between 140 and 199.

Retrospective studies generally supported the link between life events and illness. However, they were subject to frequent criticisms. Subjects who experienced serious life events might be more likely to remember and report illnesses, and subjects with serious illnesses may be more likely to recall and report serious events. Subject reports may also simply reflect their beliefs in a relationship between events and illness. Illnesses, even undiagnosed, may contribute to future life events. Finally, retrospective accounts of life events are notoriously inaccurate, with one study finding only a 25 percent overlap between events experienced and those reported after 10 months (Raphael, Cloitre, & Dohrenwend, 1991).

To answer their critics, life event researchers turned to prospective designs in which a measure of life events is taken (usually in healthy individuals) and subsequent illnesses are assessed. In an early prospective study, Rahe and Holmes (Holmes & Masuda, 1974) followed up 84 of the 88 resident physicians previously described. Here, life changes in the previous eighteen months were used to predict illness in the subsequent nine months. Forty-nine percent of those with life-change scores higher than 300 reported illness, whereas 9 percent of those with scores from 150 to 199 reported illness. A handful of prospective studies have found a relationship between life events and symptoms, generally when events and symptoms are separated by no more than a year (Andrews, 1981; Byrne, 1989; Eaton, 1978; Theorell, Lind, & Floderus, 1975).

However, perhaps the most influential prospective study took place in a rather unusual, and ideal, laboratory: three U.S. Navy cruisers. Rahe (1968), as a Navy physician, had access to such a laboratory during the Vietnam War. He examined 2,463 men on three Navy ships for six to eight months. The officers and enlisted men were all exposed to the same stressors for the period under study, thereby

TABLE 1.1 The Social Readjustment Rating Scale

Rank	Life Event	Mean Value
1	Death of spouse	100
2	Divorce	73
3	Marital separation	65
4	Jail term	63
5	Death of close family member	63
6	Personal injury or illness	53
7	Marriage	50
8	Fired at work	47
9	Marital reconciliation	45
10	Retirement	45
11	Change in health of family member	44
12	Pregnancy	40
13	Sex difficulties	39
14	Gain of new family member	39
15	Business readjustment	39
16	Change in financial state	38
17	Death of close friend	37
18	Change to different line of work	36
19	Change in number of arguments with spouse	35
20	Mortgage over $10,000	31
21	Foreclosure of mortgage or loan	30
22	Change in responsibilities at work	29
23	Son or daughter leaving home	29
24	Trouble with in-laws	29
25	Outstanding personal achievement	28
26	Wife beginning or stopping work	26
27	Beginning or ending school	26
28	Change in living conditions	25
29	Revision of personal habits	24
30	Trouble with boss	23
31	Change in work hours or conditions	20
32	Change in residence	20
33	Change in schools	20
34	Change in recreation	19
35	Change in church activities	19
36	Change in social activities	18
37	Mortgage or loan less than $10,000	17
38	Change in sleeping habits	16
39	Change in number of family get-togethers	15
40	Change in eating habits	15
41	Vacation	13
42	Christmas	12
43	Minor violations of the law	11

SOURCE   Reprinted with permission from the *Journal of Psychosomatic Research,* 11, T. H. Holmes & R. H. Rahe, "The social readjustment scale," copyright 1967, Pergamon Press.

minimizing the possibly confounding effects of life events occurring subsequent to taking a life events test. Health changes for all subjects could also be assessed by the same physicians, thus reducing the systematic biases of different physicians. Before the onset of the study, all subjects filled out the SRE for the previous six-month period. Again, a relationship between life-change scores and illness appeared. Rahe divided the subjects into the 30 percent who experienced the highest scores and the 30 percent who experienced the lowest. The greatest differences emerged in the first month. The top 30 percent group experienced 72 percent more first illnesses (201 versus 117) than the bottom 30 percent. A similar pattern emerged for the number of serious illnesses.

Both prospective and retrospective studies continued, and soon life events became the most studied dimension of stress, resulting in several thousand articles. Relationships emerged between life events and accidents, anorexia nervosa, anxiety, arthritis, athletic injuries, bipolar disorder, bulimia, cancer, depression, diabetes, family problems, fungal infections, heart disease, infectious diseases, minor health changes, poor academic performance, obsessive-compulsive disorder, psoriasis, renal disease, schizophrenia, sleep disorders, tuberculosis, and so on (for reviews, see Barrett, Rose, & Klerman, 1979; Dohrenwend & Dohrenwend, 1974; Miller, 1989; Perkins, 1982; Rabkin & Streuning, 1976; Sarason, deMonchaux, & Hunt, 1975; Thoits, 1983).

Soon, even the general public became aware of life events research. The test devised by Holmes and Rahe was reprinted in hundreds of magazine and newspaper articles as well as in virtually every major textbook in introductory and abnormal psychology, including the present text. Perhaps because of the early studies on physicians and Navy personnel, a life events score of 300 became a popular warning sign of the high likelihood of disease. One Los Angeles newspaper even warned readers not to drive on the stressful freeway if their scores were over 300. It is clear that life events research succeeded in making much of the public aware of stress. However, as we shall see in Chapter 2, researchers began encountering problems. It was time to begin thinking about stress in a new way.

APPLICATION BOX 1.1

The Five Stress Questions and You

In a sense we are all stress experts. Nearly everyone has experienced stress one time or another. In this exercise, first describe what stress means to you. It is best to use a concrete, specific example to illustrate your understanding of stress. Here is what one student, Roger, said:

What is stress? Well, whenever I'm under stress it seems someone is pressuring me. My boss is asking me to do extra work. My wife wants me to do extra household chores after a hard day of work. My children want me to help them with homework.

What is your stress experience?

_____

_____

_____

_____

_____

Now, analyze your experience in terms of the five stress questions. When most people first attempt to define stress in their lives, they focus on one or two of the stress questions. Roger, for example, focused on *external stimuli* (the boss, wife, children). Which stress question does your experience emphasize?

One of the major points of this text is the importance of examining stress from many points of view by asking all of the *five* stress questions. For example, Roger might ask what stress arousal symptoms he felt (perhaps sweaty hands or a headache), what thoughts contributed to stress (perhaps thinking in a way that takes things too seriously), how he attempted to cope (perhaps by avoiding others), and the costs and payoffs of stress (excessive demands create costly upset, but have the payoff of enabling Roger to get sympathy from others). How might you answer the five stress questions about your stress experience?

Finally, what are the benefits of asking all five stress questions, rather than relying on one or two? What important information is gained that might help you cope better in the future?

References

ANDREWS, J. G. (1981). A prospective study of life events and psychological symptoms. *Psychological Medicine, 11*, 795–801.

APPLEY, M. H., & Trumbull, R. (1986). Development of the stress concept. In M. H. Appley & R. Trumbull (Eds.), *Dynamics of stress* (pp. 3–18). New York: Plenum.

BARRETT, J. E., ROSE, R. M., & KLERMAN, G. L. (Eds.). (1979). *Stress and mental disorder.* New York: Raven.

BARTON, A. (1969). *Communities in disaster: A sociological analysis of collective stress situations.* Garden City, NY: Doubleday.

BERNARD, C. (1879). *Leçons sur les phénomènes de la vie commune aux animaux et aux vegetaux.* (Vol. 2). Paris: Bailliere.

BETTELHEIM, B. (1960). *The informed heart.* New York: The Free Press.

BIDERMAN, A. D., & ZIMMER, H. (Eds.). (1961). *The manipulation of human behavior.* New York: Wiley.

BYRNE, G. D. (1989). Personal assessments of life-event stress and the near future onset of psychological symptoms. In T. W. Miller (Ed.), *Stressful life events* (pp. 165–179). Madison, CN: International Universities Press.

CANNON, W. B. (1939). *The wisdom of the body.* New York: Norton.

CANNON, W. B. (1929). *Bodily changes in pain, hunger, fear, and rage.* New York: Appleton.

COHEN, E. A. (1953). *Human behavior in the concentration camp.* New York: Norton.

COX, T. (1978). *Stress.* New York: Macmillan.

DOHRENWEND, B. S., & DOHRENWEND, B. P. (1974). *Stressful life events: Their nature and effects.* New York: Wiley.

DOHRENWEND, B. S., & DOHRENWEND, B. P. (1982). Some issues in research on stressful life events. In T. Millon, C. Green, & R. Meagher (Eds.), *Handbook of clinical health psychology* (pp. 91–102). New York: Plenum.

EATON, W. W. (1978). Life events, social supports, and psychiatric symptoms: A re-analysis of the New Haven data. *Journal of Health and Social Behavior, 19*, 230–234.

EITINGER, L. (1964). *Concentration camp survivors in Norway and Israel.* London: Allen and Unwin.

FREUD, A., & BURLINGHAM, D. (1943). *War and children.* New York: Medical War Books.

FRIED, M. (1963). Grieving for a lost home. In L. J. Duhl (Ed.), *The urban condition* (pp. 151–171). New York: Basic Books.

GRINKER, R. R., & SPIEGAL, J. P. (1945). *Men under stress.* New York: McGraw-Hill.

HINKLE, L. E., JR. (1977). The concept of "stress" in the biological and social sciences. In Z. J. Lipowski, D. R. Lipsitt, & P. C. Whybrow (Eds.), *Psychosomatic medicine: Current trends and clinical implications* (pp. 27–49). New York: Oxford University Press.

HOLMES, T. H., & MASUDA, M. (1974). Life change and illness susceptibility. In B. S. Dohrenwend & B. P. Dohrenwend (Eds.). *Stressful life events: Their nature and effects* (pp. 45–72). New York: Wiley.

HOLMES, T. H., & RAHE, R. H. (1967). The social readjustment rating scale. *Journal of Psychosomatic Research, 11*, 213–218.

JANIS, I. L. (1951). *Air war and emotional stress.* New York: McGraw-Hill.

LAZARUS, R. S., & FOLKMAN, S. (1984). *Stress, appraisal, and coping.* New York: Springer.

LIEF, A. (1948). *The commonsense psychology of Dr. Adolf Meyer.* New York: McGraw-Hill.

LIFTON, R. J. (1968). *Death in life: Survivors of Hiroshima.* New York: Random House.

LINDEMANN, E. (1944). Symptomatology and management of acute grief. *American Journal of Psychiatry, 101,* 141–148.

MECHANIC, D. (1962). *Students under stress.* Glencoe, IL: The Free Press.

MILLER, T. W. (Ed.) (1989). *Stressful life events.* Madison, CN: International Universities Press.

PERKINS, D. V. (1982). The assessment of stress using life events scales. In L. Goldberger & S. Breznitz (Eds.), *Handbook of Stress* (pp. 320–331). New York: The Free Press.

RABKIN, J. G., & STREUNING, E. L. (1976). Life events, stress, and illness. *Science, 194,* 1013–1020.

RAHE, R. H. (1968). Life-change measurement as a predictor of illness. *Proceedings of the Royal Society of Medicine, 61,* 1124–1126.

RAHE, R. H., MEYER, M., SMITH, M., KJAER, G. & HOLMES, T. H. (1964). Social stress and illness onset. *Journal of Psychosomatic Research, 8,* 35–44.

RAPHAEL, K. G., CLOITRE, M., & DOHRENWEND, B. P. (1991). Problems of recall and misclassification with checklist methods of measuring stressful life events. *Health Psychology, 10,* 62–74.

RUFF, G. E., & KORCHIN, S. J. (1964). Psychological responses of the Mercury astronauts to stress. In G. H. Grosser, H. Wechsler, & M. Greenblatt (Eds.) *The threat of impending disaster: Contributions to the psychology of stress* (pp. 208–220). Cambridge, MA: M.I.T. Press.

SARASON, I. G., DEMONCHAUX, C., & HUNT, T. (1975). Methodological issues in the assessment of life stress. In L. Levi (Ed.), *Emotions: Their parameters and measurement* (pp. 499–509). New York: Raven.

SELYE, H. (1936). A syndrome produced by diverse nocuous agents. *Nature, 138,* 32.

SELYE, H. (1956). *The stress of life.* New York: McGraw-Hill.

SHEATSLEY, P. B., & FELDMAN, J. (1964). The assassination of President Kennedy: Public reaction. *Public Opinion Quarterly, 28,* 189–215.

SOLOMON, P., KUBZANSKY, P. E., LEIDERMAN, P. H., MENDELSON, J. H., TRUMBULL, R., & WEXLER, D. (Eds.) (1961). *Sensory deprivation. A symposium at Harvard Medical School.* Cambridge, MA: Harvard University Press.

STAR, S. A. (1949). The screening of psychoneurotics in the Army: Technical development of tests. In S. A. Stouffer, A. A. Lumsdaine, J. H. Lumsdaine, R. M. Williams, M. B. Smith, I. L. Janis, S. A. Star, & L. S. Cottress (Eds.), *Studies in social psychology in World War II* (Vol. 4), (pp. 486–547). Princeton: Princeton University Press.

SWANK, R. L. (1949). Combat exhaustion. *Journal of Nervous and Mental Disease, 109,* 475–508.

THEORELL, T. , LIND, E., & FLODERUS, B. (1975). The relationship of disturbing life changes and emotions to the early development of myocardial infarction and other serious illnesses. *International Journal of Epidemiology, 4,* 281–293.

THOITS, P. A. (1983). Dimensions of life events that influence psychological distress: An evaluation and synthesis of the literature. In H. B. Kaplan (Ed.), *Psyhosocial stress,* (pp. 33–103). New York: Academic Press.

TYHURST, J. S. (1951). Individual reactions to a community disaster: The natural history of a psychiatric projective phenomena. *American Journal of Psychiatry, 107,* 764–769.

WOLFF, H. G., WOLF, S., & HARE, C. C. (1950) *Life stress and bodily disease.* Baltimore: Williams and Wilkins.

WOLFF, H. G. (1968). *Stress and disease* 2nd ed., rev. S. Wolf & H. Goodell (Eds.). Springfield, IL: Charles C. Thomas.

CHAPTER 2

A New Look at Life Events

Stress has emerged as an important and popular area of study. This is due largely to research on life-change events and illness. However, as is often the case with ground-breaking research, the strength of the original findings were not replicated. And, after several thousand studies, one dismal fact became apparent: The relationship between life events and illness was very small, with life events accounting for between only 1 percent and 16 percent of illness (Rabkin & Streuning, 1976; Tanig, 1982). Indeed, the life events approach soon became the most widely criticized strategy for measuring stress. These criticisms have led some to discount the importance of life events as a source of stress. However, a probing examination of life events can add unexpected insights to our understanding of stress.

At first researchers noticed a serious problem in how life-change events were measured. Many of the events on life events inventories (sexual difficulties, change in recreation habits, change in sleeping habits) can also be symptoms of illness (Hudgens, 1974). It could be argued that any correlation between life events and illness is an artifact of such overlap. One study found that when illness-related events are eliminated from life events inventories, the correlation between life events and illness is no longer significant (Schroeder & Costa, 1984). At the very least, when the confound of illness events is reduced, the correlation between illness and life events is reduced (Thoits, 1983).

Partly because of such modest findings, life events researchers quickly looked for ways to improve their work. The most intense focus has been on measuring events and identifying their characteristics most related to illness. Researchers have concentrated on three general dimensions: *content* of events, including content categories, undesirability, magnitude of events; minor events and hassles; and context of events; *ambiguity* of events defined in terms of unpredictability, uncertainty, and uncontrollability; and *timing* of events, that is, imminence and duration.

Refinement of Life Events Research

Content of Events

CONTENT CATEGORIES.   One frequently cited problem of life events inventories is that their content may not be relevant to specific target populations.[1] For example, many items from the Social Readjustment Rating Scale (SRRS) (Holmes & Rahe, 1967), such as retirement from work and foreclosure on a mortgage or loan, do not usually apply to college students. However, even when researchers focus on categories of events relevant to specific populations studied (Pugh, Erickson, Rubin, Gunderson, & Rahe, 1971; Rahe, Pugh, Erickson, Gunderson, & Rubin, 1971), the link between events and illness is not strengthened (Thoits, 1983).

UNDESIRABILITY.   Although events clearly differ in their desirability, desirability is difficult to measure. Innocuous events tend to be overreported, while socially undesirable events are underreported (Caplan, 1975). The degree of event undesirability may well account for more illness variance than do any other variables (Perkins, 1982; Thoits, 1983). Furthermore, the correlation between change and disturbance drops to nearly zero when the effects of undesirable events are statistically removed (Thoits, 1983). Readjustment itself is highly correlated with undesirability, with correlations ranging from .60 to .89 (Thoits, 1983). The overlap between undesirability and change has led Ross and Mirowsky (1979) to conclude that "the correlation between absolute change and symptomatology is spurious, actually caused by undesirability" (p. 173). However, most researchers do not accept this somewhat extreme position.

MAGNITUDE OF EVENTS.   The original SRRS applied specific weights to events (for example, marriage = 50 life-change units). Do such weights have any validity? This question has important implications, since life-change theory postulates that severe (more highly weighted) events should be more stressful because of the adjustment they require. However, if one client tells you she has just started school (26 life-change units) and another has moved (20 units), should you consider the change of school a more serious problem because of its greater SRRS weight? Or should both be considered equally important? Or should you ask each client how much change or adjustment was required? Should you even be concerned about "change" or "adjustment"?

---

[1] Partly in response to this problem, the number of life events inventories has proliferated. Some simply extended the SRRS (Antonovsky & Katz, 1967; Dohrenwend & Dohrenwend, 1974; Myers, Lindenthal, & Pepper, 1975. Particularly popular has been Sarason, Johnson, and Siegal's (1978) Life Experience Inventory. Numerous highly specialized tests have appeared, including scales for culturally heterogeneous populations (Hough, 1980), schizophrenics (Brown & Birley, 1968), athletes (Bramwell, 1971), children (Beautrais, Fergusson, & Shannon, 1982; Coddington, 1972; Greene, Walker, Hickson, & Thompson, 1985; Johnson & McCutcheon, 1980), adolescents (Newcomb, Huba, & Bentler, 1981), teachers (Harrington, Burry, & Pelsma, 1989), elderly patients (Miller & Jay, 1989), hospital patients (Volicer, 1973; Volicer & Bohannon, 1975), nurses (Graffam, 1970), and lesbians (Jewell, 1990). Specialized inventories appear not to enhance greatly the finding of a link between events and illness.

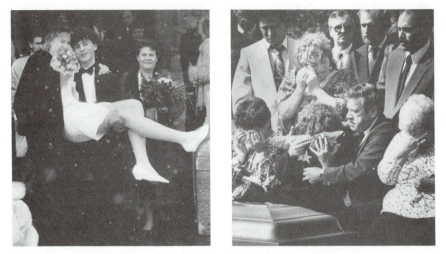

Early stress researchers believed that both desirable and undesirable life events are stressful. Which do you think is more stressful, a marriage or a funeral? (Left: *Photo by Ursula Markus*, Photo Researchers, Inc.; Right: *Photo by Tom Kelly*.)

At first, researchers found that various ways of weighting events appear to make little difference. However, this may well be a statistical artifact (Lorimor, Justice, McBee, & Weinman, 1979). Careful studies consistently find that some sort of weighting is better than no weighting; major events are indeed more related to pathology (Brown & Harris, 1978; Fava, Mundri, Pavan, & Kellner, 1981).

Some have argued that weights should be derived from the population from which they are to be applied (Perkins, 1982). For example, marriage should receive a different weight for college students than for retirees. This issue anticipates the fundamental question in life events research. Those arguing for a single set of weights for all subjects propose that this permits a "clean" measure of the stressfulness of a stimulus, unconfounded by personal perceptions (Dohrenwend & Dohrenwend, 1974). Others (Rahe & Arthur, 1978) argue that perceptions and individual differences influence the stressfulness of events, and that these subjective factors are reflected in weights tailored to specific populations.

MINOR EVENTS AND HASSLES.   Whereas some life events research has examined the impact of major events, an important and growing body of work has looked at relatively minor events. Past researchers have examined familiar daily stresses, microevents, and common annoyances (Lazarus & Folkman, 1984). However, most recent research has focused on what Lazarus and his colleagues have termed *hassles*, which are defined as "the irritating, frustrating, distressing demands that to some degree characterize everyday transactions with the environment" (Kanner, Coyne, Schaeffer, & Lazarus, 1981, p. 3). To this end these researchers developed the 117-item Daily Hassles Scale, which asks about such hassles as "trouble relaxing," "misplacing or losing things," "not enough time for family," and "too many things to do." Subjects indicate which hassles they experienced during specified times, usually from one to twelve months, and rate the severity of each on a twelve-point scale.

Research has found that hassles are only moderately correlated with major life events. Some relationship might be expected, since a serious event, such as a new job, could well contribute to a variety of hassles. However, hassles do correlate significantly with psychological symptomatology even when the impact of major life events is removed. Major life events do not add to the prediction of symptoms once hassles have been statistically removed. And substantial literature suggests that hassles negatively affect physical and mental health to a degree that exceeds the impact of life events (Kanner et al., 1981; DeLongis, Coyne, Dakof, Folkman, & Lazarus, 1982; Holahan, Holahan, & Belk, 1984; Zarski, 1984). Furthermore, central hassles, which reflect important ongoing themes or problems in a person's life, appear to be more associated with symptoms (Gruen, Folkman, & Lazarus, 1988).

Finally, the Daily Hassles Scale has been criticized for including events that are also symptoms, thus complicating any correlation between hassles and symptoms (Burks & Martin, 1985; Dohrenwend, Dohrenwend, Dodson, & Shrout, 1984). However, researchers have found nearly equal correlations when confounded items are deleted (Burks & Martin, 1985; Lazarus, DeLongis, Folkman, & Gruen, 1985; Monroe, 1983).

A different but related approach has examined patterns of stress associated with the various roles taken through life. Pearlin and Schooler (1978) defined four role areas in which people often experience strain: marriage partners, economic matters, parents, and work. Research finds a relationship between role strain and symptoms (Kandel, Davies, & Raveis, 1985; Pearlin, Menaghan, Lieberman, & Mullan, 1981).

CONTEXT OF EVENTS.   The SRRS and the Schedule of Recent Experience (SRE) (Rahe, Meyer, Smith, Kjaer, & Holmes, 1964) are simple additive scales. Weights of events are summed without regard to their context. However, a person could argue that the stressfulness of an event depends partly on the context of events in which it appears. At the simplest level, adults may adapt well to a single life event, but adapt poorly when any two events are clustered (Palmore & Erdman, 1979). Perhaps events have to be unrelated before their stressfulness adds up; losing a job and experiencing a car crash at the same time may be doubly stressful than either single event, whereas losing a job and then a car because of the inability to meet car payments may be less so (Brown & Harris, 1978). Some events may multiply the impact of others. Perhaps the weights are not constant and some "stressful" events may be growth-promoting, potentially reducing the stress of other events. Finally, negative and positive events may well provide different contexts. Linville and Fischer (1991) have proposed that people prefer experiencing two positive or two negative events some time apart, but would rather experience a positive and a negative event in close proximity to buffer losses.

Thresholds for stress may exist; a person may have to experience a minimum number of events before the risk for illness increases. Plateaus, or high levels of stress over which additional events have no impact, may also occur (Perkins, 1982). Even the order in which life events are listed may affect ratings (Hough, Fairbank, & Garcia, 1976). In spite of these many suggestions, very little research has examined the relative value of different scaling options.

What about events not on life-events scales? A *hidden event* is an experience for which no formal concept has been identified (Brim & Ryff, 1980). It is an event without a context. For example, career advances and plateaus, "male menopause," and even periods of life in which expected changes do not occur can be stressful, but are largely unrecognized by existing measurement devices.

Ambiguity of Events

UNPREDICTABILITY.   Considerable research has focused on the predictability and controllability of laboratory stress stimuli such as noise, shock, and cold (Miller, 1981). The evidence suggests that predictable, or signaled, shock is less aversive than unpredictable, or unsignaled, shock. A wide range of organisms, including rats, pigeons, and fish, prefer predictable stimuli. Indeed, subjects prefer longer, stronger, and more frequent signaled shock over shorter, weaker, and less frequent unsignaled shock (Badia, Harsh, & Abbott, 1979).

A number of theories have been proposed to explain this finding. According to the *preparatory response hypothesis*, a signaled event provides a warning that permits subjects to prepare for a stressor and thereby reduce its stressfulness (Perkins, 1968). An alternative view, the *safety signal hypothesis*, suggests that a warning signal lets subjects know when they are safe and can relax.

However, there are times when predictable stressors are not preferable (Matthews, Scheier, Brunson, & Carducci, 1989). Deliberately increasing attention to a predictable stressor may well increase stress, whereas diverting attention from an unpredictable event may reduce stress (Matthews et al., 1989).

UNCERTAINTY.   In laboratory situations, uncertainty is often defined in terms of probability. That is, a subject may have one chance out of ten of receiving an electric shock. In real life, stress often presents similar uncertainties. A patient may have a 30 percent chance of surviving surgery. In the laboratory, uncertainty often presents perplexing results. At times, stress arousal is highest when shock is least certain (Epstein & Roupenian, 1970), and at other times, when shock is most certain (Gaines, Smith, & Skolnick, 1977).

However, Lazarus and Folkman (1984) have offered a strong critique of laboratory studies of stress. Most laboratory studies employ psychology students, who usually know that ethical requirements limit the actual harm that can be inflicted on subjects. As a result, the nature of any laboratory stressors, no matter how defined by the researcher, is never entirely uncertain. In contrast, real life stressors can be highly complex and may reflect uncertainties much more serious than can be induced in any laboratory. It is highly likely that such uncertainty can have a devastating impact on conflicting coping processes and induce considerable mental confusion (Lazarus & Folkman, 1984). For example, coping strategies most appropriate for dealing with a stressor are often incompatible with strategies for coping with the prospect that a stressor will not occur. A cancer patient may deal with the prospect of death by acknowledging and mourning that possibility. However, the chance that yet-undiscovered treatments may offer a cure calls for a coping strategy that focuses on making plans for continued life as well. Similar conflicts exist for wives of men missing in war, employees with tenuous jobs in uncertain economic conditions, and so on. In addition, uncertainty can contribute to considerable mental confusion. When a person cannot decide upon a final course of action, fear, worry, anxiety, and hopelessness result (Breznitz, 1971). As we shall see in later chapters, these consequences in themselves can interfere with cognitive functioning.

UNCONTROLLABILITY.   Extensive laboratory research has examined the impact of stressor uncontrollability (Garber & Seligman, 1980; Glass & Singer, 1972; Schmale, 1972; Seligman, 1975). Strategies often supply subjects with some means of terminating or moderating an aversive stimulus, such as shock or noise. Typically, having such control, or even just believing that such control is possible, reduces stress. Uncontrollable events appear to be more strongly associated with depression. For other disorders, results are inconsistent (Thoits, 1983).

"Should I bid?" The uncertainty of an auction is one factor that makes it stressful.   *(Photo by Joel Gordon.)*

Timing of Events

IMMINENCE.   The imminence of a stressor is its latency, or the amount of time before the event occurs. In general, imminent stressors are more stressful than delayed stressors, especially when there are cues signaling stressor onset. Increased latency provides time to evaluate a stressor and to consider coping options. With imminent stressors, there may not be enough time to cope. As a result, one may apply a *hypervigilant decision-making style* (Janis & Mann, 1977) that involves being obsessed with catastrophizing thoughts, ignoring evidence that may indicate the improbability of worst-case scenarios, having an awareness of pressure, superficially scanning the most obvious alternatives, and hastily choosing the first option available while ignoring any potentially serious consequences.

The importance of event imminence is also suggested by life events research. Although most studies have focused on illnesses that develop from six months to a year after an event, some have suggested that symptom onset is most likely to begin three to four weeks after a closely spaced cluster of events (Brown & Birley, 1968; Brown & Harris, 1978). In contrast, recall of events over a year drops considerably in reliability (Thoits, 1983), thus reducing the possibility of determining a relationship between events and illness.

However, it should be noted that an increased period of time between a stressor cue and a stressor can also contribute to stress. Longer intervals permit an *incubation of threat* (Breznitz, 1967) during which subjects can become increasingly involved with worrying about a stressor. However, the pattern is not consistent. When increased time reduces to stress, a person has a greater opportunity to think through a situation and utilize various coping strategies.

DURATION.   Four types of stressors can be defined in terms of stressor duration (Elliott & Eisdorfer, 1982):

> (1) *Acute, time-limited stressors*, such as going parachute jumping, awaiting surgery, or encountering a rattlesnake; (2) *Stressor sequences*, or series of events that occur over an extended period of time as the result of an initiating event such as job loss, divorce, or bereavement; (3) *Chronic intermittent stressors* such as conflict-filled visits to in-laws or sexual difficulties, which may occur once a day, once a week, once a month; and (4) *Chronic stressors* such as permanent disabilities, parental discord, or chronic job stress, which may or may not be initiated by a discrete event and which persist continuously for a long time. (pp. 150–151)

Each pattern may be associated with a different outcome. Acute, time-limited stressors may have little lasting impact because they are limited. Stressor sequences may be associated with increased understanding of a stressor; a person knows which events will occur as a result of a stressor and can therefore plan for them. Chronic intermittent stressors may permit periods of rest and recovery between events. In contrast, chronic stressors may be most disruptive because of their ambiguous outcome and continuous nature.

We noted in Chapter 1 that Selye (1956) proposed that chronic stressors are more likely than brief stressors to evoke the general adaptation syndrome (GAS), to contribute to illness, and ultimately to lead to death. Indeed, chronic stressors are most likely to contribute to illness (Singer & Davidson, 1986). Gastric secretion, for example, often occurs with chronic demands (Mahl, 1949, 1952, 1953).

However, chronic stressors do not always lead to exhaustion. Often arousal eventually lessens, or *habituates*, in response to continued stressors (just as a person gets use to the constant drone of air conditioners, traffic, and so on). However, it may be questioned whether habituation reflects getting use to, or becoming worn down and exhausted by, a stressor. This issue is still being debated (Lazarus & Folkman, 1984; Rose, 1980). An alternative interpretation is that habituation reflects either a reappraisal of a stimulus as no longer threatening or the successful application of coping strategies.

Social Networks and Support

Our external world is not just a potential source of stress; it also provides important "resistance resources" (Antonovsky, 1979) for dealing with stress. Such resources can be financial, political, educational, geographical, and so on. However, the one resource most frequently mentioned in life events research is the support a person receives from others. There are two ways of looking at such interpersonal resources. A *social network* (Mitchell, 1969) is defined in terms of the links among people. It is simply the number and closeness of a person's friends, relatives, and acquaintances. (For example, "I have two close friends and six acquaintances.") In contrast, *social support* is more broadly defined as the quality of those relationships: how helpful they are perceived to be as well as how helpful they actually are (Sarason, Sarason, & Pierce, 1990). It can be useful to think of four kinds of social support (Cohen & Wills, 1985). *Esteem support* is provided when people are told they are valued for their own worth and are accepted despite difficulties or personal faults. Such support is also known as emotional, expressive, self-esteem, and close support as well as ventilation. *Informational support* is help in defining, understanding, and coping with stressful situations. It is also known as advice, appraisal support, and cognitive guidance. *Social companionship* involves spending leisure and recreational time with others. This has also been called diffuse support and belongingness. Finally, *instrumental support* is financial and material aid as well as needed services. Instrumental support is also termed aid as well as material and tangible support.

Think of all the ways your social networks and supports help you deal with stress. Friends, relatives, and acquaintances can help prevent stress by reducing your worry and uncertainty, enabling you to share your concerns, distracting you from needless tension, and providing you with encouragement as well as a good model for preparing for stress. They can help you deal with an ongoing problem by giving you sympathy, information, and material assistance. Such aid may directly help you to resolve stressful problems, or may give you "time off" to recover or at least divert

Social support offered through this AIDS hotline helps to reduce stress.
(Photo by Joel Gordon.)

your attention from stress. When the stress is over, your social networks and supports can help you recover by listening to your frustrations and satisfactions. Finally, even the knowledge that such support is there can enable you to perceive events as less stressful (Singer & Lord, 1984).

Indeed, research suggests the importance of perceived social support. Having few supports and relationships is associated with increased mortality from all causes (House, Landis, & Umberson, 1988; Thoits, 1982; Turner, 1981). The lack of such supports and relationships is associated with illness and symptoms (Cohen, Teresi, & Holmes, 1985), particularly for those who are especially vulnerable, such as AIDS patients and the elderly (Kennedy, Kiecolt-Glaser, & Glaser, 1990).

There are two general hypotheses as how others can help reduce stress. One hypothesis suggests that others can *buffer* the potentially destructive impact of stress. An alternative hypothesis is that social resources have a *direct beneficial effect* regardless of whether a person is under stress. To elaborate, because people need relationships, the absence of relationships can be stressful on its own. There is strong support for both points of view (Cohen & Wills, 1985). However, the relationship between the role played by others and stress is complex. First, dealing with others is not without its costs. People, even those who provide help, are a prime source of stress. Second, social support is a give-and-take proposition, a transaction. One earns love and support by giving love and support. Indeed, the process of giving may in itself serve as an important factor in helping us deal with stress by reducing destructive self-preoccupation, providing opportunities to think through our own options by helping others think through theirs, and so on. One theory even proposes that people develop something of a "social support bank" (Antonucci & Jackson, 1990) in which an ongoing account is kept of supports that have been given to and received from others. Of course, such transactions are usually done at an unconscious level. By giving support to others we "make deposits" or "rainy day investments." And, to continue with this idea, relying on others involves drawing upon and spending what we have saved. Whatever the view, social networks and supports are not so much static resources as they are coping options.

Research on social supports and networks has recently focused on certain specific issues. First, apparently the buffering impact of another is enhanced when that individual is *nonevaluative*. Laboratory studies have found that the cardiovascular reactivity of women performing stressful arithmetic was lower when they were performing in the presence of a nonevaluative female friend than when they were performing alone (Kamarck, Manuck, & Jennings, 1990). Indeed, female subjects also experienced greater reduced stress when accompanied by a companion dog than by a female friend (Allen, Blascovich, Tomaka, & Kelsey, 1991), presumably because of the appraised nonevaluative support the animal provided. This latter finding may help explain why pet ownership is associated with fewer contacts with doctors, lower blood pressure, and greater survival from coronary surgery.

Other issues in the research on social supports and networks need clarification. It is often difficult to tease out cause and effect. Do social supports and networks reduce the very occurrence of stressful life events (such as when friends and family help to prevent a divorce)? Are life events (for example, loss of work or a move) stressful because they can lead to a loss of support (Mueller, 1980; Schaefer, Coyne, & Lazarus, 1981; Thoits, 1982)? Is the perception of social support a sign of other factors that may mediate stress, such as high self-esteem and good social coping skills (Gore, 1984; Lazarus, 1990)?

One way to resolve such ambiguities is to take a highly pragmatic approach and narrow our focus to the kinds of support a person wants, and whether this help is available, offered, and received (Coyne & DeLongis, 1986; Lazarus, 1990). Using such a multifaceted strategy, Connell and D'Augelli (1990) found that people who want and enjoy social relations, seek help from others, and offer help report having larger social networks. They also receive more social support from others and perceive more support to be available.

The value of such an approach also becomes apparent when we examine social support in terms of gender, a variable often ignored in stress research. Women appear to use social supports and networks more effectively than men and to derive more from their friendships (Ratliff-Crain & Baum, 1990). Specifically, women are more likely to have more intimate relationships with their friends; they also disclose more, and offer or seek more help. Men maintain larger number of acquaintances, are often less intimate, have fewer close friends, and rely more on their spouses for support. Perhaps as a result, women appear to cope with stress by using their networks extensively and drawing from several sources of support; in contrast, men are less likely to seek support from their friends. Research has yet to show if these differences translate into lower levels of stress for women. It could be that men benefit so much from a single source of support, such as a wife or lover, that an extensive network is unnecessary. And women's involvement in an extensive social network can backfire, because sharing the problems of many others can actually increase stress; indeed, in several studies women with high social support actually show an increased risk of mortality (Shumaker & Hill, 1991).

The Status of Life Events Research

You may have the impression that this chapter has covered an enormous number of issues, but has revealed few conclusions. Indeed, one of my goals in thoroughly reviewing life events research is to show the magnitude of relatively unproductive work this area has inspired. However, Thoits (1983) has argued that thousands of life event studies appear to support one conclusion: the dimensions that increase the relationship between events and disorder are *undesirability, unpredictability, uncontrollability, event magnitude*, and *time clustering*. Of these, the most powerful appear to be undesirability, magnitude, and time clustering, and, for depression, uncontrollability. However, for all this work, the relationship between life events and illness still remains modest, with events accounting for only about 16 percent of illness.

What are we to make of the volumes of research on life events? Miller (1989) has concluded that life events research is supported more by faith than evidence. However, it is an area that has attracted several thousand studies in nearly forty years. Many other areas of psychology have attracted far less research over a much shorter period and have progressed substantially.

One conclusion is clear. The original notion of wear and tear created by a stressful world needs to be modified. The vision of Holmes and Rahe, and even Cannon and Selye, was that external events requiring change and readjustment have an automatic, cumulative, and destructive impact, much as continued use produces wear and tear on a household appliance. But the world of stress is much more complex. We must also consider physical and psychological vulnerabilities and appraisals of threat and coping options, as well as short- and long-term consequences. These topics we will cover in later chapters.

However, the dimensions we have examined can serve as a very useful starting point for understanding stress. For example, if you know nothing about another person, the stimulus characteristics of her world can suggest hypotheses about how much stress she may be under. For example, imagine you are a counselor assigned to deal with families who have survived an earthquake. You know some districts in the area have had several earthquake tremors in the last few months (time clustering), some of considerable size (event magnitude and undesirability). Furthermore, all of the earthquakes were completely unexpected (unpredictability and uncertainty) and few people were able to prepare for them (uncontrollability). Finally, you know that the earthquakes lasted unusually long (duration) and could occur again at any moment (imminence). The concepts in this chapter suggest that you may well encounter considerable stress in your clients.

In contrast, imagine you have been assigned to counsel families in a town that has been hit by a hurricane. This was the first hurricane in fifty years (no clustering of events). It was a severe hurricane, although it caused more damage in neighboring towns (relatively less magnitude and undesirability). Fortunately, the residents had a full week to prepare for the storm (predictability and certainty) and received good instructions on what to do (controllability). The storm was also relatively brief (duration). You might expect somewhat less stress in this community.

An awareness of the dimensions of stress can help us understand even everyday problems. For example, imagine a friend has told you the following:

> Everything seems to be going wrong. I lost my car keys. I didn't get the raise at work. My son got into trouble at school. And, worse yet, because I didn't get a raise, I won't be able to pay my mortgage. If I can't pay for the house, that will open a Pandora's box of problems. I'm stuck at my present job. It's not very likely that I could find work elsewhere.

The dimensions we have considered can give you some ideas as to how your friend might be experiencing stress and what you should focus on as you listen. You might want to note the clustering of hassles, the uncertainty of making the mortgage payment, and the uncontrollability of the work problems. By focusing on the core dimensions that might be creating stress, you not only increase the likelihood that you will quickly help your friend understand the source of his problem, but you help in the task of coming up with solutions.

There is another useful way of looking at the dimensions of stress we have considered. Each can be viewed as a type of *appraisal*. People differ in how they view the content of an event and the available coping resources. The perceived magnitude of an event, its undesirability, and its context are determined by a host of personal factors, including beliefs, values, and commitments as well as coping resources. The same can be said for perceived ambiguity. The unpredictability, uncertainty, and uncontrollability of an event are relative, and its timing, imminence, and duration are subjective. Perhaps life events research has taught us two things. One is that our stressful world can indeed have its costs. The second is that how we perceive this world may well determine how severe those costs are.

APPLICATION BOX 2.1

Analyzing Your Life Chart

Imagine you are constructing a life chart like those used by early life events researchers. List those events you have experienced in the last six months, noting the date for each.

Event   Date

Now, consider the major event dimensions discussed in the text: undesirability, magnitude, unpredictability, uncertainty, uncontrollability, imminence, and duration. Which dimensions increased the stressfulness of each event? Can you explain why?

Now, think of illnesses you may have had over the last six months. List them below. To what extent do you think stress contributed to these illnesses?

Did social support reduce the stressfulness of any of the events you listed? Were there times when feeling loved and valued helped? Were there times you felt better because you could count on others to help?

References

ALLEN, K. M., BLASCOVICH, J., TOMAKA, J., & KELSEY, R. M. (1991). Presence of human friends and pet dogs as moderators of autonomic responses to stress in women. *Journal of Personality and Social Psychology, 61,* 582–589.

ANTONOVSKY, A. (1979). *Health, stress, and coping.* San Francisco: Jossey-Bass.

ANTONOVSKY, A., & KATZ, R. (1967). The life crisis history as a tool in epidemiological research. *Journal of Health and Social Behavior, 8,* 15–20.

ANTONUCCI, T. C., & JACKSON, J. S. (1990). The role of reciprocity in social support. In B. R. Sarason, I. G. Sarason, & G. R. Pierce (Eds.), *Social support: An interactional view* (pp. 173–198). New York: Wiley.

BADIA, P., HARSH, J., & ABBOTT, B. (1979). Choosing between predictable and unpredictable shock conditions: Data and theory. *Psychological Bulletin, 86,* 1107–1131.

BEAUTRAIS, A. L., FERGUSSON, D. M., & SHANNON, F. T. (1982). Life events and childhood morbidity: A prospective study. *Pediatrics, 70,* 935–939.

BRAMWELL, S. T. (1971). *Personality and psychosocial variables in college athletes.* Unpublished medical thesis, University of Washington, Seattle.

BREZNITZ, S. (1967). Incubation of threat: Duration of anticipation and false alarm as determinants of the fear reaction to an unavoidable frightening event. *Journal of Experimental Research in Personality, 2,* 173–179.

BREZNITZ, S. (1971). A study of worrying. *British Journal of Social and Clinical Psychology,* 10, 271–279.

BRIM, O. G., JR., & RYFF, C. D. (1980). On the properties of life events. In P. B. Baltes & O. G. Brim (Eds.), *Life-span development and behavior* (Vol. 3, pp. 368–388). New York: Academic Press.

BROWN, G. W., & BIRLEY, J. L. (1968). Crisis and life changes and the onset of schizophrenia. *Journal of Health and Social Behavior, 9,* 203–214.

BROWN, G. W., & HARRIS, T. (1978). *Social origins of depression: A study of psychiatric disorder in women.* New York: The Free Press.

BURKS, N., & MARTIN, B. (1985). Everyday problems and life change events: Ongoing versus acute sources of stress. *Journal of Human Stress, 11,* 27–35.

CAPLAN, R. D. (1975). A less heretical view of life change and hospitalization. *Journal of Psychosomatic Research, 19,* 247–250.

CODDINGTON, E. S. (1972). The significance of life events and etiologic factors in the disease of children: Part 1. A survey of professional workers. *Journal of Psychosomatic Research, 16,* 7–18.

COHEN, C. I., TERESI, J., & HOLMES, D. (1985). Social networks, stress, and physical health: A longitudinal study of an inner-city elderly population. *Journal of Gerontology, 40,* 476–486.

COHEN, S., & WILLS, T. A. (1985). Stress, social support, and the buffering hypothesis. *Psychological Bulletin, 98,* 310–357.

CONNELL, C. M., & D'AUGELLI, A. R. (1990). The contribution of personality characteristics to the relationship between social support and perceived physical health. *Health Psychology, 9,* 192–207.

COYNE, J. C., & DELONGIS, A. (1986). Going beyond social support: The role of social relationships in adaptation. *Journal of Consulting and Clinical Psychology, 54,* 454–460.

DELONGIS, A., COYNE, J. C., DAKOF, G., FOLKMAN, S., & LAZARUS, R. S. (1982). Relationship of daily hassles, uplifts, and major life events to health status. *Health Psychology, 1,* 119–136.

DOHRENWEND, B. S., & DOHRENWEND, B. P. (1974). *Stressful life events: Their nature and effects.* New York: Wiley.

DOHRENWEND, B. S., DOHRENWEND, B. P., DODSON, M., & SHROUT, P. E. (1984). Symptoms, hassles, social supports, and life events: Problem of confounded measures. *Journal of Abnormal Psychology, 93,* 222–230.

ELLIOTT, G. R., & EISDORFER, C. (1982). *Stress and human health.* New York: Springer.

EPSTEIN, S., & ROUPENIAN, A. (1970). Heart rate and skin conductance during experimentally induced anxiety: The effect of uncertainty about receiving anoxious stimulus. *Journal of Personality and Social Psychology, 16,* 20–28.

FAVA, G. A., MUNARI, F., PAVAN, L., & KELLNER, R. (1981). Life events and depression: A replication. *Journal of Affective Disorders, 3,* 159–165.

GAINES, L. L., SMITH, B. D., & SKOLNICK, B. E. (1977). Psychological differentiation, event uncertainty, and heart rate. *Journal of Human Stress, 3,* 11–25.

GARBER, J., & SELIGMAN, M. E. P. (1980). Human helplessness: Theory and applications. New York: Academic Press.

GLASS, D. C., & SINGER, J. E. (1972). *Urban stress: Experiments on noise and social stressors.* New York: Academic Press.

GORE, S. (1984). Stress-buffering functions of social supports: An appraisal and clarification of research models. In B. S. Dohrenwend & B. P. Dohrenwend (Eds.), *Stressful life events and their contexts* (pp. 202–222). New Brunswick, NJ: Rutgers University Press.

GRAFFAM, S. R. (1970). Nurse response to the patient in distress-development of an instrument. *Nursing Research, 19,* 331–336.

GREENE, J. W., WALKER, L. S., HICKSON, G., & THOMPSON, J. (1985). Stressful life events and somatic complaints in adolescents. *Pediatrics, 75,* 19–22.

GRUEN, R. J., FOLKMAN, S., & LAZARUS, R. S. (1988). Centrality and individual differences in the meaning of daily hassles. *Journal of Personality, 56,* 743–762.

HARRINGTON, R. G., BURRY, J. A., & PELSMA, D. (1989). Factors contributing to teacher stress. In T. W. Miller (Ed.), *Stressful life events* (pp. 677–696). Madison, CT: International Universities Press.

HOLAHAN, C. K., HOLAHAN, C. J., & BELK, S. S. (1984). Adjustment in aging: The roles of life stress, hassles, and self-efficacy. *Health Psychology, 3,* 315–328.

HOLMES, T. H., & RAHE, R. H. (1967). The social readjustment rating scale. *Journal of Psychosomatic Research, 11,* 213–218.

HOUGH, R. L. (1980). *Universal and group-specific life change scales.* Unpublished manuscript. University of California at Los Angeles, Life Change and Illness Research Project.

HOUGH, R. L., FAIRBANK, D. T., & GARCIA, A. M. (1976). Problems in the ratio measurement of life stress. *Journal of Health and Social Behavior, 17,* 70–82.

HOUSE, J. S., LANDIS, K. R., & UMBERSON, D. (1988). Social relationships and health. *Science, 241,* 540–545.

HUDGENS, R. W. (1974). Personal catastrophe and depression. In B. P. Dohrenwend & B. S. Dohrenwend (Eds.), *Stressful life events: Their nature and effects* (pp. 119–134). New York: Wiley.

JANIS, I. L., & MANN, L. (1977). *Decision making.* New York: The Free Press.

JEWELL, T. L. (1990). T.J.'s stress scale for dykes. *Nightlines, 29,* 48.

JOHNSON, J. H., & McCUTCHEON, S. (1980). Assessing life stress in older children and adolescents: Preliminary findings with the life events checklist. In I. G. Sarason & C. D. Spielberger (Eds.), *Stress and anxiety (Vol. 7,* pp. 111–125). Washington, DC: Hemisphere.

KAMARCK, T. W., MANUCK, S. B., & JENNINGS, J. R. (1990). Social support reduces cardiovascular reactivity to psychological challenge: A laboratory model. *Psychosomatic Medicine, 54,* 42–58.

KANDEL, D. B., DAVIES, M., & RAVEIS, V. H. (1985). The stressfulness of daily social roles for women: Marital, occupational and household roles. *Journal of Health and Social Behavior, 26,* 64–78.

KANNER, A. D., COYNE, J. C., SCHAEFFER, C., & LAZARUS, R. S. (1981). Comparison of two modes of stress measurement: Daily hassles and uplifts versus major life events. *Journal of Behavioral Medicine, 4,* 1–39.

KENNEDY, S., KIECOLT-GLASER, J. K., & GLASER, R. (1990). Social support, stress, and the immune system. In B. R. Sarason, I. G. Sarason, & G. R. Pierce (Eds.), *Social support: An interactional view* (pp. 253–266). New York: Wiley.

LAZARUS, R. S. (1990). Stress, coping, and illness. In H. S. Friedman (Ed.), *Personality and disease* (pp. 97–120). New York: Wiley.

LAZARUS, R. S., & FOLKMAN, S. (1984). *Stress, appraisal, and coping.* New York: Springer.

LAZARUS, R. S., DeLONGIS, A., FOLKMAN, S., & GRUEN, R. (1985). Stress and adaptational outcomes: The problem of unconfounded measures. *American Psychologist, 40,* 770–779.

LINVILLE, P. W., & FISCHER, G. W. (1991). Preferences for separating or combining events. *Journal of Personality and Social Psychology, 60,* 5–23.

LORIMOR, R. J., JUSTICE, B., McBEE, G. W., & WEINMAN, M. (1979). Weighting events in life-events research (Comment on Dohrenwend et al; *Journal of Health and Social Behavior,* June, 1978). *Journal of Health and Social Behavior, 20,* 306–308.

MAHL, G. F. (1949). Anxiety, HCL secretion, and peptic ulcer etiology. *Psychosomatic Medicine, 11,* 30–44.

MAHL, G. F. (1952). Relationship between acute and chronic fear and the gastric acidity and blood sugar levels in *Macca mulatta* monkeys. *Psychosomatic Medicine, 14,* 182–210.

MAHL, G. F. (1953). Physiological changes during chronic fear. *Annals of the New York Academy of Sciences, 56,* 240–249.

MATTHEWS, K. A., SCHEIER, M. F., BRUNSON, B. I., & CARDUCCI, B. (1989). Why do unpredictable events lead to reports of physical symptoms? In T. W. Miller (Ed.), *Stressful life events* (pp. 91–100). Madison, CN: International Universities Press.

MILLER, S. M. (1981). Predictability and human stress: Toward a clarification of evidence and theory. In L. Berkowitz (Ed.), *Advances in experimental social psychology* (vol. 14, pp. 203–256). New York: Academic Press.

MILLER, T. W. (Ed.). (1989). *Stressful life events.* Madison, CT: International Universities Press.

MILLER, T. W., & JAY, L. L. (1989). Multifactoral stressors in life change events for the elderly patient. In T. W. Miller (Ed.), *Stressful life events* (pp. 729–747). Madison, CT: International Universities Press.

MITCHELL, J. C. (Ed.). (1969). *Social networks in urban situations.* Manchester, England: Manchester University Press.

MONROE, S. M. (1983). Major and minor life events as predictors of psychological distress: Further issues and findings. *Journal of Behavioral Medicine, 6,* 189–205.

MUELLER, D. P. (1980). Social networks: A promising direction for research on the relationship of the social environment to psychiatric disorder. *Social Science and Medicine, 14A,* 147–161.

MYERS, J., LINDENTHAL, J. J., & PEPPER, M. (1975). Life events, social integration and psychiatric symptomatology. *Journal of health and social behavior, 16,* 421–427.

NEWCOMB, M. D., HUBA, G. J., & BENTLER, P. M. (1981). A multidimensional assessment of stressful life events among adolescents: Derivation and correlates. *Journal of Health and Social Behavior, 22,* 400–415.

PALMORE, E., & ERDMAN, R. (1979). Stress and adaptation in late life. *Journal of Gerontology, 34,* 841–851.

PAYKEL, E. S. (1974). Life stress and psychiatric disorder: Applications of the clinical approach. B. S. Dohrenwend & B. P. Dohrenwend (Eds.), *Stressful life events: Their nature and effects* (pp. 135–149). New York: Wiley.

PEARLIN, L. I., & SCHOOLER, C. (1978). The structure of coping. *Journal of Health and Social Behavior, 19,* 2–21.

PEARLIN, L. I., MENAGHAN, E. G., LIEBERMAN, M. A., & MULLAN, J. T. (1981). The stress process. *Journal of Health and Social Behavior, 22,* 337–356.

PERKINS, C. C., Jr. (1968). An analysis of the concept of reinforcement. *Psychological Review, 76,* 155.

PERKINS, D. V. (1982). The assessment of stress using life events scales. In L. Goldberger & S. Breznitz (Eds.), *Handbook of stress* (pp. 320–331). New York: The Free Press.

PUGH, W. M., ERICKSON, J., RUBIN, R. T., GUNDERSON, E. K. E., & RAHE, R. H. (1971). Cluster analyses of life changes: II. Method and replication in Navy subpopulations. *Archives of General Psychiatry, 25,* 333–339.

RABKIN, J. G., & STREUNING, E. L. (1976). Life events, stress, and illness. *Science, 194,* 1013–1020.

RAHE, R. H., MEYER, M., SMITH, M., KJAER, G., & HOLMES, T. H. (1964). Social stress and illness on set. *Journal of Psychosomatic Research, 8,* 35–44.

RAHE, R. H., & ARTHUR, R. J. (1978). Life change and illness studies: Past history and future directions. *Journal of Human Stress, 4,* 3–15.

RAHE, R. H., PUGH, W. M., ERICKSON, J., GUNDERSON, E. K. E., & RUBIN, R. T. (1971). Cluster analyses of life changes: I. Consistency of clusters across large Navy samples. *Archives of General Psychiatry, 25,* 330–332.

RATLIFF-CRAIN, J., & BAUM, A. (1990). Individual differences and health: Gender, coping, and stress. In H. S. Friedman (Ed.), *Personality and disease* (pp. 226–253). New York: Wiley.

ROSE, R. M. (1980). Endocrine responses to stressful psychological events. *Psychiatric Clinics of North America, 3,* 1–15.

ROSS, C. E., & MIROWSKY, J. II (1979). A comparison of life event weighting schemes: Change, undesirability and effect-proportional indices. *Journal of Health and Social Behavior, 20,* 166–177.

SARASON, B. R., SARASON, I. G., & PIERCE, G. R. (1990). Traditional views of social support on their impact on assessment. In B. R. Sarason, I. G. Sarason, & G. R. Pierce (Eds.), *Social support: An interactional view* (pp. 9–25). New York: Wiley.

SARASON, I. G., JOHNSON, J. H., & SIEGAL, J. M. (1978). Assessing the impact of life changes: Development of the life experiences survey. *Journal of Consulting and Clinical Psychology, 46,* 932–946.

SCHAEFER, C., COYNE, J. C., & LAZARUS, R. S. (1981). The health-related functions of social support. *Journal of Behavioral Medicine, 4,* 381–406.

SCHMALE, A. H., JR. (1972). Giving up as a final common pathway to changes in health. *Advances in Psychosomatic Medicine, 8,* 20–40.

SCHROEDER, D. H., & COSTA, D. T. (1984). Influence of life events on physical illness: Substantive effects or methodological flaws? *Journal of Personality and Social Psychology, 46,* 853–863.

SELIGMAN, M. E. P. (1975). *Helplessness: On depression, development, and death.* San Francisco: W.H. Freeman.

SELYE, H. (1956). *The stress of life.* New York: McGraw-Hill.

SHUMAKER, S. A., & HILL, D. R. (1991). Gender differences in social support and physical health. *Health Psychology, 10,* 102–111.

SINGER, J. E., & DAVIDSON, L. M. (1986). Specificity and stress research. In M. H. Appley and R. Trumbull (Eds.), *Dynamics of stress* (pp. 47–61). New York: Plenum.

SINGER, J. E., & LORD, D. (1984). The role of social support in coping with life-threatening illness. In A. Baum, S. E. Taylor, & J. E. Singer (Eds.), *Handbook of psychology and health* (Vol. 4, pp. 383–398). Hillsdale, NJ: Lawrence Erlbaum.

TANIG, M. (1982). Measuring life events. *Journal of Health and Social Behavior, 23,* 78–108.

THOITS, P. A. (1982). Conceptual, methodological, and theoretical problems in studying social support as a buffer against life stress. *Journal of Health and Social Behavior, 23,* 145–159.

THOITS, P. A. (1983). Dimensions of life events that influence psychological distress: An evaluation and synthesis of the literature. In H. B. Kaplan (Ed.), *Psychosocial stress* (pp. 33–103). New York: Academic Press.

TURNER, R. J. (1981). Social support as a contingency in psychological well-being. *Journal of Health and Social Behavior, 22,* 357–367.

VOLICER, B. J. (1973). Perceived stress levels of events associated with the experience of hospitalization: Development and testing of a measurement tool. *Nursing Research, 22,* 491–497.

VOLICER, B. J., & BOHANNON, M. W. (1975). A hospital stress rating scale. *Nursing Research, 24,* 352–359.

ZARSKI, J. (1984). Hassles and health: A replication. *Health Psychology, 3,* 77–81.

CHAPTER 3

The Stress Arousal Response

The experience is nearly universal. Before an important interview, your hands grow cold and sweaty. You are giving a speech at work, and your heart beats hard and fast. After a near accident on the highway, your stomach is in knots and you feel nauseous. You may think of these physical symptoms as nuisances. Indeed, over time they can contribute to illness. However, they are part of an important survival response, one that has evolved through millions of years. It is called stress arousal.

The stress arousal response has two major components: the nervous system, which operates through the firing of neurons or nerve cells, and the endocrine system, which operates through the discharge of chemical hormones into the bloodstream.[1] To understand how these work, we first need to look at the structure of the nervous system.

The Nervous System

The Central and Peripheral Nervous Systems

In simplest terms, the human body has both a central and a peripheral nervous system (see Figure 3.1). The *central nervous system* (CNS) consists of the brain and spinal cord, and the *peripheral nervous system* is made up of the nerves that go to and from the CNS and the sense organs, muscles, visceral organs, and the like. The peripheral nervous system in turn consists of two parts. The *somatic nervous system* of sensory nerves transmits information from the skin, muscles, and joints to the CNS, and carries motor impulses from the CNS to the muscles, where they initiate action. The *autonomic nervous system* runs to and from internal organs, and regulates basic physical processes such as breathing, heart rate, and digestion as well as emotion. The autonomic system

---

[1] This chapter is based in part on Guyton (1991).

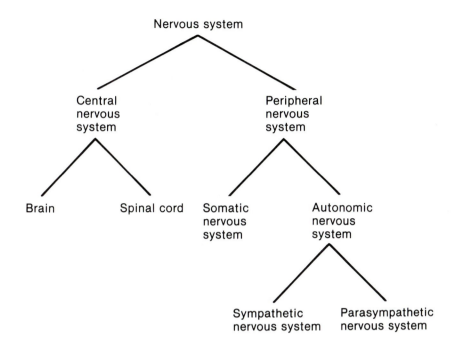

FIGURE 3.1   The nervous system.

in turn consists of the *sympathetic branch*, which contributes to stress arousal, and the *parasympathetic branch*, which generally contributes to the body's everyday "house-keeping" functions (breathing, heart rate, digestion) as well as recovery from stress. These two systems often have opposite physiological effects; for example, the sympathetic system increases heart rate, while the parasympathetic system decreases it.

The Brain

The brain is often described as having layers: a primitive *central core*, the *limbic system* that surrounds it, and the outer *cerebral hemispheres* (see Figure 3.2). Millions of years ago, the brain of dinosaurs consisted of a central core and little else. However, it was a brain that served them well. Generally, it enabled early (and contemporary) reptiles to register and respond to the physical challenges of the world automatically or "instinctively." Areas of the central core are "programmed" to control such basics as muscle coordination, heart rate, blood circulation, and respiration, as well as certain behaviors that are more or less automatic and stereotyped in lower animals (for example, hunting, homing, mating, and routine activities). Two key stress-related components of the central core are the hypothalamus and the reticular system.

The central core is surrounded by the limbic system. This system appeared more recently than the central core at about the time of mammals. It has a variety of functions, some related to the control of stereotyped "instinctive" behavior, the memory of new events, and emotion, such as aggression and pleasurable feelings including sexual excitement.

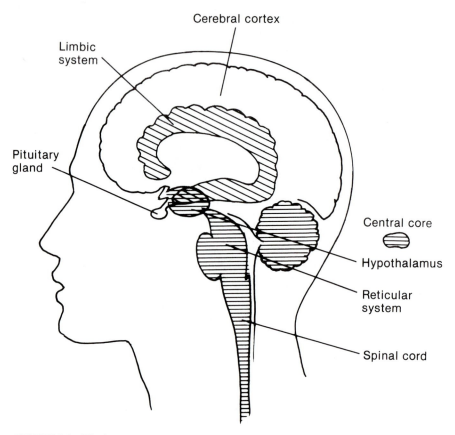

FIGURE 3.2   The brain.

The most recently evolved part of the brain, which is most fully developed in humans, is the cerebral cortex. The word *cortex* means *bark*, and the cerebral cortex is a barklike layer of neurons covering the rest of the brain. It is responsible for complex behaviors most associated with humans, such as perception, thought, language, and memory. In the cortex, stimuli are appraised as threatening or benign, and coping resources are appraised and utilized.

The Nervous System and Stress

The Hypothalamus

To understand stress, we begin with the *hypothalamus*, a part of the central core of the brain often called the "stress trigger." The hypothalamus evokes both the nervous and endocrine system responses to stress; its posterior medial (back and central) zone stimulates stress arousal, whereas the anterior lateral (front and side) zone inhibits stress. The hypothalamus is not so much a separate organ as a combination of nuclei or nerve centers with no distinct boundary. It is strategically located in the very center of the brain and communicates with the rest of the central core, as well as the limbic system and cortex. In addition, the hypothalamus has many regulatory functions that are often deeply affected by stress. It governs eating, drinking, and sexual behavior. It regulates the discharge of important hormones into the bloodstream. And it helps maintain the body's *homeostasis*, or the proper balance of activity of the various organs. Because of its central placement and many functions, the hypothalamus indeed plays a central role in stress.

The Sympathetic System

When triggered by stress, the hypothalamus sets off an alarm response through the *sympathetic branch* of the autonomic nervous system. Simultaneously, all organs associated with the sympathetic branch are aroused and energized for what Cannon (1929), an early stress expert, called the *fight-or-flight response*. Sometimes this reaction is called *mass discharge*, since so many changes are associated with it. The heart beats more quickly and pumps more blood with each beat, thus increasing blood pressure. Stored fats are broken down in the bloodstream into usable fatty acids and glycerol, while the liver increases glucose production, all essential fuels for emergency action. Breathing rate increases, and the bronchial breathing tubes dilate to facilitate the increase flow of oxygen needed to metabolize, or "burn," fuel. To conserve energy, nonessential activities are curtailed. Peripheral blood vessels, such as those in the hands, feet, and gastrointestinal tract, constrict, so that more blood is available for the brain, heart, and skeletal muscles. Salivary secretion and digestive processes decrease. The pupils of the eyes enlarge, improving the ability to see.

The Adrenal Medulla

To augment this emergency response, the hypothalamus triggers the *adrenal medulla*, the inner portion, or "kernel," of the adrenal glands found above the kidneys, to secrete two *catecholamines*: *epinephrine* (or adrenaline) and *norepinephrine* (or noradrenaline). Together the catecholamines maintain and facilitate sympathetic nervous system changes. For example, epinephrine appears to be associated with mental and emotional stress, and causes the constriction of blood vessels in the stomach and intestines, dilates vessels to the muscles, makes the heart beat faster (which you might note during an "adrenaline rush"), dilates coronary arteries in breathing tubes to increase oxygen consumption, and stimulates fat tissues and the liver to release even more glucose fuel for increased metabolism. Norepinephrine has similar functions, although it seems to require higher levels of stress to evoke and is more sensitive to physical stressors such as exercise and cold (Frankenhaeuser, 1975, 1979). In addition, norepinephrine may be less involved in the production, release, and metabolism of glucose.

The Limbic System

So far we have discussed the basic alarm, or energizing, portion of the stress response. In fact, much more is going on during stress arousal. First, the *limbic system*, responsible for many emotions as well as feelings of pleasure and displeasure, adds an important dimension of emotion and feeling to the stress response. Instead of becoming simply energized for fighting and fleeing, we also experience fear, anger, anxiety, love, and so on.

The Reticular Activation System

In addition, the reticular formation, also called the *reticular activation system* (RAS), has an important effect on arousal and awareness. The RAS is a network of neurons that extend from the spinal cord through the central core. It is a two-way communication network that carries and filters messages to and from the body and brain. But the RAS is more than a neutral telephone cable. It can contribute to increased or decreased arousal or alertness. Electrical stimulation of the RAS in different ways can lead to increased excitement or sleep; surgical lesions on the RAS can even cause an animal to go into coma. In addition, the RAS can focus or block attention of stimuli. All sense organs have nerve fibers that run through the reticular system. As a result, the RAS can let some sense messages pass to the cerebral cortex (where it can be consciously processed) and block others. The effects of this can be dramatic: during a football game or while concentrating on an exam, you might not notice the distractions around you or the pain of a toothache.

Much of this system is capable of prolonged activation, or reverberation. For example, epinephrine acts on the reticular system, which in turn excites the sympathetic nervous system, which results in the secretion of more epinephrine. Such feedback is one reason why it can take time for stress to subside even after a stressful situation has passed. In addition, the RAS awakens and arouses the brain and the body in preparation for potential action.

Finally, when one is chronically excited, transient elevations in arousal can become more enduring, and one acquires a lowered threshold for arousal. Gellhorn (1970) has termed this sympathetic, or "ergotropic," tuning (*ergo* means "work," indicating that the body is tuned for the "work" of fight or flight). In contrast, when the parasympathetic system becomes characteristically dominant, resulting in greater relaxation, the body can be said to be "trophotropically tuned" (*tropho* means "nourish," suggesting stress recovery mediated by the parasympathetic nervous system). As we shall see in Chapter 7, excessive ergotropic tuning may contribute to a wide range of illnesses. Some (Benson, 1975) have suggested that various relaxation exercises can help decrease ergotropic tuning and restore a more healthful level of trophotropic tuning.

The Parasympathetic System

In time, the *parasympathetic branch* of the autonomic system helps prepare the body for recovery. In contrast to the sympathetic system, the parasympathetic does not respond with mass discharge but acts specifically on specific organs. It increases the action of some and inhibits the action of others. Generally, parasympathetic stimulation slows the action of the heart, dilates peripheral blood vessels, increases gastrointestinal activity, constricts bronchial passages, and increases salivation. Overall, the parasympathetic system helps return the activity of organs to homeostasis after stress. There are some important exceptions. For example, during fear and excitement, the sympathetic system is usually dominant. However, at times the parasympathetic system can come into action, producing the not uncommon fear reaction of involuntary urination or defecation. Also, the sympathetic and parasympathetic systems often interact in complex ways.

The Endocrine System and Stress

The nervous system responds to stress very quickly; indeed, a nerve impulse can travel throughout the body in a few hundredths of a second. The working of epinephrine and norepinephrine is a bit slower, generally taking action from 20 to 30 seconds after stimulation and lasting an hour or so. However, the endocrine system consists of glands that react to stress by secreting hormones into the bloodstream (see Figure 3.3). This sluggish process can take minutes or hours to begin, and can persist for days or weeks. We begin again with the hypothalamus.

The Pituitary Gland

The pituitary gland is an outgrowth of the brain that lies just below the hypothalamus and is indeed triggered by the hypothalamus. It is the master gland because of the control it has on the other glands, notably the thyroid gland and the adrenal cortex. It is easy to be confused by all the Latin-derived hormone names. It can help to remember that each long name is actually a code that tells what the hormone is and does. The first part of the name generally tells where the hormone goes. This is usually followed by *tropic* or *tropin*, a word that means that the targeted organ is somehow influenced by the named hormone.

Some pituitary hormones are directly stimulated by nerve impulses from the hypothalamus and have a direct impact on the stress response. *Vasopressin*, secreted by the posterior pituitary, helps regulate kidney functioning, contributes to the constriction of the arteries, and thereby increases blood pressure. However, the major pituitary hormones are activated by hormones from the hypothalamus and have an indirect effect on stress.

In response to stress, the hypothalamus secretes the *corticotropic-releasing hormone* (CRH), which signals the anterior pituitary gland. The anterior pituitary in turn releases the *adrenocorticotropic hormone* (ACTH), the major stress hormone. ACTH travels in the blood to the adrenal cortex (the outside, or "cork," of the glands just above the kidneys) and other organs, and eventually contributes to the release of some thirty stress hormones.

The Adrenal Cortex

The adrenal cortex secretes two important hormones called *corticoids*: the *glucocorticoids* (such as cortisol) and the *mineralocorticoids* (such as aldosterone). Cortisol affects general body metabolism. Its principle function is to promote the conversion of stored proteins and fats to glucose, an essential fuel. Also, cortisol enables the muscles and fatty tissues to burn less glucose (which can be important for diabetics, because this effect makes the body insulin-resistant). The increased release of fatty acids in the bloodstream can contribute to an accumulation of fatty tissues on the arteries, which can lead to atherosclerosis and heart disease.

If stress is prolonged, glucocorticoids also affect the body's ability to respond to injury and infection. Cortisol inhibits inflammation, an important protective function of the immune system (Chapter 7). It also inhibits both the production and

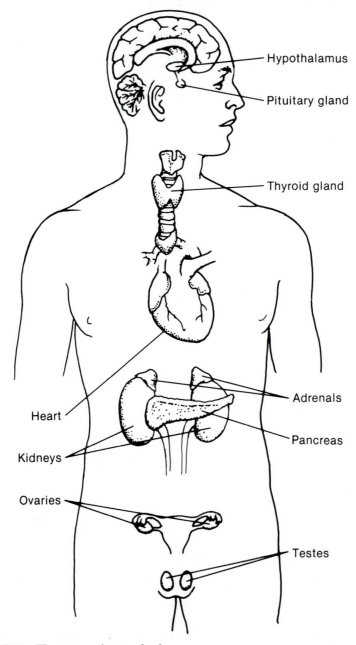

FIGURE 3.3   The major endocrine glands.

ability of illness-fighting blood cells to reach their destination, and shrinks the thymus, spleen, and lymph nodes (organs responsible for production of such cells). For these reasons, cortisol is often called an *anti-inflammatory corticoid*. As a result, muscular wasting and decreased resistance to disease can occur during prolonged stress.

Finally, one glucocorticoid, 17-hydroxycorticoid (or 17-OHCS), appears to be related to subjective feelings of anxiety associated with stress.

The mineralocorticoid aldosterone helps regulate the level of minerals in the body such as sodium, potassium, and chloride. Such minerals are retained in body tissues rather than passed through perspiration and urine. This mineral buildup contributes to the body's preparation for action during stress by increasing blood pressure and facilitating the efficient dissipation of heat and waste products and enhancing the transport of food and oxygen (just as turning up the pressure on the garden hose increases the flow of water to garden flowers). However, the risk of high blood pressure and heart disease is increased (see Chapter 7). Aldosterone is also termed a *pro-inflammatory corticoid*, since it can also promote inflammation.

The Thyroid Gland

The hypothalamus secretes other hormones as well. One is the *thyrotropin-releasing hormone* (TRH), which, as the name suggests, stimulates the anterior pituitary to secrete the *thyrotropic hormone* (TTH). TTH in turn stimulates the thyroid glands (the base of the throat) to secrete *thyroxine*. Thyroxine contributes to the stress response in many ways, including increasing the release of fatty acid fuels. The metabolism or burning of these fuels through increased breathing, heart rate, and blood pressure increases anxiety and decreases feelings of fatigue.

The Pancreas

The final gland we shall consider, the *pancreas*, is not directly controlled by the hypothalamus and pituitary gland. Located next to the stomach, it secretes glucagon and insulin in response to blood glucose levels. Glucagon stimulates the release of additional sugars into the blood. This is essential, since blood sugars are quickly burned for energy under stress and must be replenished. Insulin works in the opposite way. When blood sugar levels are too high, insulin promotes the storage of sugar in the liver, muscles, and fat tissue. When blood sugars are low, as they are when they are being burned under stress, less insulin is produced. Since epinephrine generally contributes to the release of additional blood sugars, it directly reduces insulin production.

Figure 3.4 provides a diagram of the complete stress response.

Neurotransmitters and Stress

Some exciting recent research on stress has focused on the role of *neurotransmitters*. Put simply, neurons must have a way of communicating with each other. They do not do so electrically but by means of chemical neurotransmitters. One neuron releases a neurotransmitter, and, if a receiving neuron has a matching receptor site, communication can take place. Basically, two types of messages can be sent: neurotransmitters can either excite or inhibit the firing of neurons.

There are dozens of neurotransmitters, which generally fall into three categories. The first, classical neurotransmitters, such as acetylcholine, norepinephrine (to be distinguished from the norepinephrine that is secreted by the adrenal medulla,

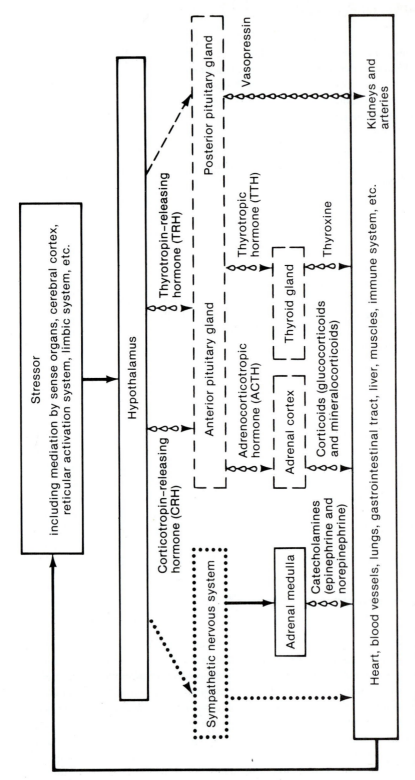

FIGURE 3.4 The complete stress response.

which generally does not cross the blood-brain barrier except in the hypothalamus), dopamine, and serotonin, have been known for quite some time. The second, amino acid neurotransmitters, are composed or derived of a single amino acid; they include glutamic acid, aspartic acid, glycine, and gamma-aminobutyric acid. The third, the neuropeptides, are composed of short amino-acid strings called peptides. One interesting type of neuropeptides, the endorphins, has been the subject of considerable research.

Neurotransmitters can help us understand one frequent stress response: depression. Depression may result from abnormally low levels of norepinephrine in the brain. The bulk of the evidence for this hypothesis is based on the observation that many drugs that relieve depression also increase brain norepinephrine levels. A second hypothesis suggests a role for serotonin, since other antidepressant drugs increase brain levels of this neurotransmitter.

Severe stress can often reduce pain. Considerable anecdotal evidence exists of injury during battle, athletics and medical emergencies that initially causes little pain. Such stress-induced analgesia may be due to the release of endorphins in the brain. Such substances have an effect very much like that of the opium family of painkillers, morphine and heroin. In fact, the term *endorphin* stands for "*endo*genous (or self-produced) mor*phine*." Research on endorphins has been extensive and exciting, and suggests that a wide range of situations, including hypnosis, acupuncture, sexual arousal, and prolonged exercise, may well contribute to self-induced analgesia.

Generality Versus Specificity

The General Adaptation Syndrome

The stress response we have been describing is general and global (Selye, 1956; Wolff, 1950). Through the principle of mass discharge, a wide array of organs are aroused simultaneously. Perhaps the most encompassing generality model is Selye's (1956) *general adaptation syndrome* (GAS). This syndrome can be evoked by a wide range of stressors, including cold, heat, poison, and trauma, and consists of three stages: alarm reaction, resistance, and exhaustion. The alarm reaction has two phases. In initial shock, temperature and blood pressure as well as blood fluid and potassium levels decline, and muscles slacken. The second phase of the alarm reaction, countershock, is essentially the stress arousal response described earlier.

The organism cannot maintain high levels of shock or countershock for long. Indeed, under severe stress, shock and countershock can lead to death. However, under less serious conditions, the organism enters a stage of resistance. Here, ACTH continues to be secreted, most notably corticoids that increase immune system functioning. The adrenal glands grow large as a result of their increased activity. As resistance to a specific stressor increases, most physiological processes return to normal, the organism appears to adapt, and the adrenal glands shrink to normal size. In the stage of resistance, the organism may appear to adapt; however, it is vulnerable. If additional stress is introduced, the animal may be unable to resist and die.

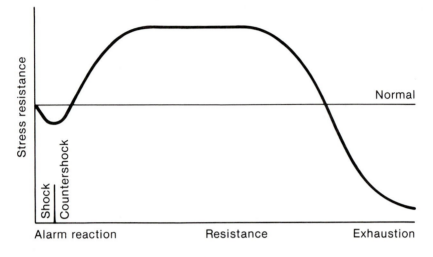

FIGURE 3.5   The stages of General Adaptation Symdrome.

With continued stress, resistance eventually collapses, and exhaustion sets in. The body attempts to deal with stress as it did in the alarm phase, through wholesale, nonspecific arousal. However, resources have already been depleted; for example, the ability of the pituitary and adrenal cortex to function is severely reduced. If stress is prolonged, death may result.

The GAS is a generality model in that Selye proposed that it is displayed by a variety of organisms in a variety of stress situations. However, it permits some specificity. Under extremely severe stress, one may experience heightened states of shock, or countershock, and die. This may well explain perplexing reports of sudden death at times associated with trauma. Others, under less severe stress, may display adaptation and resistance. Once again, the success of resistance is partly a function of the number of stressors present; resistance may be sufficient to cope with one or two stressors, but be overwhelmed by more. In other words, the specificity of Selye's model is that the pattern, stage, and severity of a stress reaction are partly a function of its severity and the number of stressors.

Distress and Eustress

Another element of Selye's theory also suggests specificity. Selye has indicated that the same arousal response can be evoked by quite different situations. *Distress* refers to the potentially destructive effects of the response, whereas the less destructive *eustress* refers to stress perceived to be agreeable or beneficial (Selye, 1975). Not only does this distinction provide for different types of stress, but it makes note of the importance of cognitive variables, a dimension we shall consider in Chapters 4 and 5.

Arousal Specificity

Many researchers believe that the intensity and pattern of stress arousal can be specific, with different types of arousal associated with different types of stress (Mason,

1974, 1975), and different individuals displaying different modes of response (Lacey, Bateman & Van Lehn, 1953).

We have already encountered the notion of specificity in our discussion of neurotransmitters. Specifically, levels of norepinephrine or serotonin may help determine if depression is part of the subjective experience of stress.

There is considerable additional evidence for the specificity of the stress response. For example, the response of the heart to stress can vary depending on whether coping is active or passive (Obrist, 1976), or avoidant or vigilant (Lacey & Lacey, 1978). In addition, different patterns of stress hormone secretion are linked with worry versus denial (Mason, 1975) and anger versus fear (Ax, 1953).

One important variable affecting the pattern of stress arousal may be how a situation evokes effort and distress. Epinephrine appears to be secreted under both conditions. This can involve a combination of effort and distress (as experienced by workers engaged in difficult and unpleasant assembly line or computer work), effort without distress (a more positive state characterized by active and successful coping, job involvement, and personal control), and distress without effort (associated with negative feelings of depression, helplessness, loss of control, and giving up). In contrast, cortisol may be more specific and appear only when there is distress, such as feelings of anxiety or depression (Frankenhaeuser, 1986; Frankenhaeuser et al; 1978). Put differently, cortisol may be more associated with situations that call for effort but for which control is not possible.

The evidence for specificity is strengthened by studies that have found low correlations among simultaneously measured autonomic nervous system organ reactions to stress (Lazarus, Speisman, Mordkof & Davison, 1962). Indeed, heart rate can even be conditioned to rise while blood pressure falls, and vice versa (Shapiro, Tursky, & Schwartz, 1970). The picture is rendered even more complex by findings that show that patterns of arousal may differ according to time. For example, Natelson, Krasnegor, and Holaday (1976) demonstrated that behavioral and cortisol measures of arousal converged and diverged, depending on at what point in a stressful situation they were measured. When monkeys are subjected to many electric shocks, they first tend to display avoidance behavior, and their performance on various tasks is poor. Here both cortisol levels and behavioral signs of arousal are high. Later, the behavioral signs may remain high, but cortisol becomes low.

Gender and Specificity

Although men and women differ in many ways, little research has been directed toward differences in stress arousal. Research has found that, compared to women, men display larger increases in blood pressure but smaller increases in heart rate when under stress (Baum & Grunberg, 1991). Men also exhibit increased levels of catecholamines during acute stress (Matthews, Davis, Stoney, Owens, & Caggiula, 1991). Injections of the corticotropin-releasing hormone appear to elicit larger pituitary responses and greater secretion of the adrenocorticotropic hormone for women (Baum & Grunberg, 1991); however, this increased ACTH appears to be associated with longer-lasting but not larger elevations of cortisol. Some of these physiological differences may be associated with the relative presence or absence of the female sex hormones estrogen and progesterone and the male sex hormone testosterone.

The overall implications of the generality versus specificity controversy are profound. At the very least they make it clear that a thorough understanding of stress must consider factors in addition to physiological arousal. For example, elevated heart rate does not tell us whether a person is responding to bad news from home or bad news in a mystery novel; the same physiological response can be associated with situations of differing degree of stressfulness. In addition, elevations in one stress response system do not enable us to predict which, if any, response systems will be elevated later. And different people can display different patterns of arousal to the same external situations. To understand stress fully, we must consider the complete picture-patterns of arousal as well as external circumstances, cognitive appraisals, and coping resources. These are issues we will consider in later chapters.

An Overview of Stress Arousal Research

The stress arousal system is indeed very complex, and is getting even more complex with new discoveries each year. However, it is useful to take an overall look at what is happening. Recall Cannon's (1929) useful observation that the stress response prepares us to *fight* or *flee*. Just what is necessary for such emergency action? First, fuels in the form of glucose sugars, fats, and proteins must be released from fatty tissues, the liver, the muscles, and so on. Second, oxygen must be taken in so the fuel can "burn" through metabolism. Breathing rate and volume increase, and bronchial air passages dilate. Third, fuel and oxygen must be efficiently transported to where they are needed: the skeletal muscles of the arms and legs that will do the fighting or fleeing. Heart rate quickens, more blood is pumped with each beat, blood pressure increases, salts are retained, and arteries to needed muscles dilate. Fourth, metabolic rate increases as body fuels are burned. Excess heat is carried away through breathing and perspiration. Fifth, functions not absolutely necessary for emergency action are reduced. Stomach and intestinal activity is limited; blood flow to the skin and the gastrointestinal system decreases. Sixth, the body prepares itself for possible injury. Surface blood vessels constrict, reducing the possibility of serious blood loss. Clotting substances are dumped into the bloodstream. The immune system increases activity in anticipation of possible infection, or reduces activity to minimize the potentially damaging effects of infection and to conserve resources for fighting and fleeing. And finally, the body readies itself for active involvement with the outside world. Skeletal muscles tighten, pupils of the eyes dilate to let in more light and enhance vision, the palms and feet become moist to increase grip and traction when running, and brain activity increases. These functions can be summarized in seven words: fuel, oxygen, transport, metabolism, conservation, protection, involvement.

Another way of looking at this complex process is through a metaphor. The nervous system enables us to process information about the world. When stressful information is present, the nervous system responds to meet the challenge, much as an army responds in battle. The emergency warning alarm is the hypothalamus, which immediately sets into motion a constellation of changes contributing to alertness and energy in preparation. Through the sympathetic nervous system, immediate storm troopers are called into action; through the somewhat slower secretion of epinephrine and norepinephrine by the adrenal medulla, reinforcements are brought in. Background music (the "feeling tone," or "drums and trumpets" of battle), is provided by the limbic system, which contributes to positive or negative feelings. The intensity of the overall response (including feeling tone) is evoked by the reticular activating system. Long-term battle preparations are mediated by changes in the endocrine system, specifically the pituitary gland, adrenal cortex, thyroid gland, and pancreas. The cerebral cortex, which acts something like the news media and commanding chiefs at the home front, assess the situation. They process physical arousal and feeling tone, sometimes amplifying them, sometimes inhibiting them, with conscious thoughts. The cortex can trigger a new threat or conclude that a threat is not present.

APPLICATION BOX 3.1

Stress Arousal Symptoms

Stress arousal is often revealed through physical stress symptoms. Often we discount such symptoms as part of life's nuisances. For example:

Roberta is bothered by cold, sweaty hands. It is a problem that seems to come and go. She puts up with it, figuring that the symptom has little meaning.

The first step in discovering the hidden meaning of symptoms is to recognize that they can be stress related. In research I conducted over the years, I examined nearly 1,500 symptoms; surprisingly, I found that virtually all could be linked to stress under certain circumstances. The most common symptoms are (Smith, 1990, 1991; Smith & Seidel, 1982; Smith & Siebert, 1984):

- My heart beats fast, hard, or irregularly.
- My breathing feels hurried, shallow, or uneven.
- My muscles feel tight, tense or clenched up (furrowed brow, making fist).
- I feel restless and fidgety (tapping fingers or feet, fingering things, pacing, shifting in seat, chewing or biting, blinking).
- I feel tense or self-conscious when I say or do something.
- I perspire too much or feel too warm.
- I feel the need to go to the rest room even when I don't have to.
- I feel uncoordinated.
- My mouth feels dry.
- I feel tired, fatigued, worn out, or exhausted.
- I have a headache.
- I feel unfit or heavy.
- My back aches.
- My shoulders, neck, or back feels tense.
- The condition of my skin seems worse (too oily, blemishes).
- My eyes are watering or teary.
- My stomach is nervous and uncomfortable.
- I have lost my appetite.

(continued)

Which symptoms (if any) have you experienced?

_____

_____

_____

_____

_____

The process of further uncovering the meaning of stress symptoms can involve asking a series of questions.

1. Symptoms can be indicators of activation of the stress arousal (for example, rapidly beating heart). Roberta's cold and sweaty hands could be the result of constriction of blood vessels to the extremities, a part of the fight or flight response. Can you explain how your symptoms might be linked to arousal?

2. Symptoms can under some circumstances actually contribute to coping, and in other circumstances cause problems. Returning to Roberta, cold sweaty hands can actually be useful in some circumstances. How? Moisture actually improves our ability to firmly grip objects. For example, baseball players often spit in their palms before grabbing a bat. If Roberta needed to grab a stick (perhaps to ward off a neighborhood dog), sweaty hands would be an asset. However, her stress symptom also has costs, primarily discomfort. What are the benefits and costs of your stress symptoms?

3. Some symptoms are immediate (hurried breathing) whereas some are somewhat more direct and delayed (headaches, fatigue). Roberta's cold and sweaty hands are rather immediate symptoms. What are yours?

4. Symptoms can be early warning indicators of a potential stress situation. And symptoms can be indicators of the lingering aftereffects of stress situations that at first appearance might be over. After charting her symptoms for a number of days, Roberta discovered a pattern: her hands became cold and sweaty before she talked with an authority figure, such as a teacher. Describe how your symptoms can be understood as an early warning sign or lingering aftereffect.

References

Ax, A. F. (1953). The physiological differentiation between fear and anger in humans. *Psychosomatic Medicine, 15*, 433–442.

BAUM, A., & GRUNBERG, N. E. (1991). Gender, stress, and health. *Health Psychology, 10*, 80–85.

BENSON, H. (1975). *The relaxation response.* New York: Avon.

CANNON, W. B. (1929). *Bodily changes in pain, hunger, fear, and rage.* New York: Appleton.

FRANKENHAEUSER, M. (1975). Experimental approaches to the study of catecholamines and emotion. In L. Levi (Ed.), *Emotions: Their parameters and measurement* (pp. 209–234). New York: Raven Press.

FRANKENHAEUSER, M. (1979). Psychoneuroendocrine approaches to the study of emotion as related to stress and coping. In H. E. Howe & R. A. Dienstbier (Eds.), *Nebraska symposium on motivation–1978* (pp. 123–161). Lincoln: University of Nebraska Press.

FRANKENHAEUSER, M. (1986). A psychobiological framework for research on human stress and coping. In M. H. Appley & R. Trumbull (Eds.), *Dynamics of stress* (pp. 101–116). New York: Plenum.

FRANKENHAEUSER, M., VON WRIGHT, M. R., COLLINS, A., VON WRIGHT, J., SEDVALL, G., & SWAHN, C. G. (1978). Sex differences in psychoendocrine reactions to examination stress. *Psychosomatic Medicine, 40*, 334–343.

GELLHORN, E. (1970). The emotions and the ergotropic and trophotropic systems. *Psychologische Forschung, 34*, 48–94.

GUYTON, A. C. (1991). *Textbook of medical physiology* (8th ed.). Philadelphia: W. B. Saunders.

LACEY, B. C., & LACEY, J. I. (1978). Two-way communication between the heart and the brain. *American Psychologist, 33*, 99–113.

LACEY, J. I., BATEMAN, D. E., & VAN LEHN, R. (1953). Autonomic response specificity: An experimental study. *Psychosomatic Medicine, 15*, 71–82.

LAZARUS, R. S., SPEISMAN, J. C., MORDKOF, A. M., & DAVISON, L. A. (1962). A laboratory study of psychological stress produced by a motion picture film. *Psychological Monographs, 76* (34, Whole No. 553).

MASON, J. W. (1974). Specificity in the organization of neuroendocrine response profiles. In P. Seeman & G. Brown (Eds.), *Frontiers in neurology and neuroscience research* (pp. 68–80). Toronto: University of Toronto.

MASON, J. W. (1975). Emotions as reflected in patterns of endocrine integration. In L. Levi (Ed.), *Emotions: Their parameters and measurement,* (pp. 143–182). New York: Raven Press.

MATTHEWS, K. A., DAVIS, M. C., STONEY, C. M., OWENS, J. F., & CAGGIULA, A. R. (1991). Does the gender relevance of the stressor influence sex differences in psychophysiological responses? *Health Psychology, 10*, 112–120.

NATELSON, B. H., KRASNEGOR, N., HOLADAY, J. W. (1976). Relations between behavioral arousal and plasma cortisol levels in monkeys performing repeated free-operant avoidance sessions. *Journal of Comparative and Physiological Psychology, 90*, 958–969.

OBRIST, P. A. (1976). The cardiovascular-behavioral interaction as it appears today. *Psychophysiology, 13*, 95–107.

SELYE, H. (1956). *The stress of life.* New York: McGraw-Hill.

SELYE, H. (1975). Confusion and controversy in the stress field. *Journal of Human Stress, 75* (1), 37–44.

SHAPIRO, D., TURSKY, B., & SCHWARTZ, G. E. (1970). Differentiation of heart rate and blood pressure in man by operant conditioning. *Psychosomatic Medicine, 32*, 417–423.

SMITH, J. C. (1990). *Cognitive-behavioral relaxation training: A new system of strategies for treatment and assessment.* New York: Springer.

SMITH, J. C. (1991). *Stress scripting: A guide to stress management.* New York: Praeger.

SMITH, J. C. & SIEBERT, J. R. (1984). Self-reported physical stress reactions: First- and second-order factors. *Biofeedback and Self-Regulation, 9,* 215–227.

SMITH, J. C. & SEIDEL, M. M. (1982). The factor structure of self-reported physical stress reactions. *Biofeedback and Self-Regulation, 7,* 35–47.

WOLFF, H. G. (1950). Life stress and body disease: A formulation. In H. G. Wolff, S. Wolf, & C. C. Hare (Eds.), *Life stress and body disease* (pp. 137–146). Baltimore: Williams & Wilkins.

CHAPTER 4

Cognitive Models of Stress: Clinical Psychology

The last decade has seen a revolution in the understanding of stress, as early stimulus and arousal theories have been subject to increasing criticism. For example, why are the same stimuli not equally stressful to different people? Why is arousal not always a reliable indicator of stress; one can be aroused while laughing, making love, or being threatened. Recent approaches to understanding stress have focused instead on cognitions, that is, thoughts, worries, perceptions, appraisals, and so on. This is a perspective that has evolved in both clinical and experimental psychology. In this chapter we shall examine theories of stress proposed by those who spend their lives treating psychopathology. We examine two general schools of clinical psychology, the psychodynamic and behavioral approaches.

Psychodynamic Approaches

Current psychodynamic approaches to stress evolved from Sigmund Freud's psychoanalysis. Briefly, psychoanalysis explains behavior in terms of the complexities of instinct, inner conflict, the unconscious, the id, the ego, the superego, and so on. Anxiety, a construct central to Freud's theory, is the result of blockage or delay in the discharge of gratification. Neurotic anxiety serves as a signal of internal conflict, whereas moral anxiety arises from a conflict with the superego, and reality anxiety is associated with threats in the external world.

Contemporary psychodynamic theories place much less emphasis on instinct and the unconscious, and more on the ego, which is the structure of the personality that, among other things, copes with stress. Anna Freud (1965), Sigmund's daughter and one of the first of the contemporary psychodynamic theorists, emphasized the ego's defense mechanisms. Horney (1945), a psychotherapist, focused on the general coping and defensive strategies of moving away from, toward, and against people; White (1959) introduced the concept of effectance motivation, or the inherent drive to master and explore the world. A complete description of these theories is beyond the scope of this book. However, one area of concern to all psychodynamic theories is directly related to stress: defense and the defense mechanisms. In addition, psychodynamic models have had much to say about crises and catastrophes, a topic we shall consider in Chapter 9.

Coping, Defense, and Fragmentation

Although Sigmund Freud focused on unconscious determinants of behavior, contemporary psychoanalytic ego psychology, following the lead of Anna Freud, concentrates more on how people cope to solve problems. Frequently, coping traits are presented in a hierarchy ranging from those that are most mature and presumed to be most healthy, followed by neurotic defenses, and ending with seriously disturbed or psychotically disorganized coping efforts (Horowitz, 1979; Menninger, 1963; Vaillant, 1977). For example, Vaillant groups defenses according to whether they are mature mechanisms (sublimation, altruism, suppression, anticipation, humor), neurotic (intellectualization, repression, reaction formation), immature (fantasy, projection, hypochondriasis, passive-aggressive behavior), or psychotic (denial of external reality, distortion, delusional projection).

Haan (1969) has offered one of the most useful ways of conceptualizing coping strategies. Like the others, she identifies a hierarchy of "ego processes"—coping, defending, and fragmentation. However, she clearly states that such processes can be understood on their own, apart from Freudian theory, and are of interest to psychodynamic and behavior therapists alike. Through coping processes for dealing with stress (Haan, 1982), a person can maintain contact with reality, openly explore a full range of options, consider the consequences of various courses of thinking and action, be creative and flexible, and realistically and appropriately manage and express feelings and desires.

Defensive processes involve some distortion of reality, are less flexible and differentiated, are more disrupted by interfering feelings, and are more likely to seek the satisfaction of urges in ineffective and indirect ways. Finally, fragmented processes are often psychotic and can involve severe distortions of reality, highly rigid behavior, and the inability to manage feelings and desires effectively.

One important feature of Haan's model is that the same generic ego processes can be involved in coping, defense, and fragmentation. For example, one generic process is means-end symbolization, a process that refers to thought about the causal relationship between means and ends. When used in coping, this process is expressed as logical analysis. The defensive use of this process is rationalization, or the application of superficially reasonable explanations that are basically incomplete or incorrect. Confabulation, or the outright invention of illogical or incorrect explanations, represents fragmentation. Similarly, the process of sensitivity, or the perception of external stimuli, is manifest in coping as empathy, as one accurately perceives the thoughts of feelings of others. When used defensively, sensitivity becomes projection, or the unconscious avoidance of anxiety-arousing thoughts and feelings by attributing them to others. Outright delusions, or systems of beliefs that seriously distort reality, represent a fragmented application of sensitivity. Perhaps the key feature distinguishing coping, defense, and fragmentation is the accurate perception of reality, including internal thoughts and feelings as well as external stimuli. In Table 4.1 we can see a further comparison of coping and defense mechanisms.

TABLE 4.1 Generic Cognitive Processes: Coping, Defense, and Fragmentation

Coping Process	Defense Process	Fragmentary Process
Discrimination (separating ideas and feelings)		
Objectivity (realistically and rationally discriminating among thoughts and feelings) EXAMPLE: John is upset over having failed an exam. He decides that such feelings are normal and are a good reason to study harder for the next exam.	Isolation (unconsciously separating thoughts and feelings that belong together so their connection is not seen) EXAMPLE: John has just failed an important exam. Rather than accept his distress, he thinks, "Well, that's how things happen," and appears quite calm and unconcerned.	Tangential concretisms (illogically following one highly concrete idea or feeling with another) EXAMPLE: John, who is under treatment for schizophrenia, utters a jumbled sequence of words, "Well, exams are paper, trees are wood."
Means-ends symbolization (making connections between causes and effects)		
Logical analysis (carefully analyzing problems and their causes). EXAMPLE: Susan is driving though a strange city and is lost. She thinks, "Let's figure out what I can do. First, I'll look for a service station. Then I'll ask for directions."	Rationalization (creating artificial explanations of cause-effect relations to obscure threatening feelings) EXAMPLE: Susan, after getting lost, thinks, "I'm not really lost. I just somehow discovered a longer route to where I am going."	Confabulation (conjuring up an illogical explanation) EXAMPLE: Susan, who is under treatment for psychotic symptoms, thinks, "I don't know where I'm going. The car has made up its mind and is taking me where it wants."
Delayed response (inhibiting an urge to complete a course of action)		
Tolerance of ambiguity (continuing to function in the face of ambiguity) EXAMPLE: Martin has to write a report at work and isn't sure what is expected. He decides to start the report anyway and fine-tune it once his questions are clarified.	Severe doubt and indecision (being unable to make decisions or act because of incomplete information) EXAMPLE: Martin, unsure of what to put in his report, spends hours considering various possibilities, even though he has no way of deciding which to use. Eventually he quits writing his report.	Immobilization ("freezing," not being able to think or act) EXAMPLE: Martin, who is quite troubled, can't figure out what to put in his report. He sits on his sofa and stares idly into space.

(continues)

TABLE 4.1 *Continued*

Coping Process	*Defense Process*	*Fragmentary Process*

Selective awareness (attending to a task and excluding distractions)

Concentration (putting aside upsetting thoughts and feelings to complete what one is doing) EXAMPLE: Julia has just broken up with her boyfriend. Although upset, she puts these feelings aside when studying.	Denial (refusing to acknowledge threatening events, thoughts and feelings) EXAMPLE: Julia, having broken up with her boyfriend, thinks, "No, I haven't really broken up. He still loves me. I'm not at all upset."	Fixation, distraction (intensely directing attention to an irrelevant stimulus or flitting from one intense concern to another) EXAMPLE: Julia becomes preoccupied with voices she hears (at times a psychotic symptom).

Sensitivity (perceiving the external reality of others' thoughts and feelings)

Empathy (accurately sensing and reporting what others are thinking and feeling) EXAMPLE: George is talking to a co-worker who has just been irritated by an irate customer. George observes, "I can tell the customer got you pissed off."	Projection (misattributing one's own threatening motives, feelings, or characteristics onto others, thereby distorting one's perception of them) EXAMPLE: George, who is angry at his co-worker for having left early last week, listens to his colleague's complaints and thinks, "Why is he so angry at me?"	Delusional thinking (holding beliefs that are seriously inconsistent with reality) EXAMPLE: George, who will see his therapist tomorrow, thinks, "Why does he want to control my thoughts through telepathy [delusion of persecution]? Boy, he'll be surprised when he discovers I can control his thoughts through telepathy [delusion of grandeur]."

Temporal reversal (reexperiencing and reenacting past experiences, including thoughts, feelings, and behaviors)

Regression in the services of the ego (engaging in adaptive, creative and childlike playfulness) EXAMPLE: Sandra is driving her friend home from work when the car breaks down. At first, neither knows what to do. Then, for a few minutes both start giggling. Sandra jokes, "Let's paint the word "HELP!" on the road. That will get us attention!" They then start brainstorming ideas.	Regression (retreating to earlier and less mature patterns of behavior to avoid present threat) EXAMPLE: Sandra, after experiencing a car breakdown, bows her head and starts crying uncontrollably.	Decompensation (acting out helplessness through seriously maladaptive behavior) EXAMPLE: Sandra starts wandering down the highway, singing gospel songs.

Impulse diversion (expressing an impulse or urge through a substitution)

Sublimation (finding satisfying and appropriate substitutions for urges that may be threatening or inappropriate if directly expressed)
EXAMPLE: John has been hiking alone for a week. He is feeling lonely and finds it helpful to spend a few hours every night writing letters to his friends.

Displacement (finding less satisfying and mal-adaptive substitutions for pent-up feelings)
EXAMPLE: John, hiking along, kicks his family photo and vents his frustration: "It's all your fault! Why did you make me such a lonely person?"

Preoccupation (reacting with considerable emotional intensity to a random assortment of people and situations)
EXAMPLE: John starts screaming at the trees, squirrels, and any other hikers he may find.

Impulse transformation (substituting one set of thoughts and feelings for what one actually thinks and feels)

Substitution (substituting one thought or feeling for another to meet the demands of the situation)
EXAMPLE: Gretchen has just been hired as a secretary. The first week her boss asks her to "do a favor" and bring him a cup of coffee. She feels insulted and enraged, but is not sure to what extent she can share her feelings without jeopardizing her new job. She politely brings him coffee and continues her work.

Reaction formation (preventing awareness of expression of threatening feelings by unconsciously adopting the opposite)
EXAMPLE: Gretchen, who is at first angry because her boss has asked her to bring him coffee, unconsciously forgets her feelings and tells him, "Just let me know what I can do to help. I like these little jobs so much."

Unstable alteration (vacillating between extremely immature uncivil expressions of feelings and more appropriate behavior
EXAMPLE: Gretchen breaks down and starts crying, "You're such a bastard! A real pig!" A minute later, she collects herself and calmly announces, "Let me bring you a cup of coffee so we can work." A minute later she begins sobbing profusely. This strange behavior continues until she is hospitalized.

Impulse restraint (withholding expression of a feeling)

Suppression (consciously putting aside uncomfortable thoughts and feelings)
EXAMPLE: Jerome has applied for a graduate program and is interviewing with the department chair. He realizes his shirt is wrinkled because his roommate had not ironed it as he had promised he would do. Jerome's first urge is to swear. He quickly puts this thought aside because of the situation.

Repression (unconsciously blocking painful thoughts and feelings)
EXAMPLE: Jerome realizes his shirt is wrinkled. The fact that this problem is his roommate's fault doesn't even cross his mind. He thinks, "Darn, why did I pick a wrinkled shirt to wear?"

Depersonalization, amnesia (restraining feelings to the point of losing track of what one is or has been doing and even of who one is)
EXAMPLE: Jerome, now getting upset in the interview, can't remember (amnesia) what he has been studying or working on for the past year.

Defensive Traits

Each defense strategy we have considered can be described as a *defensive trait*, that is, a general disposition to deal with stress in a particular way. Recent research has focused on several such traits.

DENIAL.   Denial is generally viewed as a refusal to acknowledge, a disowning or disavowal of painful stimuli. Originally, denial was viewed as an element of all defenses directed toward the external world, including projection, displacement, isolation, and undoing. It was contrasted with defenses directed toward internal stimuli, such as repression. More recent conceptualizations have loosened to include both internal and external threats. For example, Breznitz (1982) notes seven levels of denial, including denial of provided information ("No one ever warned me that this problem would happen."), denial of information about a threat ("No one told me there was something to be concerned about."), denial of personal relevance ("This problem just doesn't apply to me."), denial of urgency ("I've got plenty of time to deal with the problem."), denial of vulnerability ("So what if it does happen—it can't happen to me."), denial of emotion ("So it happened; I'm not upset."), and denial of emotion's relevance ("Gosh, I have no idea why I feel so depressed.").

REPRESSION-SENSITIZATION.   Repression-sensitization is another coping trait that has received considerable attention among researchers (Byrne, 1961). Repressors prefer to deal with stress through avoidance, that is, by knowing little and not wanting to know. In contrast, sensitizers prefer approach over avoidance. As one might expect, repressors report less distress in a stressful situation but display greater levels of stress-related skin conductance. Sensitizers report more distress and display lower skin conductance (Cook, 1985). In addition, research shows that when undergoing a stressful medical exam, sensitizers showed reduced anxiety if they were given preparatory information. In contrast, repressors did best when left alone (Shipley, Butt, & Horwitz, 1979; Shipley, Butt, Horwitz, & Farby, 1978).

A recent trend has been to consider repression and sensitization as separate coping strategies that can be applied either independently or together in different situations. Miller (1980) has found that high *monitors* (those who typically scan for threat-relevant information when under stress) and low *blunters* (those who typically do not distract themselves from threat-relevant information) both prefer to attend to information signaling the nature and onset of electric shock. In contrast, low monitors and high blunters both avoid informational cues and prefer to focus on distractions. High monitors and low blunters are also more likely to spend time attending to information about the quality of their performance in stressful situations. Miller has proposed that high blunters may benefit from distraction, while high monitors may benefit from more information when under stress.

Yet another line of thinking examines stress in terms of *private self-consciousness* (PSC), or the extent to which individuals focus on covert and hidden aspects of the self. Those high in PSC attend more closely to and more accurately detect changes in emotions and physical sensations that may indicate the presence of stress (Carver & Scheier, 1981). Such increased awareness can increase stress for problems that are persistent and perceived as beyond a person's control (see the discussion of outcome expectancies in Chapter 6; see also Frone & McFarlin, 1989).

Finally, a different line of research has suggested two constructs that bear some similarity to repression-sensitization. *Catastrophizers* focus on and exaggerate the negative aspects of a situation, a person's inability to cope, and the possible negative outcomes (Heyneman, Fremouw, Gano, Kirkland & Heiden, 1990). *Noncatastrophizers* appear to benefit from pain management strategies that involve diverting attention from pain to unrelated fantasy. However, catastrophizers find it difficult to divert attention from pain, presumably because they are continually reminded of the pain by catastrophizing thoughts. Instead, they benefit more from strategies that involve first identifying catastrophizing thoughts ("This toothache is the end of the world; I just can't cope!") and then using them as reminders to think thoughts that are less extreme and more realistic ("This is just a toothache; I'll get over it; there's a lot I can do.").

In one sense, catastrophizers are extreme sensitizers and nonblunters. One might speculate that providing them with information about a stressful situation (appropriate for sensitizers and blunters) might trigger catastrophizing thought. As we have seen, noncatastrophizers, like repressors and blunters, may well benefit from attentional diversion strategies.

In considering catastrophizers, we come to an interesting junction in our discussion of clinical approaches to understanding stress. Repression is clearly a psychodynamic construct, whereas catastrophizing comes from a behavioral tradition. Thus, two contrasting traditions consider very similar constructs using similar methodology; this convergence of traditions is a pattern we shall encounter later. But now we need to consider in full behavioral approaches to stress.

Behavioral Approaches

Behavioral approaches focus on what can be observed and measured. Traditional schools concentrated on objective behaviors, their antecedents, and their consequences, whereas more contemporary approaches examined thoughts and cognitions.

Traditional Behavioral Approaches

Traditional behavior therapy attempted to explain behavior objectively in terms of classical and operant conditioning. In *classical conditioning* (Hull, 1951; Pavlov, 1927), behavior is learned through association. A child who is reprimanded every time she approaches the stove will eventually associate the stove with the aversive stimulus. Through such classical conditioning, we may well learn to experience once neutral stimulus situations as stressful. For example, public speaking may stir anxiety because of a traumatic public speaking incident, and driving an automobile may arouse fear because of a previous automobile accident.

In *operant conditioning*, behavior is acquired not so much through association as through preceding cues as well as consequences. Behavior followed by a rewarding consequence (such as praise, money, or food) is acquired. Behavior that is either not rewarded or is punished ceases or extinguishes (Skinner, 1953). One "operates" or performs a behavior to obtain a reward or avoid punishment. Preceding cues, often called discriminative stimuli, serve as warnings as to when such behavior is best performed. A schoolchild learns to be quiet once the teacher enters the classroom (cue), providing the consequence of such behavior is praise. Such cue-behavior-consequence contingencies can also be applied to stress. The excessively driven business executive may have learned that overworking (learned behavior) in the presence of peers (cue) has in the past earned considerable praise (reward). Such stressful behavior may then generalize, or extend to other cues; that is, the business executive may overwork in the presence of family members, church members, and others.

Cognitive-Behavioral Approaches

Cognitive-behavioral therapy, a recent development in behavior therapy that integrates elements of psychodynamic and traditional behavioral thinking (Mahoney, 1977), is central to current behavioral conceptualizations of stress. Specifically, the psychodynamic approach emphasizes *internalism*; the major determinants of behavior are seen as residing inside a person in the form of impulses, desires, and the like. The behavioristic approach focuses on the influence of external events; behavior is largely learned through patterns of reward and punishment, specific signal cues become conditioned triggers for specific behaviors, and so on. The cognitive-behavioral approach accepts both internal and external causes, and maintains that both influence each other through *reciprocal determinism* (Bandura, 1978).

The work of many psychologists forms the foundation for cognitive-behavioral approaches. Rotter (1954), Kelly (1955), and Bandura (1969) emphasized the key cognitive-behavioral idea that conscious thought processes play an important role in mediating behavior. Others, such as Bandura (1969), Kanfer & Gelick-Buys (1991), Mahoney (1974), and Mischel (1973) contributed to work on the psychology of *self-control*, which emphasized that behavior change could occur through self-administered instructions (maintaining records of problem behaviors, attending to environmental stimuli that trigger problems, rewarding and punishing oneself for specific desired and undesired behavior, and so on). Although work on self-control slightly predates contemporary cognitive-behavioral approaches, most of it has progressed concurrently, so that both fields have influenced each other (Masters, Burish, Hollon & Rimm, 1987; Meichenbaum, 1985).

ELLIS AND RATIONAL EMOTIVE THERAPY. The central figures of cognitive-behavioral approaches to stress have been Albert Ellis and Aaron Beck. Ellis developed *rational emotive therapy* (RET) as a treatment for psychological disorders. The fundamental idea of RET is that disorders arise from irrational thinking. This is spelled out in what Ellis (1974; Ellis & Grieger, 1977) describes as his *A-B-C-D-E* paradigm. *A* refers to the *activating* experience, or the external stimulus to which a person is responding. *B* refers to the *beliefs*, thoughts, or self-verbalizations a person displays in response to *A*. *C* refers to the *consequences*, emotions, and behaviors that result from *A*. This portion of Ellis' paradigm holds some similarity to transactional models of stress, which also identify stimulus, intervening cognitions, and responses. In addition, *D* refers to client and therapist efforts at *disputing* beliefs when they are irrational. Such a process involves debating, discriminating, and defining, a "logico-empirical method of scientific questioning, challenging and debating" (Ellis & Grieger, 1977, p. 20). Finally, *E* refers to the *effect* of successfully confronting irrational beliefs, that is, reduced stress.

Irrational thoughts are usually defined as self-defeating, self-destructive, empirically false, or unverifiable. One interesting alternative states that all irrational thoughts are grandiose or erroneously claim evaluations to be facts (Rorer, 1989). Grandiose beliefs hold that *the world or someone or something should be different than it, she, or he is, because one wants it to be.* Examples include, "The world should be fair," "It shouldn't be so hard," "I should be able to do it perfectly," and "You should give me the love and affection I need." Central to all these is the grandiose notion that a person should be able to prescribe how the world should be.

In addition, we all apply evaluations to what we encounter in this world. People are good or bad, actions right or wrong, and subjective feelings wonderful or awful. However, it is irrational to treat our evaluations as if they were objective facts, like color and weight, rather than arbitrary and personal judgments. Put simply, it is rational to say, "You lied, and I think that's bad," when we mean "I don't like the fact that you lied." However, it is irrational to say, "You lied and are therefore an intrinsically bad person." This second judgement treats badness as if it permeates a person to the core. Such *factualized evaluations* become particularly dangerous when applied to a person's own self. Here, a person runs the risk of compromising basic self-acceptance because of specific behaviors, of thinking, "I am a worthless person because I lied," rather than, "I accept myself as basically an OK person; however, I regret my behavior of lying."

Whatever the source of their irrationality, Ellis (1962) claims that such beliefs are common in our culture. Researchers have focused on the following types of irrational thoughts (Lohr, Hamberger & Bonge, 1988):

Demand for approval. "I must be approved of and loved by all significant people in my life."

High self-expectations. "I must be thoroughly competent and adequate in all respects if I am to be worthwhile."

Blame-proneness. "If I (or others) am bad, wicked, or ignorant, then I (or others) should be blamed."

Emotional helplessness. "My unhappiness is caused by others or situations, and I have little or no ability to control my unhappiness."

Anxious overconcern. "If there's a chance that something dangerous or fearsome might happen, I should worry about it."

Problem avoidance. "It's easier to avoid than face certain difficulties and responsibilities."

Dependency. "I need someone stronger than myself to rely on."

Helplessness. "My past is an all-important determinant of my present behavior, and if something once strongly affected me, it will always affect me" (p. 175).

It should be noted that research has not clearly determined that such beliefs are indeed associated with stress and pathology. A person can imagine situations in which thinking, "I need someone stronger than myself to rely on" (dependency), and "It's easier to avoid than face certain difficulties and responsibilities (problem avoidance), could be adaptive. For example, for a patient who has just undergone heart surgery, a little problem avoidance might be a good thing. And for a religious person who is in a situation with genuinely few coping options, relying on a "greater power" may be healthy and useful. We will consider such issues further in the next chapter.

RET places considerable emphasis on *long-range hedonism*, that is, seeking a person's own satisfaction while "keeping in mind that one will achieve one's own best good, in most instances, by giving up immediate gratifications for future gains and by being courteous to and considerate of others, so that they will not sabotage one's own ends" (Ellis, 1962, p. 134).

BECK AND COGNITIVE THERAPY.   Beck's (1967, 1976) cognitive therapy evolved as a treatment for depression, but is now an important part of cognitive-behavioral approaches to understanding stress. Like Ellis, Bech accepts the *A-B-C-D-E* paradigm. Both emphasize the importance of irrational thinking. However, Beck places a greater importance on whether beliefs are adaptive or maladaptive, and on the testing of beliefs against reality through personal experimentation (Hollon & Beck, 1979). In contrast, RET emphasizes reason and persuasion.

Beck has focused on three levels of cognition. The first is *automatic thoughts* (also called internal speech, self-talk, self-statements, internal dialogues, or simply worry), which are defined as the content of a person's mind, self-verbalizations that are often fleeting and unnoticed. Stressful thoughts typically reflect an inability to cope, negative views of the future, questioning and self-doubt, and confusion and worry regarding plans (Kendall & Hollon, 1989). Typical examples include, "I can't stand it any more," "Will I make it?" and "I feel totally confused."

The second level, *cognitive processes*, are the ways in which a person processes stimuli. When cognitive processes result in conclusions that are inconsistent with some objective measure of reality, they are distortions; when they result in negative, stress-producing conclusions about a person's own self, they are biases. Most stress therapists are concerned with negative cognitive biases such as:

Personalization: Arbitrarily viewing yourself as at blame, the focus of others' attention, responsible, or somehow implicated in a stress situation. Examples: "Since my friends are looking at me, they must be thinking about me." "My son scratched the car last night, and it's all my fault."
Polarized thinking: Thinking in all-or-none, dichotomous, either/or categories. Examples: "My teachers either like me or hate me." "I'll fall completely or succeed."
Selective abstraction: Forming conclusions from an isolated detail while ignoring context. Examples: "Joey failed to return my call; therefore he doesn't like me." "I failed the first quiz; therefore I will fail the course."

Arbitrary inference: Making conclusions in the absence of supporting evidence. Examples: "I feel blue; nothing will work out right for me." "I can't walk up and talk to a stranger; they'll think I'm stupid."

Overgeneralization: Holding extreme beliefs based on specific events and inappropriately applying these beliefs to unrelated situations. Examples: "My boss wants me to mail these letters for him. Why does everyone take advantage of me?" "I didn't get that job; I won't ever get a job."

Magnification/exaggeration: Overestimating the significance of negative events. Examples: "I was late for work today; this is the end of the world." "Yesterday I made a silly remark; everyone thinks I'm stupid."

Obviously there is considerable overlap among these categories. However, some distinctions are worth noting. Perhaps selective abstraction, arbitrary inference, overgeneralization, and magnification/exaggeration are the most difficult to differentiate. It may be helpful to think of selective abstraction as drawing conclusions from a small piece of evidence ("Joey failed to return my call; therefore he doesn't like me."), while arbitrary inference involves making conclusions from *no* evidence ("I just have the feeling Joey doesn't like me."). Overgeneralization is the application of conclusions (regardless of whether they are selectively abstracted, arbitrary, or whatever) to situations for which they are irrelevant ("Joey doesn't like me. No one likes me. I just can't succeed anywhere."). Magnification/exaggeration is perhaps the most general category and involves appraising any conclusion (selective, arbitrary, overgeneralized, etc.) as more negative than it really is ("Joey doesn't like me. This is the end of the world. I can't live any more.").

Beck's third level is *cognitive schemata*, which are relatively stable cognitive patterns. These correspond to what Ellis has called beliefs and others have labeled cognitive structures. Schemata that apply only to specific situations ("I am no good at work") are *cognitive sets*, where those that are global or general are *cognitive modes*. For anxiety, a fear or danger mode appears to be overactive, leading to pervasive assessment of threat. Depressed thinking is characterized by a triad of negative views of oneself, the world, and the future.

Finally, I have modestly embellished the views of Ellis and Beck, giving particular emphasis to *cognitive structures* (Smith, 1989, 1990, 1991). Such structures help people identify stimuli quickly, categorize stimuli, obtain information that may be missing or ambiguous, and select coping strategies. In addition, I have suggested that cognitive structures provide a rationale for cognitive processes. For example, a person may overgeneralize and personalize (cognitive processes) because she believes that it is important to be perfect at all times (cognitive structure).

I and others have proposed that structures have a complex and hierarchical organization (Carver & Scheier, 1990, 1990a; Smith 1990, 1991). First, any structure comprises beliefs, values, and commitments. *Beliefs* are enduring thoughts concerning what is factual and real ("Raindrops are made of water, smoking causes cancer, and excessive stress leads to disease."), *values* are enduring thoughts about what is important ("I value my children, my job, and taking time out each day to relax."), and *commitments* are choices made about various courses of action ("I choose to give money to the lodge, eat a low-fat diet, and deal assertively with interpersonal problems.").

Attitudes and *assumptions* are structures of relatively limited domain. Most of the structures considered by Beck, Ellis, and others are at this level. More encompassing structures are *personal philosophies*, overall conceptualizations of what is most deeply real, important, and worthy of action; in addition, personal philosophies organize our attitudes and assumptions. There are at least two types of such encompassing structures: *coping philosophies* and *relaxation philosophies*. Both have a variety of functions:

> Personal philosophies serve many uses. They serve as quick reminders of the coping or relaxation paths we have chosen and inform us when action is or is not called for. They help guide our choices when we are confused. They give us courage to act, even when we may feel too comfortable, depressed, anxious, or irritated to do so. They tell us when sacrifice is needed, and when it is not. In sum, our personal philosophies give us a reason to cope assertively, and a reason to explore the depths of relaxation. And they give us a reason to persevere in the face of possible relapse (Smith, 1991, p. 125).

Empirical Support for Cognitive-Behavioral Approaches

It is important to distinguish between evidence for cognitive theories of stress and cognitive treatments (to be considered in Chapter 15). Generally, research appears to support the basic proposition of cognitive theories that cognitive processes are involved in learning and emotion (Mahoney, 1974). Studies in which subjects engage in negative or irrational thinking tend to support Ellis's *A-B-C-D-E* cognitive learning paradigm, although such work has been criticized for being short on clinical realism (Masters et. al., 1987). Additional research consistently finds that various disturbed populations are more likely to endorse irrational beliefs (Hollon & Kendall, 1980; Nelson, 1977; Rimm, Janda, Lancaster, Nahl & Dittmar, 1977). Such beliefs may contribute to increased emotional distress in the form of a greater quantity and intensity of both inappropriate and appropriate emotion.

However, research support is lacking for the stressfulness of certain beliefs proposed by Ellis (1962), such as the ideas that happiness can be achieved by inertia and inaction or by passively and uncommittedly "enjoying yourself"; a high degree of order or certainty is needed to feel comfortable; or that a reliance on some supernatural power is necessary.

As proposed by Beck (1963; see also Beck & Ward, 1961), depressed individuals do appear to describe themselves in negative terms (Blackburn, 1988) and make negative errors in thinking. In addition, anxious patients are more likely to view ambiguous situations as threatening (Butler & Mathews, 1983), themselves as vulnerable, and the future as unpredictable. Finally, researchers have found that depressed patients are more likely to engage in several forms of dysfunctional thinking and that individuals typically display patterns of dysfunctional thinking across situations (Blackburn & Eunson, 1988). Selective abstraction is most frequently associated with depressed mood and arbitrary inference with anxious mood.

Conclusion

Both psychodynamic and behavioral approaches to understanding stress have evolved somewhat from focusing on global dispositions (such as coping traits, defense mechanisms, and irrational beliefs) to traits (such as monitoring/blunting, cognitive distortions, and automatic thoughts) that are more restricted, and indeed can often be viewed as descriptions of how people actually cope in stressful situations. This focus on coping has also become the primary focus of the scientific study of stress in the laboratory and everyday life rather than in the clinic. In the following chapter we shall examine the work on coping conducted primarily by experimental psychologists.

APPLICATION BOX 4.1

Thinking and Stress

Albert Ellis and Aaron Beck have argued that our thoughts contribute to stress. This can easily be seen in the following example. Two roommates, Bart and Brad, are preparing for a major exam. Both are worried. However, Bart experiences a variety of stress symptoms, including tense shoulders and shortness of breath; Brad feels relatively calm and relaxed. The reason why these roommates are having different reactions to stress becomes clear when we examine what they are thinking. Here are the thoughts running through Bart's mind:

I must get a perfect score on this exam. Anything less than a perfect score and I will be a failure. I won't be able to face my parents.

Here are Brad's thoughts:

I would like to get a perfect score on this exam. However, I can only do my best. I will answer one question at a time, and then deal with the consequences.

How would Ellis and Beck analyze Bart's stress-producing thinking? Ellis might wonder if Bart is engaged in *perfectionistic* thinking. Beck might notice examples of all-or-none thinking. Can you see how Bart's thinking contributes to needless stress?

Now, consider a recent stressful situation in your life. Did your thinking make things worse? First, describe the thoughts that went through your mind in the stressful situation.

How did your thinking contribute to the stressfulness of this situation? Can you see examples of Ellis's irrational assumptions or beliefs, or Beck's stressful negatively biased thinking?

References

BANDURA, A. (1969). *Principles of behavior modification*. New York: Holt, Rinehart and Winston.

BANDURA, A. (1978). The self-system in reciprocal determinism. *American Psychologist, 33,* 344–358.

BECK, A. T. (1963). Thinking and depression: I. Idiosyncratic content and cognitive distortions. *Archives of General Psychiatry, 9,* 324–333.

BECK, A. T. (1967). *Depression: Causes and treatment.* Philadelphia: University of Pennsylvania Press.

BECK, A. T. (1976). *Cognitive therapy and the emotional disorders.* New York: International Universities Press.

BECK, A. T., & WARD, C. H. (1961). Dreams of depressed patients: characteristic themes in manifest content. *Archives of General Psychiatry, 5,* 462–467.

BLACKBURN, I. M. (1988). Cognitive measures of depression. In C. Perris, I. M. Blackburn, & H. Perris, (Eds.), *Cognitive psychotherapy: Theory and practice* (pp. 98–119). Neidelberg: Springer-Verlag.

BLACKBURN, I. M., & EUNSON, K. M. (1988). A content analysis of thoughts and emotions elicited from depressed patients during cognitive therapy. *British Journal of Medical Psychology, 62,* 23–33.

BREZNITZ, S. (1982). The seven kinds of denial. In S. Breznitz (Ed.), *The denial of stress* (pp. 257–280). New York: International Universities Press.

BUTLER, G., & MATHEWS, A. (1983). Cognitive processes in anxiety. *Advances in Behavior Research and Therapy, 5,* 51–62.

BYRNE, D. (1961). The repression-sensitization scale: Rationale, reliability and validity. *Journal of Personality, 29,* 334–349.

CARVER, C. S., & SCHEIER, M. F. (1981). *Attention and self-regulation: A control theory approach to human behavior.* New York: Springer-Verlag.

CARVER. C. S., & SCHEIER, M. F. (1990a). Origins and functions of positive and negative affect: A control-process view. *Psychological Review, 97,* 19–35.

CARVER, C. S., & SCHEIER, M. F. (1990b). Principles of self-regulation. In E. T. Higgins & R. M. Sorrentino (Eds.), *Handbook of motivation and cognition: Foundations of social behavior* (Vol 2, pp. 3–52). New York: Guilford.

COOK, J. R. (1985). Repression-sensitization and approach-avoidance as predictors of response to a laboratory stressor. *Journal of Personality and Social Psychology, 49,* 759–773.

ELLIS, A. (1962). *Reason and emotion in psychotherapy.* New York: Lyle Stuart.

ELLIS, A. (1974). *Humanistic psychotherapy: The rational emotive approach.* New York: McGraw-Hill.

ELLIS, A., & GRIEGER, R. (Eds.), (1977). *Handbook of rational-emotive therapy.* New York: Springer.

FREUD, A. (1965). *Normality and pathology in childhood: Vol 6. of the writings of Anna Freud.* New York: International Universities Press.

FRONE, M. R., & McFARLIN, D. B. (1989). Chronic occupational stressors, self-focused attention, and well-being: Testing a cybernetic model of stress. *Journal of Applied Psychology, 74,* 876–883.

HAAN, N. (1969). A tripartite model of ego functioning: Values and clinical research applications. *Journal of Nervous and Mental Disease, 148,* 14–30.

HAAN, N. (1982). The assessment of coping, defense, and stress. In L. Goldberger & S. Breznitz (Eds.), *Handbook of stress* (pp. 254–269). New York: The Free Press.

HEYNEMAN, N. E., FREMOUW, W. J., GANO, D., KIRKLAND, F., & HEIDEN, L. (1990). Individual differences and the effectiveness of different coping strategies for pain. *Cognitive Therapy and Research, 14*, 63–77.

HOLLON, S. D., & BECK, A. T. (1979). Cognitive therapy of depression. In P. C. Kendall & S. D. Hollon (Eds.,), *Cognitive-behavioral interventions: Theory, research, and procedures* (pp. 153–203) New York: Academic Press.

HOLLON, S. D., & KENDALL, P. C. (1980). Cognitive self-statements in depression: Development of an automatic thoughts questionnaires. *Cognitive Therapy and Research, 4*, 383–395.

HORNEY, K. (1945). *Our inner conflicts*. New York: Norton.

HOROWITZ, M. J. (1979). Psychological response to serious life events. In V. Hamilton & D. M. Warburton (Eds.), *Human stress and cognition* (pp. 235–236). New York: Wiley.

HULL, C. L. (1951). *Essentials of behavior*. New Haven: Yale University Press.

KANFER, F. H., & GAELICK-BUYS, L. (1991). Self-management methods. In F. H. Kanfer & A. P. Goldstein (Eds.), *Helping people change* (4th ed., pp. 305–360). New York: Pergamon.

KELLY, G. A. (1955). *The psychology of personal constructs*. New York: Norton.

KENDALL, P. C., & HOLLON, S. D. (1989). Anxious self-talk: Development of the anxious self-statements questionnaire (ASSQ). *Cognitive Therapy and Research, 13*, 81–93.

LOHR, J. M., HAMBERGER, L. K., & BONGE, D. (1988). The relationship of factorially validated measures of anger-proneness and irrational beliefs. *Motivation and Emotion, 12*, 171–183.

MAHONEY, M. J. (1974). *Cognition and behavior modification*. Cambridge, MA: Ballinger.

MAHONEY, M. J. (1977). Cognitive therapy and research: A question of questions. *Cognitive Therapy and Research 1*, 1–3.

MASTERS, J. C., BURISH, T. G., HOLLON, S. D., & RIMM, D. C. (1987). *Behavior therapy* (3rd ed.). San Diego: Harcourt Brace Jovanovich.

MEICHENBAUM, D. (1985). *Stress inoculation training*. New York: Pergamon Press.

MENNINGER, K. (1963). *The vital balance: The life process in mental health and illness*. New York: Viking.

MILLER, S. M. (1980). When is a little information a dangerous thing? Coping with stressful events by monitoring vs. blunting. In S. Levine & H. Ursin (Eds.), *Coping and health* (pp. 145–169). New York: Plenum.

MISCHEL, W. (1973). Toward a cognitive social learning reconceptualization of personality. *Psychological Review, 80*, 252–283.

NELSON, R. E. (1977). Irrational beliefs in depression. *Journal of Consulting and Clinical Psychology, 45*, 1190–1191.

PAVLOV, I. P. (1927). *Conditioned reflexes: An investigation into the physiological activity of the cortex* (G. V. Anrep, trans.). New York: Dover.

RIMM, D. C., JANDA, L. H., LANCASTER, D. W., NAHL, M., & DITTMAR, K. (1977). An exploratory investigation of the origin and maintenance of phobias. *Behavior Research and Therapy, 15*, 231–238.

RORER, L. G. (1989). Rational-emotive theory: An integrated psychological and philosophical basis. *Cognitive Therapy and Research, 13*, 475–492.

ROTTER, J. B. (1954). *Social learning and clinical psychology*. Englewood Cliffs, NJ: Prentice Hall.

SHIPLEY, R. H., BUTT, J. H., & HORWITZ, E. A. (1979). Preparation to reexperience a stressful medical examination: Effect of repetitious videotape exposure and coping style. *Journal of Consulting and Clinical Psychology, 47*, 485–492.

SHIPLEY, R. H., BUTT, J. H., HORWITZ, B., & FARBY, J. E. (1978). Preparation for a stressful medical procedure: Effect of amount of stimulus preexposure and coping style. *Journal of Consulting and Clinical Psychology, 46*, 499–507.

SKINNER, B. F. (1953) *Science and human behavior.* New York: Macmillan.

SMITH, J. C. (1989). *Relaxation dynamics: A cognitive-behavioral approach to relaxation.* Champaign, IL: Research Press.

SMITH, J. C. (1991). *Stress scripting: A guide to stress management.* New York: Praeger.

SMITH, J. C. (1990). *Cognitive-behavioral relaxation training: A new system of strategies for treatment and assessment.* New York: Springer.

VAILLANT, G. E. (1977). *Adaptation to life.* Boston: Little, Brown.

WHITE, R. W. (1959). Motivation reconsidered: The concept of competence. *Psychological Review, 66*, 297–333.

CHAPTER 5

The Transactional Matrix

In this chapter we complete our review of basic stress concepts. We also introduce a perspective that will serve as the guiding framework for the rest of this text. The *transactional matrix* considers stress not in terms of stimuli, responses, or even cognitions; stress is all of these, and more. But before we can explore this idea, we need to consider the study of emotion.

Why do people feel angry, depressed, or fearful? What are joy, elation, and mirth? At one level, these are emotions we all have. Such emotions are also often the first and best indicators of when we are under stress and when we are coping well. It is not surprising that the experimental psychology of stress began, and indeed continues, with the study of emotion.

Early Theories

James, Lange, and Cannon

James (1890) proposed that our emotions are determined by our perceptions of what we do. He and his contemporary Lange (1922) felt that emotion is a subjective experience determined by awareness of bodily changes in the presence of certain arousing stimuli. A threatening stimulus (an approaching wild dog) triggers physiological reactions (turning and running, a rapidly beating heart, perspiring, and heavy breathing). Our awareness of this physiological response is what we call *emotion* (for example, fear). The James-Lange theory of emotion is actually one of the earliest theories of stress, and it has a cognitive component. The emotional stress response is a *perception*.

Cannon (1927), who, as we saw in Chapter 3, helped outline the stress arousal response, was one of the first to criticize the James-Lange theory. To review, he introduced a theory of emotion that stated that sympathetic nervous system reactions to different arousing stimuli are very similar, even though our emotional reactions are quite different. Given this similarity, emotion cannot be simply the perception of physical responses. Landis and Hunt (1932) offered a similar objection. When subjects are injected with adrenalin, most experience symptoms of sympathetic nervous system activation, that is, sweaty palms, a rapidly beating heart, and so on. According to the James-Lange theory, these physical stimuli should cause specific emotions. However, in reality subjects do not report emotion, but simply physical symptoms or a strange kind of "cold emotion" in which they feel as if they are angry or afraid, but know the emotion is not the real thing.

Schachter and Singer

It is perhaps ironic that research using injected adrenalin not only contributed to the fall of the James-Lange theory but led to its replacement. Schachter and Singer (1962) argued that the situational context suggests interpretations of autonomic arousal and that the resulting cognitive evaluations lead to specific emotions. For example, you may wonder why your heart is racing. If someone has just told a joke, you may appraise the situation as humorous, and interpret your pounding heart as part of your amusement. However, if you realize that a police officer is walking in your direction and that you have double parked, you may interpret your increased heartbeat as fear.

In a famous experiment, Schachter and Singer tested their theory by injecting subjects with adrenalin, which evokes stress arousal. However, the drug was misleadingly described to the subjects as a vitamin. Furthermore, some subjects were accurately informed of what side effects to expect: increased heart rate, flushing, and so on. Thus, when these side effects began to occur, a ready interpretation was available: "it's just the vitamin." Others were misinformed that the side effects were itching and numbness. When they began to experience unexpected effects of rapid heart rate and flushing, they had no ready interpretation.

What followed was the crucial part of the experiment. Subjects were escorted into a separate room for a "test of vision." In fact, some were placed in a room in which a confederate had been secretly instructed to act sullen and irritable. Others were in a room with a confederate who acted frivolous and ebullient. He threw paper airplanes, played with a hula hoop, and played basketball with paper wads. The reason for the two situations was to cleverly suggest to subjects ways to interpret their arousal symptoms. As expected, those who already had an interpretation—that their arousal was produced by a "vitamin"—did not react to the conditions. In contrast, subjects who had no explanation for their arousal had to conclude that their reactions were caused by the situational context. Those in the euphoria condition felt joyful and happy, while those in the angry condition felt irritable. Schachter and Singer concluded that our emotions, and our feelings of stress, result from situationally suggested appraisals, which we then use to interpret arousal. In other words, emotions such as happiness and anger are handy situational explanations given to arousal.

The Schachter and Singer theory, although still quite influential, has been subject to considerable criticism (Kemper, 1978; Marshall & Zimbardo, 1979; Maslach, 1979; Plutchik & Ax, 1967). First, as we have seen, different physiological patterns may well be associated with different emotions; the Schachter and Singer theory presumes a generalized state of arousal that can be labeled in many ways. More seriously, this theory suffers from the very same problems as arousal theories of stress. In real-life situations, when individuals have not been injected with adrenalin, just what is it that induces arousal? Must appraisal come after arousal?

Transactional Approaches

The theories we have described are "cold" (Lazarus & Folkman, 1984) in that they simply describe how arousal, or appraisal, happens. The very same processes, whether they are those described by James and Lange, Cannon, or Schachter and Singer, can occur for nonstressful emotion. Parallel to these theories, a different set of approaches developed in experimental psychology. These can be described as "hot" and place central importance on motivational factors or valued wants that energize and direct our actions.

The Transactional Model of Coping and Appraisal

We shall focus on the Lazarus and Folkman's (1984) transactional model of coping and appraisal. Put simply, they state that we are under stress when something we need or want is threatened and there is not much we think we can do about the situation. Notice that this view of stress always involves some type of transaction concerning needs and wants. Stressful transactions are not unlike life's many other transactions, such as the give-and-take of dealing with problems, negotiating a complex path, bargaining, and debating. This perspective also emphasizes the complexity of a stressful encounter and the ongoing interrelationship among variables.

We can now present a formal definition of the transactional model of stress (Lazarus & Folkman, 1984, p. 19): "*A particular relationship between the person and the environment that is appraised by the person as taxing or exceeding his or her resources and endangering his or her well-being,*" [italics added]. Note that this definition sees stress in terms of cognitive appraisal and coping. Cognitive appraisal is the continuous "categorizing of an encounter, and its various facets, with respect to its significance for well-being" (Lazarus & Folkman, 1984, p. 31). There are two types of appraisal: *primary appraisal* and *secondary appraisal*. Primary appraisal concerns the stakes a person has in a stressful encounter. He asks, "What do I want?" and "Given my wants, am I in trouble or being benefited, now or in the future, and in what way?" There are four types of primary appraisal: benefit, harm/loss, threat, and challenge. An appraisal of benefit means that a person's wants are being met, limiting the possibility for stress. Harm/loss is a perception that some damage has already occurred, such as an injury, illness, or harm to social or self-esteem. An appraised threat is a harm or loss that is anticipated but has not yet taken place. Appraised challenge is similar to threat, except there is a possibility for growth or gain.

Secondary appraisal concerns the options and prospects for coping with a stressful situation. The key question of secondary appraisal is, "What, if anything, could be done about it?" At this point, it is appropriate to note Bandura's (1977, 1982) two components of *self-efficacy: efficacy expectancy*, or the perceived ability or intention (Kirsch, 1985, 1990) to perform a behavior, and *outcome expectancy*, or the belief that a particular behavior will produce a desired outcome. Outcome expectancies can include *stimulus expectancies*, or beliefs about the occurrence of external events (reinforcements such as money, grades, and social approval), and *response expectancies*, or beliefs about potentially rewarding or aversive internal reactions to events (such as joy, pleasure, pain, or fear).

A few examples can clarify these types of appraisal. Consider a student who is very anxious about an upcoming exam. Her primary appraisal may be that the exam threatens the grade point average she wants. Stress may increase if she lacks efficacy expectancy, and believes she does not have the ability to complete the exam or does not intend even to make the effort to complete it. If she believes that clearly written answers, no matter how good, will not help her exam grade, she has low stimulus outcome expectancy (the stimulus being the grade). If she believes that she will remain anxious no matter how well she does, she has low response (anxiety) outcome expectancy.

A different pattern can be illustrated by a boy dealing with the possible pain of dental surgery. His dentist has informed him that the pain will be minimal (response outcome expectancy = low pain). Furthermore, his mother has promised that they will have a special dinner the day after surgery (stimulus outcome expectancy = dinner). Just before surgery, the dentist instructs his patient in a simple pain-reduction coping strategy: "Divert your attention and think about your favorite TV show." As a result, our patient believes he is able to tolerate surgery and intends to go through with it (efficacy expectation = ability and intention to have surgery).

With appraisal a person determines the stakes of a stressful encounter as well as the prospects of coping with it. With coping, a person acts. *Problem-focused coping*

involves planful actions to change a stressful situation by acting on the environment or oneself. Examples include the use of active coping, planning, confrontive coping, self-control, and instrumental social support. *Emotion-focused coping* involves attempting to reduce the upset or discomfort associated with a stressful situation without actively trying to change the situation itself. Some emotion-focused strategies involve changing how attention is deployed. Attention can be diverted from distress through strategies involving distancing, avoidance, or escape. Attention can also be directed toward a stressful situation by accepting reality and responsibility, and by positively reinterpreting the situation.

Some of the most important recent work on coping has focused on specific coping processes applied in specific situations. Three lists of coping strategies are frequently cited in the literature: Moos (1974); Folkman, Lazarus, Dunkel-Schetter, DeLongis, and Gruen (1986); and Carver, Scheier, and Weintraub (1989). No researcher claims his or her listing to be complete; they frequently cite the need for more comprehensive lists or for lists that are tailored to certain situations. Table 5.1 presents one way of cataloging ways of coping.

It is important to recognize that any form of coping can be either problem- or emotion-focused depending on the situation. For example, planning (listed as problem-focused in Table 5.1) can reduce stressful emotion. An individual might spend the hour preceding a stressful exam planning how to approach possible questions. Even though such late-minute planning may have no effect on exam performance, it does serve to reduce anxiety. Similarly, denial (listed as emotion-focused in Table 5.1) can at times be an effective part of changing a stressful situation. A cancer patient who might be demoralized by accepting the full implications of her diagnosis may deny the severity of her disorder and optimistically make important and healthy changes in life style.

Finally, the appraisal process is constantly changing with no clear beginning or ending. A person's perception of threat may be reduced or increased depending on the coping options identified. *Reappraisal* is simply a changed appraisal brought about by new information.

One key feature of the transactional approach is that it considers many interacting variables and prompts us to look at specific stress encounters as well as their antecedents and consequences. This distinguishes the transactional approach from those that preceded it. We can see the difference in an example:

> Terry is in the study hall studying for her midterm exam. It is the night before the test. She worries about how the exam might affect her academic standing and her prospects for receiving a student loan. Although she first feels helpless and overwhelmed, Terry soon decides that such worries are getting her nowhere and that she is quite capable of coming up with a sensible study strategy. She takes a few deep breaths to clear her mind. She then organizes her review for the evening and confronts the challenge of studying for the exam. After taking action, she feels more in control and is more confident that she will pass the exam.

Knowing Terry's primary appraisal (worries about her academic standing and student loan), secondary appraisal (helplessness followed by the decision that she is

TABLE 5.1   Coping Strategies

Problem-focused coping: Attempting to alter a stressful situation through strategies such as the following (Folkman & Lazarus, 1985):

Active coping: Actively attempting to remove or circumvent a stressful situation, or ameliorate its effects. Techniques include taking direct action, increasing effort, and executing a coping plan in reasonable steps.

Planning: Thinking through how one will cope. This involves generating strategies, and selecting and deciding how to implement steps.

Confrontational coping: Standing one's ground, assertively seeking to meet one's needs and wishes, and actively attempting to change the behavior of others.

Suppression of competing activities: Putting other projects aside, trying to avoid becoming distracted by other events, even letting other things slide, if necessary, in order to deal with the stressor. Generally, this involves suppressing involvement in competing activities or thoughts.

Self-control: Trying to keep one's feelings to oneself.

Restraint coping: Waiting until an appropriate opportunity to act presents itself, holding oneself back, and not acting prematurely.

Search for social support for instrumental reasons: Seeking advice, assistance, or information for help in coping with a stressor.

Emotion-focused coping: Attempting to reduce the upset or discomfort associated with a stressful situation without actively trying to change the situation itself.

Some forms of emotion-focused coping involve retaining a more or less accurate appraisal of the facts of a situation, but changing other aspects of the appraisal. Such *reality-based reappraisals* include:

Acceptance of reality: Accepting and living with the fact that a stressful event has occurred, is real, and can't be changed.

Acceptance of responsibility (Folkman & Lazarus, 1985): Assuming that one has brought the problem on oneself.

Positive reinterpretation and growth (termed "positive reappraisal" by Folkman & Lazarus, 1985): Reappraising a stressful situation in positive terms by seeing how it might contribute to learning and growth.

Distancing (Folkman & Lazarus, 1985): Acknowledging a troubling situation but failing to deal with its emotional significance.

Other forms of emotion-focused coping involve taking action to achieve a *substitute satisfaction or tension release*. Strategies include:

Search for social support for emotional reasons: Seeking moral support, sympathy or understanding.

Search for alternative rewards (Moos, 1974): Changing one's activities to obtain satisfactions not available in a stressful encounter.

Reliance on religion: Praying as well as seeking and trusting in a higher spiritual power.

Focus on and venting of emotions: Concentrating on and expressing one's feelings of upset.

Tension reduction: Disengaging from a stressful situation through relaxation or exercise.

Humor: Laughing at and joking about a stressful situation (see also distancing).

(continued)

TABLE 5.1 *(Continued)*

Still other forms of emotion-focused coping involve some *distortion or withdrawal* from the facts of a stressful situation:

Wishful thinking (Folkman & Lazarus, 1985): Simply wishing or hoping that a stressful situation will change or go away.

Denial: Refusing to believe that a stressor exists, or acting as though it is not real or hasn't happened. The opposite of the acceptance of reality.

Behavioral disengagement: Physically giving up or withdrawing effort from attempts to attain the goal with which the stressor is interfering.

Mental disengagement: Psychologically giving up a threatened goal. This often involves engaging in attempts at obtaining substitute satisfaction through such activities as watching TV, daydreaming, sleeping, or self-distraction.

Self-isolation (Folkman & Lazarus, 1985): Avoiding people in general and keeping others from knowing how bad things are.

Alcohol or drug use: Disengaging from a stressor through alcohol or other drugs.

SOURCE   Loosely based on lists presented in Billings and Moos (1984); Carver, Scheier, and Weintraub (1989); Cohen, Reese, Kaplan, and Riggio (1986); Folkman, Lazarus, Dunkel-Schetter, DeLongis, and Gruen (1986); and Moos (1974).

capable of developing a study plan), coping (deep breaths, organizing her review, and studying), and reappraisal (feeling more in control and confident) give us a very rich understanding of her problem. In contrast, earlier stimulus-based, arousal-based, and cognitive approaches to defining stress and emotion would give a less complete portrait:

Stimulus-based account: Terry faces an exam tomorrow. Her instructor assigned the exam a month ago. Terry needs to pass this exam to pass the course. Compared with other life events, such an exam earns about 15 life-change units, not enough to contribute to subsequent illness.

Arousal-based account: Terry faces an exam tomorrow. She is perspiring and has a slight stomach ache caused by the excessive secretion of digestive fluids. If this gastric response were to continue, one might worry that Terry is at risk of developing an ulcer.

Neutral cognitive account (Schachter & Singer, 1962): Terry faces an exam tomorrow. She is sitting in the study hall with other students, who are worried about the exam, and begins perspiring and experiencing stomach discomfort. As others express their concerns and fears, Terry thinks, "Gosh, I'm anxious about this exam." Apparently, being in a room with other worried students gave Terry a ready label for her physical symptoms.

The Transactional Matrix

Lazarus and Folkman (1984) present a broader perspective that looks at appraisal and coping as well as a wide range of additional variables with which stress and coping interact. I have taken the liberty of modifying and expanding their views into a general classification system. The *transactional matrix* identifies three classes of variables involved in stress and coping: situational, personal, and external.

The understanding of stress begins with the identification of a concrete and specific stress situation, for example, the final exam, the interview, the first date, or the
argument with the spouse. With respect to such an encounter, we have already considered four *situational variables* that must be examined:

Primary appraisal
  Needs or wants
  Harm/loss, threat, challenge, benefit
Secondary appraisal
  Appraised coping potential
  Self-efficacy
  Outcome efficacy
Coping
  Problem-focused
  Emotion-focused
Reappraisal

A wide range of additional variables might also influence our understanding of a
stress encounter. Those that contribute or potentially contribute to coping are
resources; those that interfere or potentially interfere with coping are *deficits*. Some
resources and deficits are *personal variables* that exist within the individual, such as:[1]

Emotion (negative, such as fear, anger and sadness: and positive, such as joy)
Physical abilities (physical strength, flexibility, stamina, agility, etc.)
Physiological functioning (level of arousal, physical illness, etc.)
Cognitive abilities, skills, knowledge
Cognitive functioning (fatigue, mental inflexibility, distracting thoughts, nar-
  rowed attention, etc.)
Social skills (assertiveness, aggressiveness, passivity, etc.)
Beliefs, values, commitments (thoughts concerning what is real, important, and
  worthy of action)

---

[1] Stress research occasionally considers the effects of automatic patterns of processing information. Such
behaviors are usually referred to as *cognitive styles*. However, since cognitive styles can mediate reactions
to stressful situations, they are worth noting. *Field dependence-independence* (or global-analytic style) is
perhaps the most widely researched (Witkin, Goodenough, & Oltman, 1979). Field-dependent/global
individuals rely heavily on external cues when making judgments about the environment. Indeed, such
people have difficulty separating a figure from the background or field. When placed in a darkened
room and shown a tilted luminous frame surrounding a movable rod, they have problems adjusting the
rod to a true upright on the basis of bodily cues. In other words, they are so distracted by the tilted
frame that it becomes their incorrect point of reference. In contrast, field-independent/analytic individuals can see the rod as being separate from the frame and adjust it correctly. They have been more
recently viewed as possessing an analogous "disembedding," or differentiating, ability in a variety of
intellectual activities, including coping with stress. When placed in ambiguous stressful situations, field-
independent/analytic subjects appear better able to analyze and restructure a field when certainty
increases. In other words, they are not bound by previous appraisals of uncertainty and appear able to
reappraise when conditions are appropriate (Gaines, Smith, & Skolnick, 1977).
  Additional cognitive styles include *leveling* (the tendency to view stimuli in terms of characteristics they
have in common) and *sharpening* (the tendency to see stimuli in terms of their differences) as well as
focusing-scanning, flexible-constricted control, equivalence range, and *tolerance for unrealistic experiences*
(Gardner, Holzman, Klein, Linton & Spence, 1959).

Other resources and deficits are *external variables*, such as:

Objective characteristics of the situation (undesirability, unpredictability, uncontrollability, event magnitude, time clustering)
Social networks
Finances
Housing
Transportation
Work
Society (politics, social upheaval, discrimination, war, etc.)
Environment (noise, crowding, pollution, etc.)

Such personal and external variables are too complex to be discussed in full here; indeed, they form the basis of much of the rest of this book.

Situational, personal, and external variables can be viewed on two temporal dimensions: (1) *timing*, or whether the variable is concurrent with, preceding, or following a stressful encounter; and (2) *duration*, or whether the variable is immediate and short-lived, or distant and enduring. These define five general categories of stress variables:

1. *Long-term antecedent variables*: All that exist prior to the stressful situation and have endured for a relatively long time. Examples include such situational antecedents as enduring patterns of appraisal and coping with specific and concrete stress situations similar to the one under consideration; such personal variables as personality traits and dispositions, physical health, abilities, and handicaps; and such external variables as long-term friendships, financial stability, and home life.
2. *Immediate antecedent variables*: All moods, states, and transitory events and conditions that are present just before a stress encounter.
3. *Stress event variables*: All variables present during the stressful encounter.
4. *Immediate consequence variables*: All moods, states, and transitory events and conditions that are present just after a stress encounter.
5. *Long-term consequence variables*: Long-term and lasting changes that can be identified after an encounter.

To illustrate, let us examine one personal variable, the emotion *anger*, and one external variable, *tangible social support*. Both can appear at various times and for various durations. As a long-term antecedent, anger is a continuing trait, a part of a person's personality. As an immediate antecedent, it is the mood a person experiences just before a stressful situation ("Just before the exam, I was really angry."). As a part of a stress event, it is a mood a person feels during a stressful situation; as an immediate consequence, it is what a person feels after. Finally, as a long-term consequence, anger is again a continuing trait or an aspect of a person's personality.

The external variable, tangible social support (the number of friends who can supply money, physical assistance, etc.), can also exist as a long-term or immediate antecedent as well as a resource during a stressful event. An individual may have helpful friends for a long time before, just before, during, right after, and for a long time after a stressful encounter.

Finally, situational stress variables, that is, appraisal and coping, are primarily defined in terms of a stressful event. A person might appraise an exam as a threat to her overall grade, but possess the coping skills of planning and accepting responsibility. A person can display these same appraisals and coping skills immediately before ("The exam is coming up. It's a threat, but I accept responsibility for planning."), or after ("The exam is over. It's still a threat, and I still accept responsibility for planning."). These variables can exist as long-term antecedents ("All my life I have seen exams as a threat, but have accepted responsibility for planning.") and consequences ("The exam may be over, but for a long time I continued to see exams as threats and accepted responsibility for planning.").

Several principles characterize this matrix. Any single variable can be a long-term antecedent or consequence, a transitory or immediate antecedent or consequence, or part of the actual stressful encounter. Examples of situational, personal, and external variables are presented in Table 5.2.

Looking at Stress Through the Transactional Lens

The transactional matrix can be conceptualized as a lens through which a person perceives a stressful situation. The lens can focus narrowly on situational variables specific to a stressful encounter. Table 5.3 presents a narrowly focused description of a student taking an exam. However, the lens has a vertical and horizontal focus that can be broad or narrow. A broad vertical focus includes personal and external variables that accompany the stressful event, as Table 5.4 shows. A broad horizontal focus, such as that depicted in Table 5.5, includes situational variables that come before and after the event. Finally, a broad vertical and horizontal focus includes all variables. This is portrayed in Table 5.6.

The Transactional Story and the Process of Stress

As noted, the transactional perspective derives its name from what is perhaps its most important feature. Stress is not static; it is a continuous, unfolding process. Different features of this process can interrelate as a transaction. Any transaction involves back-and-forth movement. In a financial transaction, a customer may inquire about a price, then bargain, and finally pay for a desired item. In a transaction between roommates, one may ask for help in cleaning the room, the other may respond that she is too busy with homework, and both may argue until some sort of compromise is, or is not, reached. In this sense, stress is also a transaction: appraisals of resources influence how we actually cope; the emotions we experience in one encounter influence how we cope in others; illness can be both a long-term consequence of stress, and a continuing, long-term antecedent.

The transactional matrix and lens can provide something of a "snapshot" of stress, a rich but static portrait of a wide array of variables. However, we would need many

TABLE 5.2 Examples of Variables for Taking an Exam on the Transactional Matrix

Variable	Long-Term Antecedents	Immediate Antecedents	Stressful Event	Immediate Consequences	Long-Term Consequences
Personal					
Emotion (depression)	Depressed personality	Depressed mood	Depressed mood	Depressed mood	Less depressed personality
Physical abilities (physically fit)	History of being physically fit	Has stopped exercise routine before event; level of fitness lower than usual	Not physically fit	Not physically fit	Joins fitness program; increases fitness
Physiological functioning (arousal)	Chronic high blood pressure	Normal blood pressure	High blood pressure	High blood pressure	Lower chronic blood pressure
Cognitive abilities, skills, knowledge (verbal and writing skills)	Good verbal and writing skills	At peak writing ability	At peak writing ability	Less verbal	Good verbal skills
Cognitive functioning (cognitively fatigued)	History of cognitive fatigue	Not fatigued	Not fatigued	Fatigued	Generally less fatigued during stressful events
Social skills (shy)	History of being shy in most social encounters	Very sociable	Not sociable	More sociable	Still sociable during stressful events
Belief, values commitments (belief in God)	Enduring belief in God	Had not considered belief in God	Did not consider belief in God	Did not consider belief in God	Not interested in religion

(continues)

TABLE 5.2   Continued

Variable	Long-Term Antecedents	Immediate Antecedents	Stressful Event	Immediate Consequences	Long-Term Consequences
Situational					
Primary appraisal ("I want success; this is threatened.")	Generally driven to seek success, generally fearful it is threatened.	Not particularly concerned about success	Concerned about success	Less concerned about success	More concerned about living life, less concerned about success
Secondary appraisal ("I'm not prepared.")	Generally believes "I'm not prepared to deal with stress."	Feels "I'm not prepared."	Feels "I'm not prepared."	Feels "I'm not prepared about success."	Feels better prepared to deal with stress
Coping ("Plan one step at a time.")	Generally plans life activities	Has no plan	Has no plan	Has no plan	Faces stressful events with a plan
Reappraisal (fear of failure)	Generally has plan and does not fear failure	Fears failure because has no plan	Fears failure because has no plan	Still fears failure because has no plan	Learns to approach problems with plan; fears failure less
External					
Objective characteristics of situation (controllable)	Generally had little control over tests and exams	Had little control over available study time	Has control over how to take the exam	Has little control over grading of exam	Has control over taking of future exams
Social networks (many acquaintances, few friends)	Generally has had many acquaintances, few friends	Is with friends	Is with several friends	Is alone	Still maintains several good friends
Finances (little money on hand)	Generally has had considerable money	No financial problems	No financial problems	No financial problems	No financial problems
Housing, food (have place to stay and food)	Generally has had housing and food	No housing or food problems	No housing or food problems	No housing or food problems	No housing or food problems

TABLE 5.3   A Narrow Focus for Taking an Exam

Variable	Long-Term Antecedents	Immediate Antecedents	Stressful Event	Immediate Consequences	Long-Term Consequences
Personal					
Situational			"I wanted to get an *A* but, when I saw the exam, I realized it covered matter I hadn't studied. [appraisal of want and threat], and I didn't know what to do [appraisal of coping]. I pushed on, just answered the easy questions, and prayed for the best [actual coping].		
External					

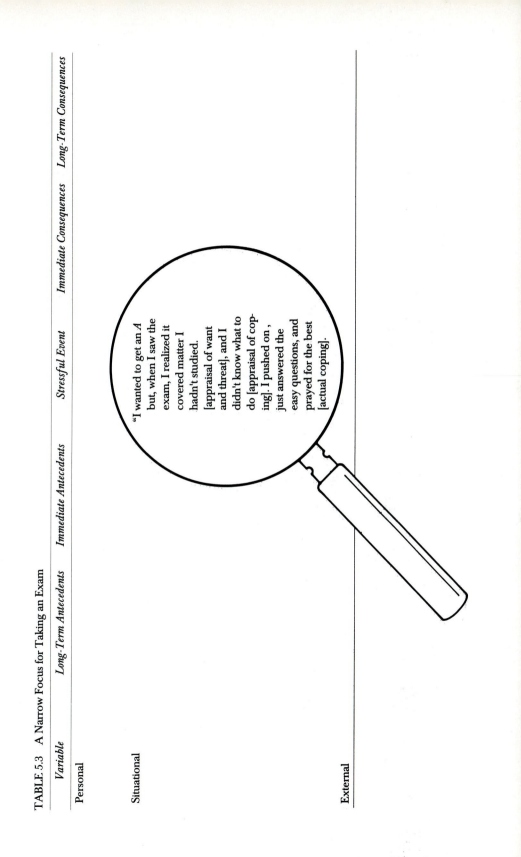

TABLE 5.4 A Broad Vertical Focus for Taking an Exam

Variable	Long-Term Antecedents	Immediate Antecedents	Stressful Event	Immediate Consequences	Long-Term Consequences
Personal			While taking this exam, I was tired and angry. This kept me awake and enabled me to keep on going.		
Situational			I wanted to get an *A* but, when I saw the exam I realized it covered matter I hadn't studied [appraisal of coping]. I pushed on, just answered the easy questions, and prayed for the best [actual coping].		
External			While taking this exam, my girlfriend was at home waiting for me. This helped me keep going.		

TABLE 5.5 A Broad Horizontal Focus for Taking an Exam

Variable	Long-Term Antecedents	Immediate Antecedents	Stressful Event	Immediate Consequences	Long-Term Consequences
Personal					
Situational	I'm the kind of person who has always wanted to get an A on exams, but I find that exams cover material I haven't studied. I just answer the easy questions and hope for the best.	Right before the exam I really wanted to get an A. I was afraid that it might cover material I hadn't studied and that I might not know what to do. Well, I decided to answer just the easy questions and pray for the best.	I wanted to get an A but, when, I saw the exam I realized it covered matter I hadn't studied [appraisal of want and threat], and I didn't know what to do [appraisal of coping]. I pushed on, just answered the easy questions and prayed for the best [actual coping].	The exam is over and I hope I got an A. It was really clear to me that it covered material I hadn't studied and I didn't know what to do. I pray for the best.	On subsequent exams, I continued to seek As and hope for the best. However, after exams I continued to realize that the exam covered material I hadn't studied for.
External					

TABLE 5.6 A Broad Vertical and Horizontal Focus for Taking an Exam

Variable	Long-Term Antecedents	Immediate Antecedents	Stressful Event	Immediate Consequences	Long-Term Consequences
Personal	People describe me as hot-headed and angry. I guess that describes part of me.	Right before this exam, I was tired and angry.	While taking this exam, I was tired and angry. This kept me awake and enabled me to keep on going.	Just after the exam, I was no longer angry. I felt a bit let down, since the worst was over.	The exam didn't change much in my life. I'm still basically an angry person.
Situational	I'm the kind of person who has always wanted to get an A on exams, but I find that exams cover material I haven't studied. I just answer the easy questions and hope for the best.	Right before the exam I really wanted to get an A. I was afraid that it might cover material I hadn't studied and that I might not know what to do. Well, I decided to answer just the easy questions and pray for the best.	I wanted to get an A but, when I saw the exam, I realized it covered matter I hadn't studied [appraisal of want and threat], and I didn't know what to do [appraisal of coping]. I pushed on, just answered the easy questions and prayed for the best [actual coping].	The exam is over and I hope I got an A. It was really clear to me that it covered material I hadn't studied and I didn't know what to do. I prayed for the best.	On subsequent exams, I continued to seek As and hope for the best. However, after exams I continued to realize that the exam covered material I had not studied for.
External	For some time before the exam, I have been living with my girlfriend. She is always around when I need her.	Just before the exam, I realized my girlfriend was at home waiting for me.	While taking this exam, my girlfriend was at home waiting for me. This helped me keep going.	Just after the exam, I realized my girlfriend was at home.	For quite some time after the exam, I continued living with my girlfriend.

snapshots to see how an event unfolds and how the variables interrelate. Such repeated glimpses of a stressful event provide something of a transactional story, complete with central and peripheral characters and interweaving plots. Of course, to study the full story of a stressful event is difficult, and requires repeated testing and complex statistics. However, as we shall see, this is one direction that stress research is taking.

Research Applications of the Transactional Matrix

Early studies that looked only at the accumulation of life events (long-term and immediate antecedents), stress-related illness (long-term consequence), or stress arousal (stressful event) had a severely restricted focus. Research is beginning to examine more elements of the transactional matrix. To illustrate, in a classic study Folkman and Lazarus (1985) examined three critical moments of a college midterm examination: anticipation, when students prepare for an exam not knowing exactly what it will be like; waiting, when the exam had been given and grades have yet to be announced; and outcome, when students deal with learning how they have done. Separate studies were conducted for each phase.

The results of the study reveal something of a changing microscopic portrait of what happens before, during, and after an exam. First, emotions change. As might be expected, threat and challenge emotions are high before and just after an exam, while harm and benefit emotions rise once the exam is taken. During the waiting period (just before receiving grades), there is considerable ambiguity, and all emotions are high, both positive and negative. How did the students cope? One surprising finding is that people cope in very complex ways. On the average, nearly seven different coping strategies were used by each student. In addition, students used both problem- and emotion-focused coping, often in combination. Before the exam, students relied on problem-focused coping (studying and seeking informational social support) as well as the emotion-focused technique of emphasizing the positive. After the exam, the use of problem-focused coping declined, and distancing and searching for emotional social support increased. Apparently, distancing is applied when waiting for an outcome.

Evaluating Coping Strategies

Which forms of coping were most useful? Generally, this question is hard to answer. Students who received poorer grades did report using more emotion-focused coping, probably to manage their disappointment. However, at times emotion-focused coping can reduce interfering emotion and thereby facilitate problem-focused coping. Perhaps this is the reason problem-focused coping correlated highly with emphasizing the positive and seeking social support. Generally, people use a wide variety of coping strategies, which change as a stressful situation unfolds (see Table 5.7).

TABLE 5.7 The Transactional Matrix Applied to Exam Research

Variable	Long-Term Antecedents	Immediate Antecedents	Stressful Event	Immediate Consequences	Long-Term Consequences
Personal		Threat and challenge emotions.		Threat and challenge emotions, harm and benefit emotions. All emotions are high just before receiving grade.	
Situational		Problem-focused coping (studying and seeking information-al social support) as well as emphasizing the positive.		Problem-focused coping declined, and distancing and searching for emotional social support increased. Students who received poorer grades reported using more emotion-focused coping, probably to manage their disappointment.	
External					

We have described one study in detail because it represents an important direction in which stress research is progressing. Instead of examining global consequences or antecedents, the emphasis is on a microanalysis of process and what people actually do in stressful situations; put simply, the aim is to discover important stress stories. The potential of this line of research is considerable. In time, we may learn which coping strategies are most appropriate for which people in which situations.

This research model is beginning to yield some tantalizing results:

- Most people use nearly all forms of coping in every stressful encounter, although some may be emphasized more than others (Lazarus, 1990).
- The pattern of coping changes from one stage of a stressful encounter to another. Students coping with an examination tend to seek information before the exam, but use distancing after the exam and before grades are announced (Lazarus, 1990).
- Some forms of coping are relatively stable, whereas others are unstable. For example, problem-focused approaches tend to vary highly from one situation to another, whereas some emotion-focused strategies, such as positive reappraisal and self-control, are more stable and used in a wide variety of situations (Lazarus, 1990).
- Problem-focused and reality-based emotion-focused coping (particularly confrontive coping, acceptance of responsibility, and planning) as well as positive reappraisal predominates when people feel that something constructive can be done. In contrast, emotion-focused coping, such as distancing and disengagement from a situation, predominates when people appraise a stressor as something that cannot be changed (Folkman & Lazarus, 1980; Folkman, et al., 1986). In addition, the suppression of competing activities and search for instrumental support are also more likely to be applied in controllable situations (Carver et al., 1989).
- Unsuccessful coping appears to be more associated with confrontational and avoidant strategies as well as wishful thinking and self-blame, whereas successful coping is more associated with planful problem-solving (Folkman et al., 1986; Folton, Revenson, & Hinrichsen, 1989).
- Emotions play a complex role in stress, and can inhibit, instigate, and maintain coping behavior. Emotion is also one important consequence of coping, and different emotions are associated with failure, success, and uncertain outcome (Folkman & Lazarus, 1991).
- Depressed people appear to feel they have more at stake in stressful encounters and use more confrontive coping and self-control (keeping feelings to themselves). They also seek more social support, yet report more anger and hostility in their encounters. One is tempted to speculate that such strategies are counterproductive. Keeping feelings to oneself and using confrontive coping may not be conducive to the development of social support such individuals seek, thus contributing to further depression (Coyne, Aldwin, & Lazarus, 1981; Folkman & Lazarus, 1986; Folkman & Lazarus, 1988).
- Rational, planful problem-solving may be less likely to communicate hostility than confrontive coping, and may well invite the cooperation and support of others. Indeed, one study found that planful problem-solving elicited all types

of support (emotional, tangible, and informational), whereas confrontive coping elicited primarily information (Dunkel-Schetter, Folkman, & Lazarus, 1987).

· Finally, causal antecedents (such as life events and personality) are poor predictors of how people actually cope during a stressful encounter as well as of the short and long-term consequences they will experience (Folkman & Lazarus, 1980; Lazarus & Folkman, 1984). What a person actually does in a stressful situation is determined by a complex array of factors, including situational constraints, resources, personality, appraisals, and past coping successes and failures.

The Relativity of Coping: The Case of Denial

It should be clear that the stress research we have described does not assume that any coping strategies are either good or bad. Any particular strategy works differently for different individuals, and generalizations concerning the overall utility of coping strategies may be hard to come by. This can be seen very clearly with respect to denial, a strategy about which psychotherapists have had much to say. For example, psychodynamic therapists see denial as a sign of neurosis, and rational emotive therapists view it as irrational. However, experimental stress researchers note that people frequently engage in benign self-deceptions, such as faith in the existence (or nonexistence) of God or an afterlife, feelings of virtual immortality, and belief in unproven remedies for illness and techniques for self-improvement. Such illusions foster a sense of self-efficacy and optimism that may well be conducive to health (see Chapter 6).

In fact, there are both costs and benefits to denial. In chapters to come we will explore this notion more fully in a variety of contexts, including illness (Chapter 6), catastrophe and disaster (Chapter 9), and developmental tasks (Chapter 10). In general, Lazarus and Folkman (1984) and others have proposed a variety of conditions under which denial and denial-like forms of coping might have favorable or unfavorable outcomes:

· When nothing can be done to overcome a threat, denial can reduce distress without causing harm. ("I am terminally ill and that cannot be changed.")
· When certain facets of a situation can be denied, others can be attended to and managed with less disruption. ("My diabetes isn't really a serious disorder; however, I will very diligently keep up with my medications and diet.")
· When a given stressful situation must be encountered again and again, denial can interfere with mastery and increase stress.
· Denial may be valuable at an early stage of coping if a person's resources are insufficient for managing a problem, such as the beginning of a crisis, a sudden illness, incapacitation, or loss of a loved one. Such denial may provide the breathing room needed to develop coping resources.
· Some kinds of denial may be more or less dangerous or helpful than others. Weisman (1972) has suggested that it may be more dangerous to deny fact (that a person has cancer) than implication (that cancer can lead to death). In addition, it may be more dangerous to deny what is clear and unambiguous (that a person is

overweight, has heart disease, and should go on a diet) than what cannot be known for certain (working hard may contribute to stress).
· When an uncontrollable situation is changing and may become controllable, denial can be risky and prevent timely action.

Lazarus and Folkman (1984) have also suggested that denial that is "partial, tentative or minimal" should be less destructive and potentially more useful. Such denial is closer to a "working fiction," a sense of "as if" that is often difficult to challenge empirically (p. 137). This can serve to maintain morale and even motivate a person to cope. There comes a point when minimal denial ceases to be denial and instead becomes an accurate reappraisal, a shift of emphasis. An individual may well first view his situation as a threat and thus experience considerable stress. However, it can be just as realistic but much more adaptive to view the same situation as a challenge.

Clinical and Experimental Approaches to Stress

Coping research in general and the example of denial in particular shows how complex stress can be. A wide range of variables may determine when any particular strategy is constructive or destructive. One overall lesson of coping research is the *importance of assessing the costs and payoffs of any coping strategies that an individual may apply*. This is the core of contemporary clinical approaches to stress management (see Chapters 13–15).

In addition, coping research may help the clinical process of experimenting with a wide range of coping strategies in a search for those that work. This becomes obvious when we phrase empirical questions as personal concerns:

· "An exam is coming up. How do successful students cope with their anxiety? I tend to be shy and overanxious. Are there coping strategies that would apply well to my situation?"
· "Next week I have surgery. I want to do everything possible to hasten my recovery. I know that a certain amount of fear is normal, but how can I learn to keep my fear in check? I'm the kind of person who likes to know all the details about what is going on. Are there coping strategies that are better for me?"
· "I play on the school basketball team and have to deal with many types of pressure. Sometimes I have to worry about the crowd (and my date) watching me. Sometimes it is an important game, and I think about not making the one mistake that loses the game. Sometimes we are just practicing. Are different strategies for dealing with pressure better for different situations or for my type of personality?"
· "My job is really tense. I want to do my best, but this is impossible given the enormous amount of work I must do. My concern is that heart disease runs in my family, and I don't want work stress to increase my chances of becoming ill. Should I learn to relax? Should I lower my standards? Should I just learn to

accept what can't be changed? It would be helpful to know what works for other people in my situation."

The transactional matrix represents a step closer to behavioral approaches to clinical stress assessment. Typically, the clinician identifies the specifics of a problem situation, and then examines the consequences to determine problem behaviors, their seriousness, client motivation to change, and so on. An examination of antecedents helps determine coping resources that have been applied in similar situations, difficulties a client may have in learning and applying new skills, and the probability of change. In other words, clinical stress assessment begins with a narrow focus and then expands to apply a broad horizontal focus in exploring the vast array of variables suggested by the transactional matrix. Whey do stress clinicians initially tend to pay less attention to personal and external antecedents and consequences? From the research examined, it appears that such variables may not provide as much predictive power as do the concrete and specific situational variables (although they can enrichen our understanding of a situation). For example, to understand how John may fare on his next interview, the first task would be to ask how he fared on previous interviews rather than to explore his overall situation, personality, and so on.

In sum, just as clinical approaches to stress have become more experimental, experimental models have become more clinical. The transactional matrix represents something of a meeting of the two worlds of research.

Conclusion

This chapter completes our review of current research and thinking on the basics of stress. Much of this work can be organized in terms of the transactional matrix. In chapters to come we will continue our exploration using what we have learned as a foundation.

We continue our journey in Chapter 6 with a topic that has received considerably urgent attention: stress and health. People's personalities consist of enduring patterns of behaviors, including how they habitually cope and defend themselves, and their ongoing reactions to patterns of coping failures and successes. Is there an illness-prone or health-prone personality? How do specific patterns of stress contribute to specific illnesses? And what is the link between stress, illness, and risk behaviors such as lack of exercise, poor eating habits, smoking, alcoholism, and substance abuse?

After probing these questions, we shall step back and discuss more general contexts that have attracted considerable research: disasters, catastrophes, and crises; development and the family; work stress; and environment and the society. We shall conclude by examining the major approaches to stress management used in clinics.

APPLICATION BOX 5.1

Analyzing Stress with the Transactional Lens

Think of a recent stress situation. Try to recall all of the specifics. When did it happen? What did you think, do, and say? Where were you? Now try to identify examples of primary appraisal, secondary appraisal, and coping in your example. Describe these below:

Primary appraisal _____

_____

Secondary appraisal _____

_____

Coping _____

_____

   Now, let's see if we can understand your stress situation more deeply. What are all the elements in the "stress story" of this situation? Below is an empty transactional matrix. Try to identify what came before and after the stress situation. What were your personal and external resources and deficits? What were the short and long-term costs and payoffs?

Variables	Long-term Antecedents	Immediate Antecedents	Stress Event	Immediate Consequences	Long-term Consequences
Personal	_____	_____	____	_____	_____
	_____	_____	____	_____	_____
Situational	_____	_____	____	_____	_____
	_____	_____	____	_____	_____
External	_____	_____	____	_____	_____
	_____	_____	____	_____	_____

References

BANDURA, A. (1977). Self-efficacy: Toward a unifying theory of behavioral change. *Psychological Review, 84,* 191–215.

BANDURA, A. (1982). Self-efficacy mechanism in human agency. *American Psychologist, 37,* 122–147.

BILLINGS, A. G., & MOOS, R. H. (1984). Coping, stress, and social resources among adults with unipolar depression. *Journal of Personality and Social Psychology, 46,* 877–891.

CANNON, W. B. (1927). The James-Lange theory of emotions: A critical examination and an alternative theory. *American Journal of Psychology, 39,* 106–124.

CARVER, C. S., SCHEIER, M. F., & WEINTRAUB, J. K. (1989). Assessing coping strategies. A theoretically based approach. *Journal of Personality and Social Psychology, 56,* 267–283.

COHEN, F., REESE, L. B., KAPLAN, G. A., & RIGGIO, R. E. (1986). Coping with the stresses of arthritis. In R. W. Moskowitz & M. R. Haug (Eds.), *Arthritis and the elderly* (pp. 47–56). New York: Springer.

COYNE, J. C., ALDWIN, C., & LAZARUS, R. S. (1981). Depression and coping in stressful episodes. *Journal of Abnormal Psychology, 90,* 439–447.

DUNKEL-SCHETTER, C., FOLKMAN, S., & LAZARUS, R. S. (1987). Correlates of social support receipt. *Journal of Personality and Social Psychology, 53,* 71–80.

FOLKMAN, S., & LAZARUS, R. S. (1980). An analysis of coping in a middle-aged community sample. *Journal of Health and Social Behavior, 21,* 219–239.

FOLKMAN, S., & LAZARUS, R. S. (1985). If it changes it must be a process: Study of emotion and coping during three stages of a college examination. *Journal of Personality and Social Psychology, 48,* 150–170.

FOLKMAN, S., & LAZARUS, R. S. (1986). Stress processes and depressive symptomatology. *Journal of Abnormal Psychology, 95,* 107–113.

FOLKMAN, S., & LAZARUS, R. S. (1988). Coping as a mediator of emotion. *Journal of Personality and Social Psychology, 54,* 466–475.

FOLKMAN, S., & LAZARUS, R. S. (1991). Coping and emotion. In A. Monat & R. S. Lazarus (Eds.), *Stress and Coping (3rd ed.*, pp. 207–227): New York: Columbia University Press.

FOLKMAN, S., LAZARUS, R. S., DUNKEL-SCHETTER, C., DELONGIS, A., & GRUEN, R. J. (1986). Dynamics of a stressful encounter: Cognitive appraisal, coping, and encounter outcomes. *Journal of Personality and Social Psychology, 50,* 992–1003

FOLTON, B. J., REVENSON, T. A., & HINRICHSEN, G. A. (1989). Stress and coping in the explanation of psychological adjustment among chronically ill patients. *Social Science and Medicine, 18,* 889–898.

GAINES, L. L., SMITH, B. D., & SKOLNICK, B. E. (1977). Psychological differentiation, event uncertainty, and heart rate. *Journal of Human Stress, 3,* 11–25.

GARDNER, R. W., HOLZMAN, P. S., KLEIN, G. S., LINTON, H. B., & SPENCE, D. P. (1959). Cognitive control: A study of individual consistencies in cognitive behavior. *Psychological Issues, 1,* (4).

JAMES, W. (1890). *Principles of psychology.* New York: Henry Holt.

KEMPER, T. D. (1978). *A social interaction theory of emotions.* New York: Wiley.

KIRSCH, I. (1985). Response expectancy as a determinant of experience and behavior. *American Psychologist, 40,* 1189–1202.

KIRSCH, I. (1990). *Changing expectations: A key to effective psychotherapy.* Pacific Grove, CA: Brooks/Cole.

LANDIS, C., & HUNT, W. A. (1932). Adrenalin and emotion. *Psychological Review, 39,* 467–485.

LANGE, C. G. (1922). *The emotions.* Baltimore: Williams & Wilkins.

LAZARUS, R. S. (1990). Stress, coping, and illness. In H. S. Friedman (Ed.), *Personality and disease* (pp. 97–120). New York: Wiley.

LAZARUS, R. S., & FOLKMAN, S. (1984). *Stress, appraisal, and coping.* New York: Springer.

MARSHALL, G. D., & ZIMBARDO, P. G. (1979). Affective consequences of inadequately explained physiological arousal. *Journal of Personality and Social Psychology, 37,* 970–985.

MASLACH, C. (1979). Negative emotional biasing of unexplained arousal. *Journal of Personality and Social Psychology, 37,* 953–969.

MOOS, R. H. (1974). Psychological techniques in the assessment of adaptive behavior. In G. V. Coehlo, D. A. Hamburg, & J. E. Adams (Eds.), *Coping and adaptation* (pp. 334–399). New York: Basic Books.

PLUTCHIK, R., & AX, A. F. (1967). A critique of determinants of emotional state by Schachter and Singer (1962). *Psychophysiology, 4,* 79–82.

SCHACHTER, S., & SINGER, J. (1962). Cognitive, social and physiological determinants of emotional state. *Psychological Review, 69,* 379–399.

WEISMAN, A. D. (1972). *On dying and denying: A psychiatric study of terminality.* New York: Behavioral Publications.

YAKUBOVICH, I. S., RAGLAND, D. R., BRAND, R. J., & SYME, S. L. (1988). Type A behavior pattern and health status after 22 years of follow-up in the Western Collaborative Group Study. *American Journal of Epidemiology, 128,* 579–588.

ZUCKERMAN, M. (1974). The sensation seeking motive. In B. Haher (Ed.), *Progress in experimental personality research (vol. 7).* New York: Academic Press.

PART II

Stress, Health, and Illness

In this section we consider the topic that has perhaps received greatest attention from stress researchers: stress, health, and illness. We begin with a continuation of Chapter 5 as we examine personality traits and behavior patterns associated with disease. We then focus on specific stress-related physiological processes associated with major categories of illness. Finally, we consider various risk behaviors and their link to stress, health, and illness.

CHAPTER 6

Personality and Illness

Is there such a thing as an health-prone or illness-prone personality? To the casual observer, the answer may seem to be an obvious "yes." The popular press abounds with miraculous accounts of recovery. Note, for example, what Norman Cousins (1977) wrote after recovering from what seemed to be a fatal disease by using laughter and positive emotion:

> I have learned never to underestimate the capacity of the human mind and body to regenerate—even when the prospects seem most wretched. The life-force may be the least understood force on earth. William James said that human beings tend to live too far within self-imposed limits. It is possible that these limits will recede when we respect more fully the natural drive of the human mind and body toward perfectibility and regeneration. Protecting and cherishing that natural drive may well represent the finest exercise of human freedom (p. 51).

Often, physicians face the brutal facts of illness and death, which all too frequently occur in spite of virtue, laughter, and positive emotion. Such realities have prompted the editor of the prestigious *New England Journal of Medicine* to brand psychological treatments of illness as cruel "folklore" that often burdens patients who fail to get well, in spite of heroic psychological efforts, with needless guilt (Angell, 1985). The fact is that we now understand more about personality and illness than both Cousins and many medical skeptics surmise.

In Chapter 5, we saw that a broadly focused transactional consideration of stress must include long-term antecedents and consequences of stressful events. This is the realm of personality. Specifically, a personality trait is a long-term pattern of thought and behavior, an enduring predisposition to think and act in a particular way. Enduring patterns of defense, such as denial and repression, are traits considered in Chapter 4. In Chapter 5 we examined the process of appraisal and coping. Successful coping is associated with a set of coping traits we will consider first in this chapter. Such traits have been considered at two levels. Some researchers have focused on the relatively abstract dimension of beliefs, values, and commitments presumed to be consistent with coping; others have examined specific patterns of coping presumed to be desirable. After considering coping traits, we shall examine specific traits postulated to be associated with illness.

Coping Traits I: General Beliefs, Values, and Commitments

The first set of coping traits we shall consider reflect philosophical views concerning oneself and the world, that is, general beliefs about what works and what or who is responsible for life's problems, values concerning what is important, and commitments reflecting global choices.

Work on such traits evolved from studies on helplessness. Over three decades ago, researchers suggested that people at times display a *giving up–given up complex* in response to losses (Engel, 1968; Engel & Schmale, 1967; Schmale, 1972; Schmale & Engel, 1967). This complex has five characteristics: (1) helplessness or hopelessness; (2) lower sense of worth; (3) loss of gratification, roles, or relationships in life; (4) confusion or loss of continuity about the past, present, and future; and (5) recall and reactivation of earlier periods of giving up. Engle (1968) describes this complex as a "sense of psychological impotence, a feeling that for briefer or longer periods of time one is unable to cope with the changes in the environment" (pp. 359–360). Retrospective evidence suggests the link between giving up–given up and illness as well as death (Schmale, 1972).

More recent researchers have examined helplessness and depression. The *learned helplessness theory* of depression originated from Seligman's (1975) research on animals. His studies found that a dog placed in an aversive situation, such as an electrified cage, will quickly learn to avoid shock (by jumping into a "safe" cage) in response to a warning light. However, if this avoidance strategy has been mastered and the shock is then made inescapable (the safe cage is no longer available), something interesting happens: the animal simply sits and endures the shock. It learns that its efforts are futile and gives up, even when the safe cage is again made available.

The learned helplessness model did not work particularly well for humans, however. Most seriously, helplessness in humans is often highly circumscribed. The original theory posited an across-the-board helplessness brought about by general expectations that responses will no longer produce desired outcomes. In reality, humans display helplessness in some situations and not others. Such observations have led to a revised model of learned helplessness that focuses on cognitive appraisal.

Explanatory Style

Explanatory style (Abramson, Garber, & Seligman, 1980) is a coping trait that reflects the subjective perception of helplessness versus resourcefulness. A pessimistic explanatory style has three dimensions (Peterson & Seligman, 1987):

An *internal explanation* points to something about the self, (e.g., "It's me") and makes loss of self-esteem following a bad event more likely. A *stable explanation* refers to long-lasting causes (e.g., "It's the way the world is") and is apt to produce chronic difficulties in the wake of bad events. A *global explanation* specifies a pervasive determinant (e.g., "It's going to undermine everything I do") and increases the likelihood that bad events will produce widespread problems (p. 240 [italics added]).

Thus, a pessimistic explanatory style of bad events, one that is internal, stable, and global, is debilitating, ("I failed the test because I have deep and long-lasting deficiencies that will interfere with everything I do.") Whereas external, unstable, and specific explanations are less troublesome. ("I failed the test because my roommate forgot to return my textbook—that won't happen again!") An impressive series of prospective studies links pessimistic explanatory style in early adulthood with illness and death twenty to thirty-five years later as well as with lower performance in academics, athletics, and work (Kamen-Siegel, Rodin, Seligman, & Dwyer, 1991; Peterson, Seligman, & Vaillant, 1988).

Locus of Control

A variety of theories have focused on general and relatively enduring beliefs concerning control. Although several constructs have been introduced, including fatalism, mastery, and personal competence, the best known is Rotter's (1966) notion of *locus of control.* An internal locus of control is the belief that reinforcements are contingent on a person's behavior, while an external locus of control is the belief that events are contingent on such external factors as chance, fate, God, luck, powerful others, and society. Locus of control is a trait, and an enduring predisposition to think and act in a certain way; it is most likely to be salient in situations of ambiguity. That is, when it is unclear what an outcome will be or what a person can do about it, locus of control can determine perceptions of control (Rotter, 1975). Attempts have been made to associate an internal locus of control with "good coping" (Lefcourt, 1985). Support for this notion is modest at best (Cohen & Edwards, 1989; Janoff-Bulman & Wortman, 1977; Nagy & Wolfe, 1983; Taylor, Lichtman, & Wood, 1984). Also, it is possible that those with an internal locus of control may respond better to relaxation training (Lewis, Biglan, & Steinbock, 1978) than those with an external locus of control to biofeedback (Prager-Decker, 1979). However, in general, the proposed link between locus of control and stress is now often seen as an overly simplistic concept that obscures the possibility that it is more adaptive to view situations externally at certain times and internally at others (Lazarus & Folkman, 1984).

A variety of attempts have been made to create locus of control scales of greater specificity by focusing, for example, on crowding, academic achievement, economic success, and control over personal versus social-political systems. Generally, such scales have not improved the predictive power of locus of control. The one exception is locus of control measures targeted to health-related behaviors. For example, the Multidimensional Health Locus of Control scales tap the belief that health is determined by a person's own behavior, the reliance on powerful others (health professionals) for health maintenance, and the belief that health or illness are due to chance (Wallston, Wallston, & DeVellis, 1978). Such health-related scales may provide insight into a person's perception of responsibility for illness and treatment (Lefcourt, 1981). Indeed, there is some evidence that people with an internal locus of health control and those with an external locus may respond to different treatments. The latter may have difficulty assuming responsibility for their problems; it may be more appropriate to direct their therapy toward altering external circumstances rather than internal responses.

Coherence

According to Antonovsky (1979), stress-resistant people have access to *resistance resources* with which to manage their tensions and acquire a feeling of social belongingness. Generally, such people have a *sense of coherence*, which Antonovsky (1987) defined as confidence that the world is *comprehensible* (structured, predictable, and explicable); *manageable* (resources are available to meet the demands); and *meaningful* (demands are challenges, worthy of investment and engagement).

Hardiness

Hardiness is a trait that consists of three characteristics: *control*, or a belief in a person's ability to influence events; *commitment*, or an approach to life marked by curiosity and a sense of meaningfulness; and *challenge*, or the expectation that change is normal and stimulates development (Kobasa, Maddi, & Courington, 1981). Maddi, Kobasa, and their colleagues propose that hardy individuals are more likely to utilize *transformational coping* by which they reduce the threat of a stressor by viewing it in broader perspective, analyzing it into its component parts, and identifying and completing specific solutions (Maddi & Kobasa, 1984).

In a widely cited prospective study, Kobasa, Maddi, and Courington (1981) examined 259 executives over a period of years. Both hardiness and life events predicted their subsequent illness. However, the results of other studies have not been consistent with their findings. Indeed, although hardiness is widely discussed in the stress research as a buffer, the evidence is weak at best. (Cohen & Edwards, 1989). One reason for this inconsistency is that hardiness is frequently assessed through personality measures of alienation from stress, locus of control, and life goals evaluation. Yet that these measures accurately test control, commitment, and challenge is open to question (Lazarus & Folkman, 1984). Also, hardiness may simply be another name for psychological health or high self-esteem, variables that are occasionally, and somewhat inconsistently, found to be associated with stress (Cohen & Edwards, 1989). We shall consider this point later in this chapter when we discuss negative affectivity.

Coping Traits II: Specific Beliefs Concerning Secondary Appraisal

The coping traits we have considered so far—explanatory style, locus of control, coherence, and hardiness—reflect abstract beliefs, values, and commitments concerning oneself and the world. A second set of coping traits concerns a specific group of beliefs about a person's options and prospects for coping. As we saw in Chapter 5, such beliefs form a person's secondary appraisal of a stressful situation.

Self-Efficacy

As we have noted, self-efficacy is part of secondary appraisal of a specific stressful situation. Self-efficacy can also be considered as a general disposition or trait. To review, Bandura (1977) has proposed that enduring beliefs concerning efficacy can often make the difference between success and failure. *Efficacy expectancy* is the belief that a person can and has the intention to complete a specific behavior required to produce a desired outcome, and *outcome expectancy* is the estimate that a given behavior will lead to the outcome. Given the right incentives, efficacy expectancies play an important part in determining how a person copes. Research suggests that people who believe they cannot cope tend to dwell on personal deficiencies and exaggerate potential difficulties. Such *self-referent misgivings* create fear and anxiety, impair performance by diverting attention from effective action, and contribute to giving up. In contrast, high efficacy expectancies can contribute to a willingness to take on challenges and persist in the face of obstacles and frustration (Bandura, 1982). An important question (Baker & Kirsch, 1991; Kirsch, 1985) in self-efficacy research is the extent to which efficacy expectancies reflect beliefs concerning *ability* ("I can cope.") or *intention* ("I will cope.").

Optimism and Pessimism

Optimism and *pessimism* are constructs that bear some similarity to self-efficacy. Generally, Scheier and Carver (1987) define optimists as having favorable expectations for their future, and pessimists as having unfavorable expectations. Compared to self-efficacy theory, optimism/pessimism theory focuses on the importance of outcome expectancy, that is, the confidence that an outcome will occur regardless of whether it is due to personal efforts or outside assistance; we have seen that Bandura's notion of self-efficacy concentrates on personal expectations that an individual can attain a specific outcome. Research suggests that optimists are less likely to disengage from threat and experience distress, and more likely to engage in active coping (Carver & Scheier, 1990, 1990a; Carver, Scheier, & Weintraub, 1989; Scheier, Weintraub, & Carver, 1986).

Hope

Hope (Snyder et al., 1991) is a newly operationalized construct that also bears considerable similarity to self-efficacy. Snyder and his colleagues have identified two components of hope: (1) successful *agency*, or a positive sense of determination to meet goals ("I can find a way to solve the problem; I meet the goals that I set for myself."); and (2) successful *pathways*, or a sense of being able to generate successful plans to meet goals ("I can think of many ways to get out of a jam; I know I can find a way to solve the problem."). Both are required for successful coping. A determined person without a path has nowhere to go; a person lacking determination will not move even when a path is present. Research on hope has just begun.

Constructive Thinking

Epstein (Epstein, 1990; Epstein & Meier, 1989) has defined *constructive thinking* as a person's ability to think in a manner that solves everyday problems at a minimal cost in stress. Specifically, it is defined in terms of automatic constructive thoughts ("When doing an unpleasant chore, I make the best of it by thinking pleasant or interesting thoughts; if I do poorly on a test, I realize it is only a single test, and it doesn't make me feel generally incompetent.") and destructive thoughts that one might encounter ("When something bad happens to me, I feel that more bad things are likely to follow; I spend a lot of time thinking about my mistakes, even if there is nothing I can do about them."). Research on this construct has also just started.

Social Problem-Solving

One of the most concrete conceptualizations of positive traits has focused both on relatively general coping beliefs and specific coping patterns. D'Zurilla and Nezu's (D'Zurilla, 1986, 1990; Nezu & D'Zurilla, 1989) social problem-solving model of stress and coping consists of two components. The first, *problem orientation* includes the general tendency to perceive a problem as a challenge or an opportunity for benefit, respond with positive emotions, and actively approach and handle a problem with dispatch. In contrast, a more negative orientation views a problem as a threat, responds with negative emotions, and avoids coping. Second, *problem-solving skills* include problem definition and formulation, generation of alternative solutions, decision-making, and solution implementation and verification. Research suggests that problem orientation and problem-solving skills are somewhat distinct (people may have strengths in one and weaknesses in the other). A person might speculate from this that the more general traits we first considered—*i.e.*, explanatory style, locus of control, hardiness, and coherence—may be distinct from more specific patterns of coping. Initial research suggests a negative relation between problem orientation and problem-solving skills and subsequent depression and stress (D'Zurilla & Sheedy, 1991).

You may have noticed a similarity between the research on positive patterns of coping and the research discussed in Chapter 5. To recall, Lazarus and others (Folkman & Lazarus, 1985) have developed comprehensive lexicons of coping strategies, most of which include notions considered here, such as defining a problem, actively approaching a problem, and seeing a problem as a challenge. However, there is a fundamental distinction between the theories discussed in this chapter and the work on coping presented in Chapter 5. Research on positive patterns of coping derive from initial hypotheses concerning what constitutes effective coping, whereas the coping research of Lazarus and his colleagues makes no initial assumptions. To elaborate, self-efficacy, optimism, hope, constructive thinking, and problem-solving are proposed by their promoters to be positive, effective general coping strategies. By contrast, the transactional researchers of the previous chapter treat these strategies with utter neutrality and indeed are even open to the possibility that they may be destructive in certain circumstances.

Finally, another domain of coping research has focused on specific and isolated coping strategies. For example, there are literatures (complete with theories and assessment inventories) on assertiveness, negotiation, relaxation, and rational thinking. Since most of this work has evolved from clinical stress management and is applied to stress management, we shall consider it in Part IV.

Truth Versus Illusion

An important issue concerning the models we have been considering is the difference between perception and reality. Which is more important: perceived or actual self-efficacy, resourcefulness, hardiness, coherence, and optimism? When provided with an *illusion of control*, people often find stressful situations less aversive. If, for example, a laboratory subject is threatened with a loud noise and is told incorrectly that pushing a certain button will reduce the noise, then stress is reduced (Pennebaker, Burnam, Schaeffer, & Harper, 1977). In addition, people often perceive that they are in control when in fact they are not. In a classic series of studies, Langer (1975) presented subjects with a selection of lottery tickets. Of course, chance alone determines which ticket wins. Yet, subjects were willing to pay more when given the opportunity to choose among several tickets. Langer concluded that when a chance situation (winning the lottery) is made to resemble a situation in which skill is usually called for (making choices), people take on a *skill orientation*, that is, they assume that they have control even when no control is possible.

Traits Associated with Illness

Negative Affectivity and Neuroticism

Hundreds of terms are used when describing personalities. A friend may be thought of as "warm, friendly, kind, and generous," a teacher as "hard-working, thoughtful, cool, and intellectual," and so on. Through complex statistical procedures, researchers have been able to sort the broad lexicon of personality traits into five general factors (Digman & Takemoto-Chock, 1981; Goldberg, 1982; McCrae & Costa, 1984). These include three factors that are linked with stress (neuroticism, extroversion, and agreeableness), and two that have not yet been clearly linked with stress (openness to experience and conscientiousness).

As the name suggests, *neuroticism* refers to general emotional instability, maladjustment, and distress. Six specific traits that are often seen as typical of neuroticism are anxiety, hostility, depression, self-consciousness, impulsiveness, and vulnerability. Of these, anxiety, depression, and hostility are most consistently associated with a variety of illnesses (Friedman & Booth-Kewley, 1987). Indeed, one important debate in personality research concerns whether such constructs are in fact distinct or part of a global construct, *negative affectivity* (Watson & Clark, 1984). To elaborate, those with negative affectivity tend to be self-preoccupied, have a negative view of themselves and the world, experience discomfort at all times and across situations even in the absence of stress, and are highly reactive to even minor stressors. Indeed, such individuals appear to be more highly disposed to respond negatively to almost any test or questionnaire item, resulting in spurious correlations between negative affectivity and job stress, satisfaction, health, and a host of other variables (Watson, Pennebaker, & Folger, 1987).

HOSTILITY.   The pattern becomes more complex when we examine the involvement of other traits, particularly with respect to hostility. A number of researchers distinguish between three types of expression of hostility: *anger-in*, or keeping feelings within; *anger-out*, or confrontively expressing anger; and *problem-solving*, or directing attention toward solving anger-provoking problems (Funkenstein, King, & Drolette, 1957; Harburg, Blakelock, & Roeper, 1979; Spielberger, Jacobs, Russell, & Crane, 1983). There is tentative evidence that both anger-in and anger-out strategies contribute to higher blood pressure and perhaps other illnesses.

Stone and Costa (1990) have also pointed out the importance of distinguishing *antagonistic hostility* from neurotic hostility. Antagonistic hostility is essentially mean-spiritedness, or cold-blooded and callous hostility. In terms of the five general personality factors mentioned, individuals low on agreeableness tend not to be soft-hearted, trusting, helpful, and forgiving, but instead are antagonistic, cynical, rude, uncooperative, and manipulative. The relationship between antagonistic hostility and illness is fairly well established; research on disagreeableness and illness is still in its infancy.

INTROVERSION AND NEUROTICISM.   The link between extroversion and health has received some attention. Eysenck (1967) has focused on the interaction of extroversion-introversion and normality-neuroticism. The extrovert is a person who likes people and is sociable and easygoing. In contrast, the introvert is shy, quiet, withdrawn, and detached from social involvement. Generally, the extrovert seeks and the introvert avoids stimulation, possibly because introverts have higher levels of internally generated stimuli because of higher levels of a ascending reticular activating system arousal. Eysenck has also related neuroticism to arousal, particularly in the sympathetic nervous system. Those high in both neuroticism and introversions are prone to exaggerated responses to stress, presumably because they are prone to stress arousal from two sources, the ascending reticular activating system and the sympathetic nervous system.

Sensation- or arousal-seeking is a construct similar to extroversion. High-sensation-seekers prefer increased levels of stimulation (Zuckerman, 1974). They look for and enjoy activities that are exciting, stimulating, and arousing, such as traveling, motorcycling, and skiing. Low-sensation-seekers shy away from such activities and look for less arousing activities. You might expect high-sensation-seekers to be better able to cope with the increased arousal that might be associated with life change events. Evidence for this association is modest, however (Smith, Johnson, & Sarason, 1978).

Reactivity is yet another related concept associated with stress. Specifically, reactivity is defined in terms of a preference for low levels of stimulation and arousal, accompanied by high sensitivity to weak stimulation, heightened distractibility, and a lack of functional endurance or the ability to adapt to increasingly intense, prolonged, or repetitive stimulation (Kohn, 1985, 1987; Strelau, 1983). Reactivity appears to increase sensitivity to pain and to augment the impact of hassles on minor physical ailments (Kohn, Lafreniere, & Gurevich, 1991).

Finally, extroversion (and related traits) may well be part of a more general construct, *positive affectivity* consisting of psychological well-being, extroversion, energy, and enthusiasm (Tellegen, 1985). Those with positive affectivity lead full, happy, and interesting lives, and maintain high activity levels (Costa & McCrae, 1980; Tellegen, 1985; Watson & Clark, 1984).

Expression of Needs

Many of the positive traits we have considered, such as hope and optimism, reflect enduring beliefs, values, and commitments concerning control over life's stressors. Decades of research have examined a somewhat similar construct: the successfulness in expressing various needs. In terms of Lazarus's transactional model (Lazarus & Folkman, 1984), enduring thoughts about control are secondary appraisals; enduring thoughts about the frustration of needs are appraisals of threat, or primary appraisals. One of the earliest theories linking personality and disease has focused on needs and wishes that may be in conflict.

Alexander (1950) proposed that specific unconscious conflicts could lead to specific diseases. For example, he speculated that a patient with a peptic duodenal ulcer has an unconscious wish to be fed and nurtured. Ashamed of this wish, the ulcer patient displays a façade of independence. Patients with essential hypertension repress their own aggressiveness, fearing retaliation. Bronchial asthma patients desire to be enveloped and protected by their mother and fear rejection. Colitis patients experience frustration over their wish or hope of carrying out an obligation. Arthritis patients repress their rebellious and hostile tendencies. As might be expected, much controversy has surrounded Alexander's speculative links between specific conflicts and illnesses. However, his work pointed to the link among personality, stress, and disease, and anticipated much of the research being conducted today.

A somewhat different line of research has focused on *social motives*, or personality characteristics that energize, direct, and select behavior and experience (McClelland, 1980, 1985). McClelland and his colleagues concentrated on two such motives: power and affiliation. The power motivation is the desire to have an impact on others by influencing, persuading, helping, arguing with, or attacking them. The affiliation motive is the desire to establish, maintain, or restore warm relationships with other people not as a means to an end but as an end in its own right (Jemmott, 1987). In and of themselves, neither motive is strongly linked to disease. However, illness does appear to be linked to power motivation that is stressed by external events that block its expression (failing an exam) or inhibited by an internal hesitation to experience or express power. For example, a power-motivated executive who is constantly rebuffed in her attempts at promotion (stressed power motive) and feels that such needs are wrong and should be suppressed (inhibited power motive) would be at risk for illness. Similarly, unstressed and relaxed affiliation appears to be associated with lower illness. For example, an individual with such affiliation needs would likely want and freely acknowledge and act on a desire for warm relationships (relaxed affiliation), and not be blocked by external circumstances in making friends (unstressed).

An impressive body of research generally confirms the expected relationship between power and affiliation and elevated sympathetic nervous and endocrine system arousal, impaired immune system functioning, and illness. Such impairments can be both long- and, as indicated by recent research, short-term. In one clever and often misquoted study, McClelland and Kirshnit (1986) played documentaries of World War II battles (designed to arouse power motive) and Mother Theresa of Calcutta caring for the sick and dying (designed to arouse the affiliation motive). Saliva samples revealed that subjects with an inhibited power motive manifested lower immune system antibody levels after watching the war film (see Chapter 7). The Mother Theresa documentary had no such effect.

Type A and B Behavior Patterns

Heart disease is the leading cause of death in the West. Perhaps this is one reason researchers have spent considerable time and effort exploring the link between stress and heart disease. An enormous amount of this research has focused on one pattern, the *Type A behavior pattern* (TABP). Health professionals have long suspected a link between heart disease and stress. As early as the turn of the century, Canadian physician Sir William Osler (1910) noted that "in the worry and strain of modern life, arterial degeneration is not only very common but develops at a relatively early age. For this, I believe that the high pressure at which men live, and the habit of working the machine to its maximum capacity are responsible for coronary disease." Furthermore, he proposed that the person at greatest risk was not the "delicate neurotic" but the "robust, the vigorous in mind and body, the keen and ambitious man, the indicator of whose machine is always at full speed ahead" (Osler, 1910, p. 840).

Two cardiologists, Friedman and Rosenman (1974), were the first to explore this pattern systematically. Their work began with an unexpected observation: cardiac patients appeared to show a consistent set of unusual behaviors. Often they would sit on the edges of their seats during examinations. Their wives would often complain about the degree of stress their husbands experienced. Eventually, Friedman and Rosenman offered the classic definition of the TABP:

> a characteristic action-emotion complex which is exhibited by those individuals who are engaged in a relatively *chronic struggle* to obtain an *unlimited* number of *poorly defined* things from their environment in *the shortest period of time* and, if necessary, against the opposing efforts of other things and persons (Friedman, 1969, p. 84).

This pattern often includes a degree of hostility, both repressed and expressed.

The TABP is often seen in contrast to the *Type B behavior pattern*, which typically includes being relaxed, easygoing, readily satisfied, and less concerned with achievement and acquisition needs. In general, the Type B behavior pattern has been poorly and inconsistently defined, and probably represents a trait that is separate and distinct from the TABP, rather than being just the opposite of the TABP.

Three methods evolved for assessing the TABP: a formal, structured interview (Chesney, Eagleston, & Rosenman, 1981); the Framingham Scale (Haynes, Levine, Scotch, Feinleib, & Kannel, 1978); and the Jenkins Activity Survey (Jenkins, Zyzanski, & Rosenman, 1971). Of these, the structured interview may be the best predictor of heart disease. Indeed, people who score high on one assessment tool do not necessarily score high on another (Matthews, Krantz, Dembroski, & Mac-Dougall, 1982). This serious problem anticipated a history of research troubles.

At first, it appeared that different assessment tools were simply tapping different behaviors. A close examination of the tests in question suggested that this interpretation made some sense. The structured interview lasts from fifteen to twenty minutes and involves a series of questions about daily activities. The interviewer might ask, for example, "What irritates you most about your work or the people with whom you work?" The interviewer tends to be challenging and deliberately interrupt or challenge a response, or may even ask an obvious question in a deliberately slow manner. The point is to provoke the interviewee into displaying TABP. Indeed, the scoring of the structured interview is based only on such behaviors as explosiveness of answers, firmness of handshake, and loudness of voice (see Table 6.1) rather than on the actual content of responses.

The structured interview is essentially a measure of reactivity to events that are frustrating, difficult, or moderately competitive. In contrast, the Jenkins Activity Survey appears to measure two factors, Achievement Strivings and Impatience and

TABLE 6.1   Type A Behaviors Measured by the Structured Interview

- Expressions of vigor, energy, alertness, and confidence
- Firm handshake
- Brisk walking pace
- Loud, vigorous voice
- Terse speech
- Clipped speech (failure to pronounce the ending sounds of words)
- Rapid speech
- Acceleration of speech at the end of a long sentence
- Explosive speech
- Interrupting examiner
- Hurrying examiner by saying "yes, yes," "right, right," etc.
- Vehement reactions to questions relating to impedance of time
- Clenching fists or pointing fingers
- Sighing
- Hostility
- Frequent, abrupt, emphatic, one-word responses to questions ("Yes! Never!")

SOURCE   Adapted from Chesney, Eagleston, and Rosenman (1981), pp. 40–41.

Irritability (Pred, Spence, & Helmreich, 1986). Finally, the Framington Scale misses many of the behaviors originally thought be part of the TABP; instead, it focuses on dissatisfaction and discomfort with competition and work.

Two classic studies have offered strong support for a link between TABP and heart disease. In the first, known as the Western Collaborative Group Study (WCGS), 3,524 men were initially given a complete medical exam and the structured interview (Rosenman et al., 1975). At the outset, 113 had coronary heart disease, 71 percent of whom displayed the TABP. The remaining subjects were followed for eight and one-half years. During this period, another 257 men developed coronary disease, 69 percent of whom were Type As. The Type As had a risk of heart disease that was 2.37 times greater than that of the Type Bs. When other risk factors (age, systolic blood pressure, cigarette smoking, and serum cholesterol) were taken into account, the estimated relative risk was reduced, but was still 1.97 times greater for Type As.

The second project, the Framingham Heart Study, lasted more than eight years, and involved long-term follow-up of 1,700 coronary-free males and females who had been classified as Type As and Type Bs in the 1960s. The findings of the WCGS were replicated and extended to women. Indeed, Type A women were nearly twice as likely as Type Bs to experience heart disease (Haynes, Feinleib, & Kannel, 1980).

This coach shows the signs of Type A behavior.
(Photo by Joel Gordon.)

Clearly there is a relationship between Type A behavior and heart disease. Indeed, it is quite possible that the link has been understated; in a twenty-two year follow-up of the WCGS sample, the TABP was a risk factors for all forms of morbidity (Yakubovich, Ragland, Brand, & Syme, 1988). However, a number of studies have revealed several serious inconsistencies in that finding. At times the TABP is not related to illness. Perhaps part of the inconsistency is due to the fact that different measures are used to examine the connection between the TABP and disease, measures that, as we have seen, are relatively unrelated. However, this points to a deeper problem: just what *is* the crucial component of the TABP?

Hostility has most frequently been identified as the "toxic" component of the TABP (Dembroski & Costa, 1987; Williams, Barefoot, & Shekelle, 1985). Indeed, acute anger, rather than fear and anxiety, does tend to be associated with sympathetic nervous system arousal and increased diastolic blood pressure. Furthermore, Type A hostility could well contribute to distrustful hypervigilance, which in experimental studies is associated with increased muscle vasoconstriction and norepinephrine, which are also associated with hypertension (Williams et al., 1982). And chronic hostility may well contribute to chronic sympathetic nervous system arousal, which in turn could contribute to illness (Julius, Schneider, & Egan, 1985). This pattern of arousal may well be complicated by Type As tendency not to note fatigue and illness, and presumably not to take preventive action (Carver, Coleman, & Glass, 1976).

From the onset, the TABP was conceptualized as occurring in response to certain environmental stimuli. Early researchers postulated that Type As have a heightened need to exert control over their environment and find the prospect of a loss of that control particularly threatening (Glass, 1977). Specifically, a potentially destructive component of the TABP may be a tendency to exhibit swings from an excessive desire for control to a surrendering of control in the face of the frustration of excessive control. Much of the situational research on the TABP can be interpreted in light of this theory. When Type A males are presented with annoying or harassing conditions, or pressure to accomplish something in a short time, they respond with elevated physical stress. Type As select faster work paces and heavier work paces perhaps contributing to stress. However, they cope better than Type Bs with a lighter work load, and their superior performance appears not to have physiological costs. Consistent with this finding, Lazarus and Folkman (1984) have proposed that the TABP is potentially stressful when combined with low coping skills; that is, Type As who are poor copers and who view what they are doing as threatening are under greater risk for heart disease than other Type As.

Type C Cancer-Prone Coping Style

A constellation of traits has been suggested as associated with cancer development and progression (Morris & Greer, 1980; Temoshok & Heller, 1984; Temoshok et al., 1985). The "Type C" cancer-prone individual has been described as "nice," stoic or self-sacrificing, cooperative and appeasing, unassertive, patient, compliant with external authorities, and unexpressive of negative emotions, particularly anger

(Temoshok, 1990). One process central to this pattern may be the nonexpression of emotion (Gross, 1989).

Temoshok (1987) has proposed a model that specifies different processes for cancer initiation and progression. At first, the cancer-prone individual utilizes a Type C coping style to accommodate to everyday stressors. By keeping a "stiff upper lip," only certain stressors are dealt with, while personal needs and feelings are minimized and not expressed. However, when rigidly applied to all of life's problems, this strategy is not completely successful; problems tend to be put aside rather than solved. Eventually, stress increases, perhaps aggravated by severe life events.

In time, perhaps because of increased levels of stress, cancer takes hold and is diagnosed and the Type C coping style is no longer successful. It is no longer possible to suppress needs, feelings, and disappointments completely and carry on with a happy façade. At this crisis point, there are three possible outcomes: (1) the individual may develop a more stable and adequate coping style, hopefully involving the appropriate expression of needs and feelings and the recruitment of genuine social support; (2) the Type C façade breaks down, exposing feelings of hopelessness and helplessness; or (3) the individual continues to cope using the same Type C style. Thus, according to this model, Type C coping should be predictive early in the development of cancer, whereas once cancer is diagnosed, factors such as hopelessness, helplessness, and inadequate emotional expression may assume more importance as predictors.

Personality and Disease: A Complex Relationship

Any consideration of personality and illness must examine an important issue that has perhaps been most vigorously stated in terms of the construct *negative affectivity*, or the general disposition to see oneself and the world in negative terms. The argument is that correlations between various stress measures, for example, life events and illness, lack of exercise and fitness, hassles and illness, and social support and health, really reflect the operation of underlying negative affectivity. Those who view themselves and the world negatively, will, because of their negativity, *claim* more negative life events and hassles, lower levels of fitness, less social support, greater illness, and so on. In other words, they are prone to think negatively just about anything (Costa & McCrae, 1987; Watson & Clark, 1984; Watson & Pennebaker, 1989).

Actually, the same problem exists for any enduring disposition we have considered in this and the previous chapter, especially if it is measured through self-report. Those who report Type A or Type C behavior, general defensiveness, hopelessness, or low self-efficacy may display a similarly negative propensity to describe life events, hassles, illness, and so forth.

This problem clearly points to the need for a broadly focused transactional assessment of stress, one that considers all antecedent, process, and consequence variables. If any one variable is left out of the stress equation, its role will never be known. Recent studies on Type A behavior have begun to take this direction. If extended, this line of research may well yield a full portrait of the stress dynamics of heart disease.

To illustrate, one proposed component of Type A behavior—hostility, or negative affectivity,—can be viewed as a causal personal antecedent, a self-reported trait. In addition, assume that this Type A person generally finds himself in work situations with poorly defined goals but urgent deadlines. These can be introduced as causal situational antecedents. In such situations he desires to be in control and know what is going on; however, since these desires are threatened, he fears losing control. Each of these is an appraisal. This person tries to cope by working harder and longer, and putting his feelings of fatigue and frustration aside. His physiological reactions include activation of his sympathetic nervous system. Emotionally, he occasionally experiences fatigue. The long-term consequences of such behavior are varied. First, he is setting himself up for heart disease. He also experiences a general dissatisfaction with life. He functions adequately at work but is not particularly creative. As a result, he is often passed by for promotion. Table 6.2 organizes these variables in terms of the transactional matrix.

Close examination of this matrix reveals that *any component* can be either a cause or an effect. For example, perhaps the Type A subject's hostile behavior irritates his superiors, who in turn are less inclined to spend extra time clearly defining his goals or checking to see if his deadlines are reasonable. Of course, poorly defined work goals and urgent deadlines could contribute to hostility. Furthermore, his coping attempts of working harder and putting his feelings of fatigue and frustration aside may either result from or contribute to his hostility and work ambiguities. Even the long-term result, heart disease, could be either a result of any of the preceding patterns or a contributing cause. For example, wishing to prove that he does not have heart disease, the subject may work even harder and suppress his feelings even more. This consideration of personality and illness makes one lesson clear: when considering the many variables of stress, no specific cause-effect link should be assumed. Instead, we must be open to the possibility that numerous such links exist and that many of them may be mutually reinforcing *feedback loops*. In short, complete understanding of stress must consider all of its variables.

TABLE 6.2   Transactional Matrix for a Type A Individual

Variable	Long-Term Antecedents	Immediate Antecedents	Stressful Event	Immediate Consequences	Long-Term Consequences
Personal	General hostility, sympathetic nervous system arousal	Sympathetic nervous system arousal	Sympathetic nervous system arousal	Sympathetic nervous system arousal	Sympathetic nervous system arousal, heart disease, chronic dissatisfaction, adequate function at work
Situational	Poorly defined goals		Appraisals: Wants to have control and to know what's going on, fears losing control Coping: Works harder and longer, puts feelings of fatigue and frustration aside		
External	Urgent deadlines	Urgent deadlines	Urgent deadlines		Passed by for promotion

APPLICATION BOX 6.1

Your Personality and Stress

This chapter has considered a large number of personality traits. In understanding these, it can be useful to examine your own life and ask which bests describes what you are generally like.

The traits discussed in this chapter can be understood in terms of Ellis's irrational beliefs, Beck's negative thinking biases, as well as the many forms of coping and defense we have considered. For example, the Type A individual is often seen as engaging in *overcontrol*. He or she can be seen as engaged in a constant struggle to master even those things that cannot be mastered. Can you recognize how Ellis might see this behavior as reflecting an irrational belief that one must be in control at all times? What would Beck say? How could such overcontrol be a form of *denial* (perhaps denial that one is at times helpless)?

See if you can interpret other traits introduced in this chapter in terms of irrational beliefs, negative biases, defense, and coping.

Trait	Irrational Belief	Negative Bias	Defense	Coping
————	————	————	————	————
————	————	————	————	————
————	————	————	————	————
————	————	————	————	————
————	————	————	————	————
————	————	————	————	————

References

ABRAMSON, L., GARBER, G., & SELIGMAN, M. E. P. (1980). Learned helplessness in humans: An attributional analysis. In J. Garber & M. E. P. Seligman (Eds.), *Human helplessness: Theory and applications* (pp. 3–34). New York: Academic Press.

ALEXANDER, F. (1950). *Psychosomatic Medicine.* New York: Norton.

ANGELL, M. (1985). Disease as a reflection of the psyche. *The New England Journal of Medicine, 312,* 1570–1572.

ANTONOVSKY, A. (1979). *Health, stress, and coping.* San Francisco: Jossey-Bass.

ANTONOVKSY, A. (1987). *Unraveling the mystery of health.* San Francisco: Jossey-Bass.

BAKER, S. L., & KIRSCH, I. (1991). Cognitive mediators of pain perception and tolerance. *Journal of Personality and Social Psychology, 61,* 504–510.

BANDURA, A. (1977). Self-efficacy: Toward a unifying theory of behavioral change. *Psychological Review, 84,* 191–215.

BANDURA, A. (1982). Self-efficacy mechanism in human agency. *American Psychologist, 37,* 122–147.

CARVER, C. S., COLEMAN, A. E., & GLASS, D. C. (1976). The coronary-prone behavior pattern and the suppression of fatigue on a treadmill test. *Journal of Personality and Social Psychology, 33,* 460–466.

CARVER, C. S., & SCHEIER, M. F. (1990). Origins and functions of positive and negative affect: A control-process view. *Psychological Review, 97,* 19–35.

CARVER, C. S., & SCHEIER, M. F. (1990a). Principles of self-regulation. In E. T. Higgins & R. M. Sorrentino (Eds.), *Handbook of motivation and cognition: Foundations of social behavior* (vol 2, pp. 3–52). New York: Guilford.

CARVER, C. S., SCHEIER, M. F., & WEINTRAUB, J. K. (1989). Assessing coping strategies. A theoretically based approach. *Journal of Personality and Social Psychology, 56,* 267–283.

CHESNEY, M. A., EAGLESTON, J. R., & ROSENMAN, R. H. (1981). Type A behavior: Assessment and intervention. In C. K. Prokop & L. A. Bradley (Eds.), *Medical psychology: Contributions to behavioral medicine* (pp. 34–67). New York: Academic Press.

COHEN, S., & EDWARDS, J. R. (1989). Personality characteristics as moderators of the relationship between stress and disorder. In R. W. J. Neufeld (Ed.), *Advances in the investigation of psychological stress* (pp. 235–283). New York: Wiley.

COSTA, P. T., JR., & MCCRAE, R. R. (1980). Influence of extraversion and neuroticism on subjective well-being: Happy and unhappy people. *Journal of Personality and Social Psychology, 38,* 668–678.

COSTA, P. T., JR., & MCCRAE, R. R. (1987). Neuroticism, somatic complaints, and disease: Is the bark worse than the bite? *Journal of Personality, 55,* 299–316.

COUSINS, N. (1977). Anatomy of an illness (as perceived by the patient). *Saturday Review* (May 28, pp. 4–6, 48–51).

D'ZURILLA, T. J. (1986). *Problem-solving therapy: A social competence approach to clinical intervention.* New York: Springer.

D'ZURILLA, T. J. (1990). Problem-solving training for effective stress management and prevention. *Journal of Cognitive Psychotherapy: An International Quarterly, 4,* 327–354.

D'ZURILLA, T. J., & SHEEDY, C. F. (1991). Relation between social problem-solving ability and subsequent level of psychological stress in college students. *Journal of Personality and Social Psychology, 61,* 841–846.

DEMBROSKI, T. M., & COSTA, P. T. (1987). Coronary-prone behavior: Components of the Type A pattern and hostility. *Journal of Personality, 55,* 211–236.

DIGMAN, J. M., & TAKEMOTO-CHOCK, N. K. (1981). Factors in the natural language of personality: Re-analysis, comparison, and interpretation of six major studies. *Multivariate Behavioral Research, 16,* 149–170.

ENGEL, G. L. (1968). A life setting conducive to illness: The giving up–given up complex. *Bulletin of the Menninger Clinic, 32,* 355–365.

ENGEL, G. L., & SCHMALE, A. H. (1967). Psychoanalytic theory of somatic disorder. *Journal of the American Psychoanalytic Association, 15,* 344–363.

EPSTEIN, S. (1990). Cognitive-experiential self-theory. In L. Pervin (Ed.), *Handbook of personality theory and research* (pp. 165–191). New York: Guilford Press.

EPSTEIN, S., & MEIER, P. (1989). Constructive thinking: A broad coping variable with specific components. *Journal of Personality and Social Psychology, 53,* 572–578.

EYSENCK, H. (1967). *The Biological basis of personality.* Springfield, IL: Charles C Thomas.

FOLKMAN, S., & LAZARUS, R. S. (1985). If it changes it must be a process: Study of emotion and coping during three stages of a college examination. *Journal of Personality and Social Psychology, 48,* 150–170.

FRIEDMAN, H. S., & BOOTH-KEWLEY, S. (1987). The "disease-prone personality": A meta-analytic view of the construct. *American Psychologist, 42,* 539–555.

FRIEDMAN, M. (1969). *Pathogenesis of coronary artery disease.* New York: McGraw-Hill.

FRIEDMAN, M., & ROSENMAN, R. F. (1974). *Type A behavior and your heart.* New York: Knopf.

FUNKENSTEIN, D. H., KING, S. H., & DROLETTE, M. E. (1957). *Mastery of stress.* Cambridge, MA: Harvard University Press.

GLASS, D. C. (1977). *Behavior patterns, stress and coronary disease.* Hillsdale, NJ: Erlbaum.

GOLDBERG, L. R. (1982). From ace to zombie: Some explorations in the language of personality. In C. D. Spielberger & J. N. Butcher (Eds.) *Advances in personality assessment* (vol. 1, pp. 203–234). Hillsdale, NJ: Erlbaum.

GROSS, J. (1989). Emotional expression in cancer onset and progression. *Social Science and Medicine, 28,* 1239–1248.

HARBURG, E., BLAKELOCK, E. H., & ROEPER, P. J. (1979). Resentful and reflective coping with arbitrary authority and blood pressure: Detroit. *Psychosomatic Medicine, 41,* 189–202.

HAYNES, S. G., FEINLEIB, M., & KANNEL, W. B. (1980). The relationship of psychosocial factors to coronary heart disease in the Framingham study: III. Eight-year incidence of coronary heart disease. *American Journal of Epidemiology, 111,* 37–58.

HAYNES, S. G., LEVINE, S., SCOTCH, N., FEINLEIB, M., & KANNEL, W. (1978). The relationship of psychosocial factors to coronary heart disease in the Framingham study. *American Journal of Epidemiology, 107,* 362–383.

JANOFF-BULMAN, R., & WORTMAN, C. B. (1977). Attributions of blame and coping in the `real world': Severe accident victims react to their lot. *Journal of Personality and Social Psychology, 35,* 351–363.

JEMMOTT III, J. B. (1987). Social motives and susceptibility to disease: Stalking individual differences in health risks. *Journal of Personality, 55,* 267–298.

JENKINS, C. D., ZYZANSKI, S. J., & ROSENMAN, R. H. (1971). Progress toward validation of a computer-scored test for the type A coronary-prone behavior pattern. *Psychosomatic Medicine, 33,* 193–202.

JULIUS, S., SCHNEIDER, R., & EGAN, B. (1985). Suppressed anger in hypertension: Facts and problems. In M. Chesney & R. H. Rosenman (Eds.), *Anger and hostility in cardiovascular and behavioral disorders* (pp. 127–138). Washington, DC: Hemisphere.

KAMEN-SIEGEL, L., RODIN, J., SELIGMAN, M. E. P., DWYER, J. (1991). Explanatory style and cell-mediated immunity in elderly men and women. *Health Psychology, 10,* 229–235.

KIRSCH, I. (1985). Response expectancy as a determinant of experience and behavior. *American Psychologist, 40,* 1189–1202.

KOBASA, S. C., MADDI, S. R., & COURINGTON, S. (1981). Personality and constitution as mediators in the stress-illness relationship. *Journal of Health and Social Behavior, 22,* 368–378.

KOHN, P. M. (1985). Sensation seeking, augmenting-reducing, and strength of the nervous system. In J. T. Spence & C. Izard (Eds.), *Motivation, emotion, and personality: Proceedings of the XXIII International Congress of Psychology* (pp. 167–173). Amsterdam: North Holland.

KOHN, P. M., LAFRENIERE, K., & GUREVICH, M. (1991). Hassles, health, and personality. *Journal of Personality and Social Psychology, 61,* 478–482.

LANGER, E. J. (1975). The illusion of control. *Journal of Personality and Social Psychology, 32,* 311–328.

LAZARUS, R. S., & FOLKMAN, S. (1984). *Stress, appraisal, and coping.* New York: Springer.

LEFCOURT, H. (1981). *Research with the locus of control construct* (vol. I). New York: Academic Press.

LEFCOURT, H. M. (1985). Intimacy, social support, and locus of control as moderators of stress. In I. G. Sarason & B. R. Sarason (Eds.), *Social support: Theory, research, and applications* (pp. 155–172). Dordrecht: Martinus Nijhoff.

LEWIS, C. E., BIGLAN, A., & STEINBOCK, E. (1978). Self-administered relaxation training and money deposits in the treatment of recurrent anxiety. *Journal of Consulting and Clinical Psychology 4,* 1274–1283.

MADDI, S. R., & KOBASA, S. C. (1984). *The hardy executive: Health under stress.* Homewood, IL: Dow Jones-Irwin.

MATTHEWS, K. A., KRANTZ, D. S., DEMBROSKI, T. M., & MACDOUGALL, J. M. (1982). Unique and common variance in structured interview and Jenkins activity survey measures of the type A behavior pattern. *Journal of Personality and Social Psychology, 42,* 303–313.

McCLELLAND, D. C. (1980). Motive dispositions: The merits of operant and respondent measures. In L. Wheeler (Ed.), *Review of personality and social psychology* (vol. 1, pp. 10–41). Beverly Hills, CA: Sage.

McCLELLAND, D. C. (1985). *Human motivation.* Glenview, IL: Scott, Foresman.

McCLELLAND, D. C., & KIRSHNIT, C. (1986). The effect of motivational arousal through films on salivary immunoglobulin A. Unpublished manuscript, Boston University.

McCRAE, R. R., & COSTA, P. T., JR. (1984). *Emerging lives, enduring dispositions: Personality in adulthood.* Boston: Little, Brown.

MORRIS, T., & GREER, S. (1980). A "Type C" for cancer? Low trait anxiety in the pathogenesis of breast cancer. *Cancer Detection and Prevention, 3* (abstract no. 102).

NAGY, V. T., & WOLFE, G. R. (1983). Chronic illness and locus of control beliefs. *Journal of Social and Clinical Psychology, 1,* 58–65.

NEZU, A. M., & D'ZURILLA, T. J. (1989). Social problem solving and negative affective conditions. In P. C. Kendall & D. Watson (Eds.), *Anxiety and depression: Distinctive and overlapping features* (pp. 285–315). San Diego, CA: Academic Press.

OSLER, W. (1910). The Lumlein Lectures on angina pectoris. *Lancet, 1,* 839–844.

PENNEBAKER, J. W., BURNAM, M. A., SCHAEFFER, M. A., & HARPER, D. C. (1977). Lack of control as a determinant of perceived physical symptoms. *Journal of Personality and Social Psychology, 35,* 167–174.

PETERSON, C., & SELIGMAN, M. E. P. (1987). Explanatory style and illness. *Journal of Personality, 55,* 237–265.

PETERSON, C., SELIGMAN, M. E. P., & VAILLANT, G. E. (1988). Pessimistic explanatory style is a risk factor for physical illness: A thirty-five-year longitudinal study. *Journal of Personality and Social Psychology, 55,* 23–27.

PRAGER-DECKER, I. J. (1979). The relative efficacy of progressive relaxation, EMG biofeedback and music for reducing stress arousal of internally versus externally controlled individuals. *Dissertation Abstracts International, 39,* 3177B.

PRED, R., SPENCE, J., & HELMREICH, R. (1986). The development of new scales for the Jenkins Activity Survey measure of the Type A construct. *Social and Behavioral Documents, 16,* 51–52. (Ms. no. 2769).

ROSENMAN, R. H., BRAND, R. J., JENKINS, C. D., FRIEDMAN, M., STRAUSS, R., & WURM, M. (1975). Coronary heart disease in the Western Collaborative Group Study: Final follow-up experience of 8 1/2 years. *Journal of the American Medical Association, 233,* 872–877.

ROTTER, J. B. (1975). Some problems and misconceptions related to the construct of internal versus external control of reinforcement. *Journal of Consulting and Clinical Psychology, 43,* 56–67.

SCHEIER, M. F., & CARVER, C. S. (1987). Dispositional and physical well being: The influence of generalized expectances on health. *Journal of Personality, 55,* 169–210.

SCHEIER, M. F., WEINTRAUB, J. K., & CARVER, C. S. (1986). Coping with stress: Divergent strategies of optimists and pessimists. *Journal of Personality and Social Psychology, 51,* 1257–1264.

SCHMALE, A. H., JR. (1972). Giving up as a final common pathway to changes in health. *Advances in psychosomatic medicine, 8,* 20–40.

SCHMALE, A. H., JR., & ENGEL, G. L. (1967). The giving up–given up complex illustrated on film. *Archives of General Psychiatry, 17,* 135–145.

SELIGMAN, M. P. E. (1975). *Helplessness: On depression, development, and death.* San Francisco: Freeman.

SMITH, R. E., JOHNSON, J. G., & SARASON, I. G. (1978). Life change, the sensation seeking motive, and psychological distress. *Journal of Consulting and Clinical Psychology, 46,* 348–349.

SNYDER, C. R., HARRIS, C., ANDERSON, J. R., HOLLERAN, S. A., IRVING, L. M., SIGMON, S. T., YOSHINOBU, L., GIBB, J., LANGELLE, C., & HARNEY, P. (1991). The will and the ways: Development and validation of an individual-differences measure of hope. *Journal of Personality and Social Psychology, 60,* 570–585.

SPIELBERGER, C. D., JACOBS, G., RUSSELL, S., & CRANE, R. (1983). Assessment of anger: The State-Trait Anger Scale. In J. N. Butcher & C. D. Spielberger (Eds.), *Advances in personality assessment: Vol. 2* (pp. 161–189). Hillsdale, NJ: Erlbaum.

STONE, S. V., & COSTA, JR., P. T. (1990). Disease-prone personality or distress-prone personality? The role of neuroticism in coronary heart disease. In H. S. Friedman (Ed.), *Personality and disease* (pp. 178–202). New York: Wiley.

STRELAU, J. (1983). *Temperament, personality, activity.* San Diego, CA: Academic Press.

TAYLOR, S. E., LICHTMAN, R. R., & WOOD, J. V. (1984). Attributions, beliefs about control, and adjustment to breast cancer. *Journal of Personality and Social Psychology, 46,* 489–502.

TELLEGEN, A. (1985). Structures of mood and personality and their relevance to assessing anxiety, with an emphasis on self-report. In A. H. Tuma & J. D. Maser (Eds.), *Anxiety and anxiety disorders* (pp. 681–706). Hillsdale, NJ: Erlbaum.

TEMOSHOK, L. (1987). Personality, coping style, emotion, and cancer: Toward an integrative model. *Cancer Surveys, 6,* 837–909.

TEMOSHOK, L. (1990). On attempting to articulate the biopsychosocial model: Psychological-physiological homeostasis. In H. S. Friedman (Ed.), *Personality and disease* (pp. 203–225). New York: Wiley.

TEMOSHOK, L., & HELLER, B. W. (1984). On comparing apples, oranges, and fruit salad: A methodological overview of medical outcome studies in psychosocial oncology. In C. L. Cooper (Ed.), *Psychosocial stress and cancer* (pp. 231–261). Chichester, England: Wiley.

TEMOSHOK, L., HELLER, B. W., SAGEBIEL, R. W., BLOIS, M. S., SWEET, D. M., DiCLEMENTE, R. J., & GOLD, M. L. (1985). The relationship of psychosocial factors to prognostic indicators in cutaneous malignant melanoma. *Journal of Psychosomatic Research, 29,* 139–154.

WALLSTON, K. A., WALLSTON, B. S., & DeVELLIS, R. (1978). Development of the Multidimensional Health Locus of Control (MHLC) scales. *Health Education Monographs, 6,* 160–170.

WATSON, D., & CLARK, L. A. (1984). Negative affectivity: The disposition to experience aversive emotional states. *Psychological Bulletin, 96,* 465–490.

WATSON, D., & PENNEBAKER, J. W. (1989). Health complaints, stress, and distress: Exploring the central role of negative affectivity. *Psychological Review, 96,* 234–254.

WATSON, D., PENNEBAKER, J. W., & FOLGER, R. (1987). Beyond negative affectivity: Measuring stress and satisfaction in the work place. In J. M. Ivancevich & D. C. Ganster (Eds.), *Job stress: From theory to suggestion* (pp. 141–157). New York: Haworth Press.

WILLIAMS, R. B., BAREFOOT, J., & SHEKELLE, R. B. (1985). The health consequences of hostility. In M. Chesney & R. H. Rosenman (Eds.), *Anger and hostility in cardiovascular and behavioral disorders* (pp. 173-186). Washington, DC: Hemisphere.

WILLIAMS, R. B., LANE, J. D., KUHN, C. M., MELOSH, W., WHITE, A. D., & SCHANBERG, R. E. (1982). Type A behavior and elevated physiological and neuroendocrine responses to cognitive tasks. *Science, 218,* 483–485.

YAKUBOVICH, I. S., RAGLAND, D. R., BRAND, R. J., & SYME, S. L. (1988). Type A behavior pattern and health status after 22 years of follow-up in the Western Collaborative Group Study. *American Journal of Epidemiology, 128,* 579–588.

ZUCKERMAN, M. (1974). The sensation-seeking motive. In B. Maher (Ed.), *Progress in experimental personality research: (Vol. 7)* (pp. 80–148). New York: Academic Press.

CHAPTER 7

Stress and Illness

The link between stress and disease has been headline news for several decades. At first, the biological model introduced the concept of "one germ, one disease, one therapy." This view is now seen as too simplistic. Medical textbooks in the 1960s often spoke of a limited number of "stress-related" and "psychosomatic" illnesses. Even this expanded view is no longer accepted by most researchers. The harsh (or hopeful) reality appears to be that all diseases can be stress related, and that perhaps all of the stress dimensions we have considered, notably life events, social support, coping, and personality, are potential risk factors for illness. In this chapter we shall examine the physiological mechanisms whereby stress contributes to illness. We begin with the immune system.

The Immune System

We are constantly exposed to bacteria, viruses, fungi, parasites, and poisons. At times, these assaults can cause serious illness and even death. However, our bodies are usually able to defend against such organisms and toxins.

The body's *immune system* is a powerful defense against illness. However, immunity can be seriously compromised, and occasionally augmented, by stress. For this reason, any serious consideration of stress must examine the complexities of the immune system.

The immune system has two general components. One, called *innate immunity*, has a nonspecific protective value against a wide range of assaults. In contrast, *acquired immunity* is targeted toward specific organisms or toxins (Guyton, 1991).

Innate Immunity

Our bodies are built for self-protection against many general forms of assault. This capacity is called innate immunity. The skin is a tough protective barrier against infection. Secretions of harsh acids and digestive fluids in the stomach destroy many forms of bacteria and viruses. The blood itself contains many chemical compounds that can attach to foreign organisms or toxins to destroy them. However, the most complex form of innate immunity involves a special type of blood cell.

Most people know that blood consists of red and white blood cells. Red blood cells carry oxygen throughout the body. White blood cells, also known as leukocytes, have a variety of functions related to immunity. Leukocytes are mobile units of the body's immune system that are formed in the bone marrow and lymph tissue, and then transported in the bloodstream to where they are needed.

NEUTROPHILS AND MONOCYTE-MACROPHAGES.   Of the many types of leukocytes, the most important are *neutrophils* and *monocyte-macrophages*. These cells attack and destroy bacteria, viruses, and other potentially destructive substances. Neutrophils are adult cells that are fully capable of defending the body. Monocytes are immature cells that must develop and greatly expand into powerful, giant white blood cells called macrophages. Together, neutrophils and macrophages are able defenders indeed. Specifically, they destroy or eat, or as it is technically called, *phagocytize* (from the Greek word *phagein*, meaning "eat" or "destroy"). Because of this function, such cells are often called *phagocytes*.

Phagocytes are transported through the blood from the bone marrow or lymphoid tissue to areas of the body where they are needed. Macrophages can even reside as strategic reserves in the skin, lungs, liver, spleen, and bone marrow, waiting to be called into action. For example, this is what happens in the process of inflammation.

INFLAMMATION.   When the body is injured, whether by a bacterial infection, a cut, chemicals, or a burn, a variety of changes take place to protect the body and facilitate healing. A red, "inflamed" sore may appear, which is a sign that local blood vessels are dilating or expanding to increase blood flow to the injured area. Then, the blood vessels become more permeable, allowing needed fluids to leak into the spaces between cells. Special clotting substances seep into these spaces to form a protective scar. Large numbers of white blood cells migrate to the tissue to combat disease (once these cells do their work and die, they form a white substance called "pus"). In addition, as cells rupture, additional substances are discharged that call neutrophils and macrophages into action to destroy viruses, bacteria, or toxins that may be present. Finally, the entire neutrophil-macrophage response is regulated by a complex array of substances released by the macrophages and inflamed tissue, the most important perhaps being tumor necrosis factor and interleukin-one. As we shall see in the following section, the role of neutrophils and macrophages goes far beyond inflammation.

Acquired Immunity

Acquired immunity is a truly remarkable defense. When activated, it can protect the body against doses of certain toxins 100,000 times the lethal level. There are two basic types of acquired immunity: (1) humoral, or B cell, immunity; and (2) cell-mediated, or T cell, immunity. Both involve the protective activity of specialized white blood cells that are called *antibodies* for humoral immunity and *sensitized lym-*

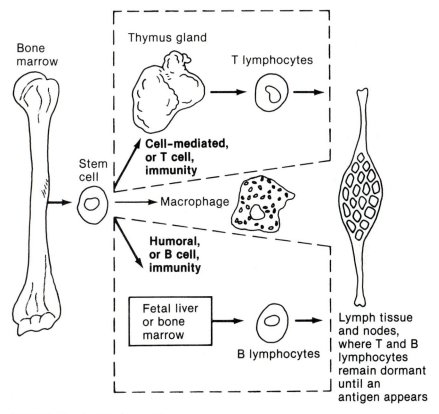

FIGURE 7.1   Acquired immunity.

phocytes for cell-mediated immunity. The viruses, bacteria, and toxins that attack the body are called *antigens*.

ORIGINS OF ACQUIRED IMMUNITY.   Acquired immunity begins from one type of cell, called the stem cell (see Figure 7.1). Originating from bone marrow (soft tissue within the bones), stem cells migrate to the thymus gland at the base of the neck, where they are preprocessed into T lymphocytes. Other stem cells migrate in fetal life to the liver and bone marrow (also called the B-processing area), where they are preprocessed into B lymphocytes. Eventually, T and B lymphocytes migrate through the blood and settle in lymph tissue and nodes.[1] However, at this point, T and B lymphocytes are still immature and cannot protect the body against illness.

---

[1] The body's cardiac circulatory system transports life-sustaining blood through the veins and arteries. The *lymph system* is the body's second circulatory system. Unlike the cardiac system, the lymph system has no heart and blood; instead, a special fluid, lymph, carries away cell wastes and houses special immune system cells. Special bulbs of lymph tissue, called lymph nodes, are strategically placed so they can attack disease in early stages.

ACTIVITY OF ANTIBODIES AND SENSITIZED LYMPHOCYTES.   T and B lymphocytes remain dormant in lymph tissue, like troops in reserve. Macrophages, which
are giant white blood cells, ingest an invading agent and discharge the partially
digested remains. In turn, these remains activate specific T and B lymphocytes to
produce vast quantities of sensitized T cells and antibodies, the "storm troopers" of
acquired immunity. Some of these activated cells fight off the invading agent.

When activated, B lymphocytes produce plasma cells that then secrete "killer protein" substances called antibodies including: IgM, IgG, IgA, IgD, and IgE (*Ig* stands
for *immunoglobulin protein*). Antibodies protect against invading agents by destroying
them or rendering them inactive. The immunoglobulin IgA is found in bodily fluids
such as tears, saliva, and respiratory and gastrointestinal tract secretions. IgE is
involved in allergic reactions.

In contrast, T lymphocytes do not secrete antibodies, but themselves proliferate
into three groups of sensitized T cells: helper T cells, killer T cells, and suppressor
T cells. Of these, the killer T cell is a direct attack cell, capable of killing foreign
agents. Both killer T cells and antibodies have the capacity to recruit macrophages
to destroy additional antigens.

Helper T cells are the most numerous and serve as the major regulator of virtually all immune functions. They do this by producing a series of "messenger substances," including the interleukins, the granulocyte-monocyte colony stimulating
factor, and interferon. These substances stimulate the activity of macrophages, antibodies, and killer, suppressor, and even helper T cells. Finally, the suppressor T cell
appears to have a regulatory function, and to turn off the immune system before it
becomes too active and begins to attack the body itself.

Amazingly, antibodies and T cells are highly specific; the body produces only
one type of immune cell for any one type of antigen, much as a single key fits
a single keyhole. In general, antibodies appear to target bacteria and certain viruses that appear outside of cells; T cells appear to target intracellular viruses, cancer cells, and transplant tissue (thus contributing to an occasional unfortunate
transplant rejection).

VACCINATION.   The body's first response to an antigen is relatively sluggish, but it
prepares the body for a more massive and rapid response to subsequent exposures.
This happens when, in addition to producing antibodies and sensitized T cells to
fight off an initial antigen exposure, the body creates vast quantities of reserve
"memory" B and T lymphocytes. When again exposed to the same antigen, memory
cell B lymphocytes produce additional antibody-generating plasma cells, and the
stored quantities of T lymphocytes are sensitized for a more powerful response (see
Figure 7.2).

This crucial step in the development of cellular immunity is activated every time
we are inoculated against a disease such as the flu, polio, and chicken pox. An inoculation involves the introduction into the body of an artificially produced antigen, a
harmless fragment (or thoroughly killed version) of a bacteria or virus. Once
injected into the body, this artificial antigen triggers the appropriate B or T lympho-

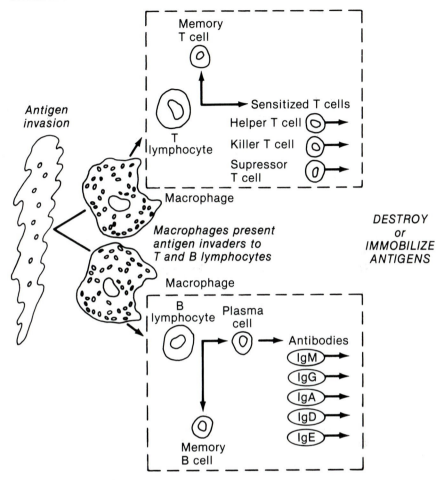

FIGURE 7.2   Activation of acquired immunity.

cytes (remember, these cells are highly specialized) to produce more B and T lymphocytes and enormous reserves of memory B and T lymphocytes. Now stocked with armies of highly targeted memory lymphocytes, the body is prepared to fight off future invading antigens with much greater efficiency.

Psychoneuroimmunology

It may appear that we have presented a great deal of detail about the functioning of the immune system, perhaps more than you wanted to know. However, the immune system is indeed extremely complex. Also, hardly a month goes by without research revealing that another component is linked to stress. Indeed, such research has given birth to a new area of study, *psychoneuroimmunology*.

Immune functions are known to be affected by many factors, including age, sex, race, nutrition, genetics, sunlight, temperature, circadian rhythms, trauma, drug and alcohol use, and many medications (Borsyenko, 1984). The effect of stress on these immune functions is complex and extensive (Ader, 1981; Ader, Felten, & Cohen, 1991; Jemmott & Locke, 1984). A variety of both experimentally and naturally occurring stressful situations have been examined, including space flight, sleep deprivation, academic exams, vigilance tasks, life-change events, bereavement, negative mood, and loneliness. Nearly all have been associated with the alternation of such components of immune functioning as macrophage and killer cell activity, leukocyte count, antibody levels, T cell transformation, and even atrophy of the thymus gland. Another line of evidence has shown that immune responses can be classically conditioned. Rats given an immune-suppressing drug and sweetened water eventually show immune suppression to the water only. In addition, hypnosis can enhance or inhibit immune system activity in some individuals. Clearly, a wide range of stress-related factors can affect the immune system. Most often, this impact is negative, although occasionally research finds that acute stress has an enhancing effect.

Several physiological mechanisms appear to mediate the impact of stress on immune functioning. First, elevated levels of catecholamines and corticoids associated with the general adaptation syndrome appear to contribute to the inhibition of inflammation, suppression of the immune system, and illness. Second, the autonomic nervous system connects with several major components of the immune system, including the thymus, spleen, and lymph nodes. Through such connections, the fight-or-flight response may well have a direct impact on immune functioning. Third, various neurotransmitters may well do more than serve as nerve-to-nerve messenger substances. Endorphins may decrease killer T cell activity and alter T cell production. Low levels of epinephrine and norepinephrine are also associated with immune system suppression, although high levels of dopamine and metenkephalin are associated with immune system enhancement. Some have hypothesized that there may be a family of sixty to one hundred neurotransmitters that carry messages back and forth between the central nervous system, endocrine system, and immune system (Vollhardt, 1991). Finally, to make matters more complex, various components of the immune system may in turn have an impact on the nervous and endocrine systems.

Gender Differences in Immune Functioning

Men and women are at risk for different illnesses. Women are more likely to be victimized by autoimmune diseases and men, by cardiovascular disorders. It is not surprising there are gender differences in immune functioning (Baum & Grunberg, 1991). Women display higher resting immunoglobulin levels and greater antibody responses to antigens. In contrast, women's cell-mediated immune responses appear to be weaker, although probably not enough to have an impact on health. These differences seem to be mediated by sex hormones. Boys in puberty show a greater disposition to allergies, but these gender differences decrease when levels of the male sex hormone testosterone and female sex hormone estrogen increase.

Estrogen appears to stimulate B cell and inhibit suppressor T cell function (Schuurs & Verheul, 1990). Male sex hormones appear to interfere with the maturation of both B cells and some T cells (Grossman, 1984).

The functioning of the human immune system can have an impact on a wide range of illnesses. In addition, various stress processes can directly contribute to illness. We shall now consider major categories of illness and their link to stress.

The Muscles

The fight-or-flight response can result in many types of physical movement, including walking, lifting, throwing, talking, expressing emotion, and even bracing and grimacing. All movement involves two general types of muscles: skeletal and smooth. *Skeletal muscles* are connected to bones (hence the term *skeletal*) and are responsible for deliberate movement. *Smooth muscles* surround the intestines, blood vessels, bladder, sweat glands, bronchial passages, and so on. They are generally controlled by the autonomic nervous system. Whatever the type, all muscles can do only two things: contract and relax.

Continuous and extreme muscle contraction can contribute to a variety of problems, including pain, fatigue, and organ dysfunction. When a contraction is partial, tension develops, but usually no actual work is done. For example, when blood vessels are partially closed, blood flow is constricted, a condition that can contribute to pain. Pain can also result when a chronically tense muscle exerts continuous pressure on a joint, or even contributes to improper posture or alignment of backbone vertebrae. Clearly, pain can also occur when a muscle is injured or torn through overexertion. Fatigue, a problem often associated with chronic muscle contraction, can be the result of the accumulation of lactic acid (a byproduct of continuous vigorous muscle activity), the depletion of fuel (glycogen) and oxygen, and even incomplete breathing because of tightened chest muscles and poor posture. Finally, the disruption of smooth muscles can contribute to disorders of the organs to which they are attached, including diarrhea and constipation (abnormal activity or inactivity of the colon), colitis (spasms of the lower colon), and esophageal spasms.

Often skeletal muscles are constricted unknowingly. People often tap their feet, fidget, clench their fists, shrug their shoulders, and tighten their jaws unwittingly. In addition, simply thinking of making a fist can result in subtle increases in tension detectable only through electromyograph (EMG) equipment. Such equipment senses minute electrical activity associated with the firing of muscle fibers. In addition, people often become used to and tune out continuous stimulation, such as the drone of air conditioners, traffic noises, and chronic muscle tension. Even though we may be unaware of it, muscle tension is still there. For this reason, one of the first tasks of relaxation programs designed to reduce muscle tension is to increase awareness of hidden sources of tension.

Cardiovascular Problems

Stress can contribute a variety of problems in the heart and circulatory system. Two major cardiovascular problems are hypertension and coronary artery disease. It has been estimated that from 15 to 20 percent of the adult population suffers from hypertension. About 90 percent of all cases involve essential hypertension, for which there is no known medical cause. Essential hypertension is associated with a range of risk factors, including poor diet, lack of exercise, smoking, alcohol consumption, and stress.

Hypertension is simply increased blood pressure caused by narrowed or blocked blood vessels, or an increased volume of blood pumped. The basic process is much like what would happen to water pressure in a hose if the hose were squeezed or blocked, or if the flow of water were increased. Technically, when the body is under stress, particularly in situations requiring active coping, the cardiac output increases, and supplies more blood and oxygen to tissues than is often needed (Turner & Carroll, 1985). As a result, homeostatic mechanisms attempt to return blood and oxygen supplies to normal, partly by narrowing peripheral arteries. This in turn increases blood pressure. In addition, sodium excretion (through urine and perspiration) is inhibited, resulting in increased sodium content in the blood and increased blood volume and pressure (Koepke, Light, Grignolo, & Obrist, 1983). The entire process is aggravated by the blocking of arteries caused by the accumulation of fats and cholesterol. Since hypertension, and many of its associated stress processes, contribute to coronary disease, we will consider this disease in detail.

Coronary artery disease is the leading cause of death in this country. It is estimated that among a group of men in their forties, in ten years 15 percent will develop symptoms of heart disease, 7.5 percent will have a heart attack, 5 percent will have angina pains, and 5 percent will die from heart disease. Only 4.5 percent will die from other causes (Stokes, Froelicher, & Brown, 1981).

Coronary disease is a general term for a variety of illnesses associated with the narrowing or occlusion of coronary arteries supplying blood to the heart muscle. Two major forms of the disease are angina pectoris and myocardial infarction, or heart attack. Angina is chest pain that results when the heart muscle is deprived of oxygen because of narrowed arteries. Myocardial infarction is more serious, and involves the injury and death of heart tissue from the sustained deprivation of blood that is caused when the coronary arteries leading to the heart narrow or become clogged by a clot.

Central to both forms of coronary disease is the narrowing of coronary arteries through atherosclerosis. Generally, this occurs when plaques consisting of mounds of fat and scar tissue accumulate in the arteries. Plaque accumulation is much more common than most people think. Seventy-seven percent of American soldiers killed in the Korean War had observable atherosclerosis; indeed, more than fifteen percent had at least one coronary artery that was more than 50 percent blocked. All were young, appeared to be perfectly healthy, and had no signs of coronary disease (*Essentials of Life and Health*, 1977). People can experience up to an 85 percent blockage of coronary arteries without symptoms.

Many factors appear to be related to the development of coronary disease (Stokes et al., 1981). A *high fat diet* contributes to high levels of low-density lipoproteins and cholesterol in the blood and low levels of *high-density* lipoproteins (the "good" cholesterol); these in turn supply the fats that form plaque. High blood pressure, or *hypertension*, pushes fats into artery walls and damages the lining of the arteries by creating tiny fissures that attract plaque, which acts as scar tissue on a wound. *Nicotine* from tobacco use constricts coronary arteries, thereby reducing blood supply to the heart, and also contributes to the development of plaques and clots. *Lack of physical exercise* reduces the network of cardiac blood vessels, increasing a greater demand for blood and reducing the reliability of the blood supply. Changes in metabolism associated with a sedentary life increase the levels of low-density lipoproteins and cholesterol and decrease the levels of high-density lipoproteins. Other risk factors include being a *male*, increased *age*, *genetic predisposition*, *diabetes*, *alcohol consumption*, and the use of *oral contraceptives*. However, the startling fact is that the highest concentration of all traditional risk factors accounts for only about half of coronary disease (Keys, 1966).

As shown in Chapter 6, Type A behavior first emerged as a risk factor for coronary disease. However, this behavior pattern is more realistically viewed as a risk for all disease, and perhaps most stress is a risk factor for coronary disease. Acute stress can lead to a sudden constriction of coronary arteries, which, if already partially blocked, can lead to angina or myocardial infarction. Elevated blood pressure can injure the lining of the arteries, attracting the accumulation of plaque. A variety of stress hormones lead to the increased release of fatty substances in the blood to fuel the fight-or-flight response, which can contribute to plaque; these same hormones increase the supply of blood-clotting substances to protect against possible injury from the fight-or-flight reaction, which in turn can contribute to plaque. Plaques are relatively stable as long as tiny blood vessels keep them alive by supplying them with food and oxygen. However, under stress, peripheral blood vessels, including those in plaques, constrict. As a result, the plaques die, break off artery walls, lodge in narrowed arteries, and cause a heart attack or, if they lodge in the brain, a stroke (see Figure 7.3). Recent research suggests that this process might be aggravated by the tendency of partially blocked arteries to constrict more than unblocked arteries under stress. One theory indicates that the inner lining of blood vessels produces a natural vessel-relaxing substance when exposed to epinephrine; because blocked vessels are less likely to produce this substance, they are less able to adjust to the vessel-constricting impact of epinephrine (Fackelman, 1991).

Cancer

About 30 percent of Americans will have cancer in their lifetime, and approximately 15 percent of all deaths in the U.S. are due to cancer (American Cancer Society, 1989). In fact, there are over one hundred types of cancer (Table 7.1), the most common for men being lung, colon, and prostate, and for women, breast, lung, and colon. All have several things in common. A normal cell or group of cells alters

1. Normal artery

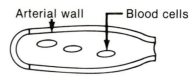

Arterial wall — Blood cells

2. Stress-induced blood pressure stretches arterial wall, creating small fissures

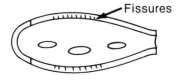

Fissures

3. Stress-induced increases in cholesterol, fatty substances, and clotting substances form scarlike plaques

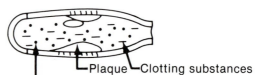

Plaque — Clotting substances
Cholesterol and fatty substances

4. Plaques grow and are kept alive by tiny capillaries

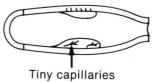

Tiny capillaries

5. Stress causes tiny plaque capillaries to shrink depriving plaques of blood

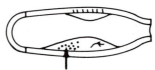

Shrunken capillary

6. Deprived of blood, plaque dies and breaks off of artery wall

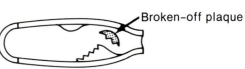

Broken-off plaque

7. Plaque floats in bloodstream blocking narrowed arteries, or stress causes arteries to constrict. Either can cause a heart attack or stroke.

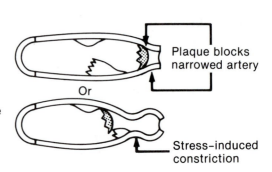

Plaque blocks narrowed artery

Or

Stress-induced constriction

FIGURE 7.3   The progress of coronary disease.

TABLE 7.1   Common Types of Cancer in
the U.S.

Breast	Mouth and pharnyx
Colon	Prostate
Esophagus	Rectum
Hodgkin's disease	Skin
Leukemia	Stomach
Lung	

and proliferates wildly because normal mechanisms that inhibit cell growth are impaired. Eventually, these cancer cells spread to adjacent tissue and, if the environment is suitable, proliferate wildly through a process called metastasis. A cancer tumor is something of a factory, producing additional cells that obstruct and starve surrounding tissue.

Cancer development, or the *neoplastic process*, occurs through several stages. First, normal cells are exposed to a variety of "hits" or insults that alter normal cellular structure or function (Miller, 1980). Of those cells that are hit, some die, some are altered, and a few become precursor cells that are potentially cancerous. Altered by additional hits, precursor cells may become malignant and die, or continue to grow and spread throughout the body.

Two factors can influence the neoplastic process: exposure to carcinogens and stress. The list of known carcinogens is impressive and growing, and includes tobacco, sun exposure, fat, air pollution, x-rays, asbestos, and polyvinyl chloride. Substances and other factors speculated to contribute to cancer include alcohol, coffee, tea, marriage at an early age, number of sexual partners, circumcision, refined food, food additives, pesticides, water pollution, and ionizing radiation.

Whether environmental hits result in cancer partly depends on host resistance. Certain genetic factors can increase susceptibility to cancer. In addition, the immune system treats cancer cells as antigens and usually destroys them. The innate immune system appears to help guard against the initial appearance of cancer cells. Macrophages and killer T cells may well be the body's first line of defense. Acquired immunity is thought to inhibit tumor growth and metastasis rather than the inception of cancer. As discussed, life events and certain personality factors, such as the Type C coping style, may also contribute to cancer, possibly through suppression of the immune system.

Other Disorders

Gastrointestinal Disorders

Most areas of the gastrointestinal tract are responsive to stress. A host of minor complaints are common stress symptoms, including dry mouth, loss of appetite, nausea, heartburn, and alterations in bowel habits. Two more serious disorders are peptic ulcers and irritable bowel syndrome.

PEPTIC ULCERS.   The stomach and intestines are covered with a mucus membrane. Ulcers are sores or lesions that occur most often in the intestinal duodenum and somewhat less often in the stomach. A *peptic ulcer* seems to occur when hydrochloric acid and the enzyme pepsin override the protective resistance of mucus membranes. Tissues are initially irritated, and eventually lesions may form. It is estimated that in their lifetime about 5 percent of people in the United States will develop an ulcer (Blumenthal, 1960).

Risk factors for ulcers include genetic predisposition, cigarette smoking, anti-inflammatory drugs, and possibly alcohol and caffeine. In addition, stress increases stomach acid secretion and possibly contributes to the reduction of blood flow, which may weaken stomach and intestinal linings (Weiss, 1984).

IRRITABLE BOWEL SYNDROME.   *Irritable bowel syndrome* (IBS) is the most common disorder of digestive tract functioning. Indeed, it accounts for up to 50 percent of referrals to gastrointestinal clinics (Sammons & Karoly, 1987). Symptoms are reported by from 8 percent to 19 percent of adults yearly (Thompson, Dotevale, Drossman, Heaton, & Kruis, 1989). IBS is characterized by chronic constipation or diarrhea, sometimes accompanied by abdominal distention and discomfort. Basically, it is caused by altered bowel activity or motility rather than any objective physiological abnormality. Its causes include diet and stress; sympathetic nervous system arousal can significantly alter bowel motility.

Asthma

Bronchial *asthma* affects about 5 percent of Americans (McFadden, 1987). With this condition, air exchange in the lungs is obstructed by muscle spasms and tissue swelling in the bronchial tubes. Specifically, overreactive IgE antibodies cause non-specific hyperirritability of the tracheobronchial tree. A wide range of substances can then cause an asthmatic attack, including pollen, dust, drugs, respiratory infections, and exercise. As we have seen, the production of antibodies can be influenced by stress hormones, thus increasing the potential for asthma in someone prone to this disorder. In addition, constrictions of the bronchial tubes are partly mediated by the autonomic nervous system.

Rheumatoid Arthritis

Rheumatoid arthritis is chronic inflammation of the joints experienced by about 1 percent of the population (Anderson, Bradley, Young, McDaniel, & Wise, 1983). Its symptoms include pain and stiffness, usually starting in the hands and feet. The inflammatory process affects cartilage and the surrounding joint tissues, resulting in deformity and tissue damage. Rheumatoid arthritis is at least in part an autoimmune disease. Perhaps because of earlier joint damage or an overactive immune response aggravated by stress, the immune system mistakenly recognizes joint tissue, particularly the surrounding synovial membrane, as foreign and eventually damages it. The joint tissue tries to heal, which produces more tissue. This new tissue is recognized as yet more foreign tissue, and the inflammatory response continues. Eventually, inflamed tissue grows to create considerable pain and impairment of movement.

Eczema or Dermatitis

Eczema or *dermatitis* is an inflammatory skin reaction to a wide range of external and internal stimuli. The skin itches, reddens, swells, and blisters. There are many causes and kinds of eczema, including those caused by allergies, asthma, and exposure to irritants. Stress may well play an important role in causing eczema. Numerous changes in the skin occur as a result of autonomic and endocrine arousal. Perspiration increases, blood flow decreases, and the propensity for inflammation may grow, all of which can upset the environment of the skin, rendering it more subject to irritation.

Migraine and Tension Headaches

Up to 80 percent of Americans suffer from at least one *migraine or tension headache* a year, and for from 10 percent to 15 percent of the people, the problem can be severe and recurring (Ziegler, 1984). Typically, a migraine attack is characterized by throbbing pain, often in the forehead, frequently accompanied by nausea, vomiting, sensitivity to light and sound, and diarrhea. This is preceded by a prodromal phase, consisting of mood alterations or increased hunger and thirst for a day or more before the headache, and a neurological symptom stage, characterized by such sensory symptoms as visions of flashing lights, partial loss of sight, and pricking or tingling sensations on one side of the body. These neurological symptoms rarely last more than thirty minutes. A popular but still questioned theory states that premigraine symptoms are created by arterial constriction and reduced blood flow to the brain and skull. Reduced oxygen to the brain does cause many of the prodromal and neurological symptoms. This is followed by a sudden rush of blood to previously deprived areas. The resulting vascular dilation is the source of the intense, throbbing migraine pain.

Stress may contribute to migraine headaches in a variety of ways. General sympathetic arousal may evoke changes in blood flow that initiate the migraine process. Stress-mediated changes in blood flow and muscle tension can also moderate the intensity and duration of the headaches.

Most headaches are simple tension headaches. These also involve stress and vascular changes, but the processes are somewhat different from those for migraine. Here, stress leads to the contraction of muscles surrounding the skull, which in turn create vascular constrictions and headaches. The physiological differences between migraine and tension headaches are now being examined.

AIDS

Acquired Immune Deficiency Syndrome (AIDS) is caused by the human immunodeficiency virus (HIV), which is also called the human T cell lymphocytic virus III (HTL-III). Initial exposure can cause a brief period of flu-like symptoms, including fatigue, fever, and swollen glands. The virus then usually becomes dormant for up to twelve years, during which the patient remains asymptomatic but capable of infecting others. When the virus becomes active it attacks the immune system, particularly helper T cells, and interferes with humoral and cell-mediated immunity. Although antibodies are produced, they are not enough to eliminate the virus.

Once the immune system is seriously impaired, the individual is vulnerable to multiple opportunistic infections that would likely have been resisted if the immune system were intact. The most debilitating of these are pneumocystisis pneumonia, Karposi's cancer, tuberculosis, and toxoplasmosis.

AIDS is transmitted through unprotected sex (carried by blood or semen) or contaminated blood transfusions. Casual contact does not transmit AIDS. As with cancer, the immune system may well succeed in fighting off the virus for a period of time, especially when supplemented by a variety of antiviral drugs such as AZT, DDC, or DDI. Progression from infection to the appearance of AIDS may well hasten for those whose immune systems are already suppressed through stress. Indeed, the diagnosis of AIDS may in itself create sufficient chronic stress to hasten the appearance of opportunistic infections.

Summary

We have considered a wide range of disorders, many of which have clear links to stress. However, the transactional matrix warns us not to think simplistically that stress directly causes any particular disorder. The story of stress and illness is much more complex. True, stress can be a contributing factor to disease. However, although much research has attempted to link specific personality factors to specific illnesses, for such as the Type A personality and heart disease, and the Type C personality and cancer, the findings have not been conclusive. At this point, it is perhaps more important to recognize specific disease processes that may be influenced by general physiological stress processes and the psychological factors that can in turn contribute to such processes.

APPLICATION BOX 7.1

Stress, Illness, and You

Often we ignore warning signs that stress may be contributing to illness. However, upon reflection, most people can think of an instance in which stress contributed to illness and illness contributed to stress. Can you think of an illness you recently experienced that was aggravated by any of the stress dimensions we have considered so far in this book (life events, lack of social support, continuous stress arousal, appraisal of threat, appraisal of lack of coping resources, poor coping strategies, personality disposition, etc.)?

References

ADER, R. (Ed.). (1981). *Psychoneuroimmunology*. New York: Academic Press.

ADER, R., FELTEN, D. L., & COHEN, N. (1991). *Psychoneuroimmunology* (2nd ed.). San Diego: Academic Press.

AMERICAN CANCER SOCIETY. (1989). *Cancer Facts and figures: 1989*. New York: American Cancer Society.

ANDERSON, K. O., BRADLEY, L. A., YOUNG, L. D., McDANIEL, L. K., & WISE, C. (1985). Rheumatoid arthritis: Review of psychological factors related to etiology, effects, and treatment. *Psychological Bulletin, 98,* 358–387.

BAUM, A., & GRUNBERG, N. E. (1991). Gender, stress, and health. *Health Psychology, 10,* 80–85.

BLUMENTHAL, I. S. (1960). *Research and the ulcer problem*. Santa Monica, CA: The Rand Corporation.

BORYSENKO, J. (1984). The immune system: An overview. *Annals of Behavioral Medicine, 9,* 3–10.

Essentials of life and health. (1977). New York: Random House.

FACKELMANN, K. A. (1991, November 16). Stress puts squeeze on clogged vessels. *Science News*, p. 309.

GROSSMAN, C. J. (1984). Regulation of the immune system by sex steroids. *Endocrinology Review, 5,* 435–455.

GUYTON, A. C. (1991). *Textbook of medical physiology* (8th ed.). Philadelphia: W. B. Saunders.

JEMMOTT, J. B., & LOCKE, S. E. (1984). Psychosocial factors, immunological mediation, and human susceptibility to infectious diseases: How much do we know? *Psychological Bulletin, 95,* 78–108.

KEYS, A. (1966). The individual risk of coronary heart disease. *Annals of the New York Academy of Sciences, 134,* 1046–1063.

KOEPKE, J. P., LIGHT, K. C., GRIGNOLO, A., & OBRIST, P. A. (1983). Neural control of renal excretory function during behavioral stress in dogs. *American Journal of Physiology, 254,* 251–258.

McFADDEN, E. R., JR. (1987). Asthma. In E. Braunwald, K. J. Isselbacher, R. G. Petersdorf, J. D. Wilson, J. B. Martin, & A. S. Fauci (Eds.), *Harrison's principles of internal medicine* (11th ed., pp. 1060–1065). New York: McGraw-Hill.

MILLER, D. G. (1980). On the nature of susceptibility to cancer. *Cancer, 46,* 1307–1318.

SAMMONS, M. T., & KAROLY, P. (1987). Psychosocial variables in irritable bowel syndrome: A review and proposal. *Clinical Psychology Review, 7,* 187–204.

SCHUURS, A. H., & VERHEUL, H. M. (1990). Effects of gender and sex steroids on the immune response. *Journal of Steroid Biochemistry, 35,* 157–172.

STOKES, J., FROELICHER, V. F., & BROWN, P. (1981). Prevention of cardiovascular disease. In L. J. Schneiderman (Ed.), *The practice of preventative health care* (pp. 213–245). New York: Wiley.

THOMPSON, W. G., DOTEVALE, G., DROSSMAN, D. A., HEATON, K. W., & KRUIS, W. (1989). Irritable bowel syndrome: Guidelines for the diagnosis. *Gastroenterology International, 2,* 92–95.

TURNER, J. R., & CARROLL, D. (1985). Heart rate and oxygen consumption during mental arithmetic, a video game, and graded exercise: Further evidence of metabolically-exaggerated cardiac adjustments? *Psychophysiology, 4,* 261–267.

VOLLHARDT, L. T. (1991). Psychoneuroimmunology: A literature review. *American Journal of Orthopsychiatry, 6,* 35–47.

WEISS, J. M. (1984). Behavioral and psychological influences on gastrointestinal pathology: Experimental techniques and findings. In W. D. Gentry (Ed.), *Handbook of behavioral medicine* (pp. 174–221). New York: Guilford.

ZIEGLER, D. K. (1984). An overview of the classification, causes, and treatment of headache. *Hospital and Community Psychiatry, 35,* 263–267.

CHAPTER 8

Stress, Risk Behaviors, and Health

There are many ways in which people injure their health. Belloc and Breslow (1972), after surveying nearly 7,000 individuals, identified seven behaviors related to the maintenance of personal health:

1. Sleeping seven to eight hours daily.
2. Eating breakfast almost every day.
3. Never or rarely eating between meals.
4. Being at or near prescribed height-adjusted weight.
5. Never smoking cigarettes.
6. Moderate or no use of alcohol.
7. Regular physical activity.

Any of these, if not maintained, can become a *risk behavior* that contributes to illness and death. In this chapter we shall see that many of these same behaviors are closely tied to stress. We will focus on three that have received the most research attention: fitness and exercise, eating and nutrition, and addiction and substance abuse.

Fitness and Exercise

Many people believe that exercise helps to manage stress. Often such notions are either downplayed or overemphasized in stress clinics. But what are the facts? Are athletes better prepared to manage stress? Can daily exercise aid in stress management at work and home? Before exploring these questions, it is important to review some basic concepts concerning fitness.

Physical fitness is defined in terms of several variables. *Muscular strength* is the maximum force a muscle can generate; *muscular endurance* is the ability of a muscle to sustain continuous work; *cardiorespiratory endurance* is the ability of the heart, lungs, and blood vessels to sustain continuous work by supplying oxygen and food and removing waste products; *flexibility* is the ability to exercise and move joints fully; *body composition* is the proportion of lean body mass (bone and muscle) to fat; and *agility* is the ability to work with speed and balance. *Aerobic fitness* is related to endurance and involves the efficiency with which one uses oxygen; aerobically fit individuals, compared with those who are unfit, use up a greater percentage of the oxygen they breathe.

To achieve fitness, a person must engage in some form of regular physical activity, including exercise. Most exercises can be classified as *isotonic, isometric*, or *isokinetic*. In addition, exercises vary the extent to which they are *aerobic*. Isotonic exercises (weight lifting, push-ups, and many calisthenics) involve moving a heavy object (including a person's own body weight) in one direction, contributing to strength and endurance. Isometric exercises involve exerting force against an immovable object, such as a wall, and are better for building strength than endurance. Isokinetic exercises involve exerting effort in more than one direction, for example, by pushing and pulling a heavy object. This type of exercise builds strength and endurance. Finally, aerobic exercises are vigorous activities that require high levels of oxygen consumption. Heart and breathing rates increase, contributing to endurance and aerobic fitness.

Exercise, particularly aerobic, has several general benefits that can indirectly help reduce the possible costs of stress on health. Exercise burns calories, which can lead to sustained weight loss. Increased metabolism that results from exercise suppresses appetite. Aerobic exercise strengthens the heart, enhances muscle tone, strength, and elasticity, and has desirable effects on blood pressure, heart pumping efficiency,

Left: Weightlifting is a form of isotonic exercise. (*Photo by Mimi Forsyth,* Monkmeyer Press Photo Service.) *Right:* Businessmen read while working out on exercise bikes, a good form of aerobic exercise. (*Photo by Spencer Grant,* Stock Boston.)

and cholesterol (Brownell, 1980). Partly because of these effects, aerobic exercise decreases the risk of many diseases that can be aggravated by stress, including coronary disease, diabetes, and hypertension.

People who exercise report less anxiety, depression, and tension (Folkins & Sime, 1981). Exercise improves sleep (Folkins, Lynch, & Gardner, 1972) as well as self-concept (Hughes, 1974). Such findings, although common, leave unanswered the question of causality. Does exercise contribute to reduced stress, do people with lower stress have more time and energy to exercise, or does some third variable contribute to both? In one experiment, Goldwater and Collis (1985) randomly assigned male subjects to a six-week vigorous (five days a week) aerobic exercise program and a moderate (two days a week) aerobic exercise program. The vigorous exercise increased the subject's fitness and reduced their anxiety.

In addition, those who exercise or are fit show less cardiovascular reactivity to stress and are less likely to be hypertensive (Crews & Landers, 1987). Again, questions can be asked about causal links. Research clarifies the situation. Both retrospective (Kobasa, Maddi, & Puccetti, 1982) and prospective (Roth & Holmes, 1985) studies show that people experiencing high levels of stress are much less likely to report and experience illness if they exercise. Brown (1991) found that aerobic fitness had a clear buffering effect. For unfit subjects, high life stress was strongly related to illness (measured by visits to a health center); however, for fit subjects, life stress had little ill effect.

Six mechanisms have been proposed to explain the impact of fitness and exercise on stress:

1. Exercise may *change cognitive appraisals* of a person's self image and the world. Improved physical appearance resulting from exercise can increase self-esteem (Folkins & Sime, 1981). Observable improvements in strength, flexibility, and endurance can contribute to feelings of self-efficacy and mastery (Rodin, 1986). However, Folkins and Sime (1981) suggest that participants in an exercise program feel more confident and able, even though changes in aerobic fitness may be unrelated to confidence and ability ratings. A variety of factors can contribute to such perceptions, including social support, increased feelings of control and mastery, expectations of improvement, and satisfaction with personal improvement (King, Taylor, Haskell & DeBusk, 1989).
2. Exercise may *reduce affective states*, such as anger and hostility, implicated in stress disorders (Czajkowski et al., 1990).
3. Physical fitness may *divert attention* form stressful situations and cognitions (Bahrke & Morgan, 1978). Simply taking time off from a hectic day removes one source of potentially stressful stimulation. And becoming absorbed in a vigorous sport leaves less attention for stressful worry.
4. Exercise *increases the flow of blood and oxygen to the brain*, possibly contributing to feelings of greater energy and alertness (Kostrubala, 1977).
5. Exercise (especially aerobic) may *enhance the production of certain neurotransmitters*, including catecholamines and endorphins, leading to a positive mood and feelings of euphoria.

6. Highly-fit people *show less physiological reactivity* to stress than those that are not fit. Specifically, they show lower arousal on some physiological dimensions and more rapid recovery on others. To explain, the cardiovascular and biochemical changes associated with aerobic fitness enable the body to respond more efficiently to physical stress (Sinyor, Schwartz, Peronnet, Brisson, & Seraganian, 1983). The long-distance runner, swimmer, and biker are physically conditioned to sustain the demands of running, swimming, and biking. Physiologically, their heart rate is lower, the volume of blood pumped with each stroke is increased, their heart rate returns more rapidly to normal after exercise, and their glucose, insulin, norepinephrine, and cortisol levels are lower.

It should be clear that many of the physical changes evoked by physical exertion are similar to those associated with psychological stress, even in the absence of exertion. This suggests that people who are fit may show less arousal and quicker recovery in response not only to the demands of running, swimming, and biking but also to the demands of psychological stress. Recent research is beginning to support this thinking. Holmes and Roth (1985) found that highly-fit women show lower elevations in heart rate in response to laboratory stress.

Eating and Nutrition

Stress and eating are related in at least four ways. Poor nutrition can make a person more vulnerable to stress-related illnesses; stress can deplete the body of certain nutrients; some foods can evoke or aggravate the stress arousal response; and specific eating disorders may have a stress component.

Good Nutrition

First, what is good nutrition? The United States Department of Agriculture's *food pyramid* suggests a balance of six food groups emphasizing bread and grains, vegetables, and fruit, while placing less importance on meat, milk products, and fats and sweets. Perhaps the best way of avoiding stress-related nutrition problems is to maintain a responsible diet.

EATING AND ILLNESS.   Poor nutrition can contribute to illnesses that have been linked with stress. For example, a diet high in saturated fats (found in red meats, whole milk, and butter) and cholesterol can increase the level of cholesterol in the blood, contributing to heart disease. Diets low in fiber (found in whole wheat grains, fruit, and vegetables) or high in saturated fat can contribute to breast, colon, and prostate cancers. Adequate levels of vitamins A and C may be needed to help prevent cancer of the larynx, esophagus, stomach, and lung. Cruciferous vegetables (such as broccoli, carrots, cauliflower, and spinach) contain fiber and beta carotene, which may also help prevent cancer. Finally, excess salt (sodium) can aggravate the risk of hypertension for those already at risk.

DEPLETION OF NUTRIENTS.   Many components of the stress arousal response, such as cortisol production and the metabolism of carbohydrates and glucose, require the use of B complex vitamins (thiamine, riboflavin, niacin, pantothenic acid, and pyridoxine hydrochloride) as well as vitamin C. People who experience vitamin deficiencies can feel anxious, depressed, and weak, and suffer from insomnia and an upset stomach. In addition, when the "stress" vitamins are depleted, the body's ability to manufacture certain stress hormones and mount an effective stress response is impaired. Stress may also interfere with the absorption of important minerals, such as calcium, potassium, zinc, copper, and magnesium. Finally, an excessive ingestion of certain nutrients can aggravate the depletion of important stress-related vitamins and minerals. To metabolize sugar and processed (unenriched) flour, the body requires B complex vitamins, leaving less available for the production of stress hormones.

NUTRITION AND THE STRESS AROUSAL RESPONSE.   Certain food substances called *pseudostressors*, or *sympathomimetics*, can mimic the sympathetic nervous system arousal response. Caffeine (contained in colas, coffee, tea, and chocolate) as well as theobromine and theophylline (found in tea) increase metabolism and stress hormone secretion. In addition, they increase the arousability of the nervous system, resulting in an exaggerated stress response to other stimuli. Caffeine's best documented physiological effect is its ability to increase blood pressure both at rest and under stress, particularly for those at risk for hypertension (Lovallo et al., 1991). However, caffeine may well have different effects and operate through different mechanisms than stress; for example, some studies show that caffeine produces a decreased heart *rate*. The debate over whether caffeine is actually a stimulant continues (Pincomb, Lovallo, Passey, Brackett, & Wilson, 1987; Robertson et al., 1978).

Excessive sugar intake can contribute to *hypoglycemia*, a condition of low blood sugar preceded by elevated blood sugar. Some people who experience "midmorning slump" or increased irritability after a breakfast or lunch consisting of a doughnut may be displaying the symptoms of hypoglycemia. For some, this disorder can be triggered by having a high intake of sugar in a short period or missing meals. Paradoxically, temporary high levels of blood sugar stimulate the release of insulin, which causes sugar to be removed form the blood into body tissue. The result is hypoglycemic sugar depletion. Symptoms of hypoglycemia, such as anxiety, headaches, dizziness, rapid heartbeat, and irritability, can intensify the stress arousal response.

Finally, excessive salt intake may not only aggravate hypertension in some, but may well contribute to stress symptoms. The sodium in salt is important for regulating water balance, but too much sodium results in excessive fluid retention. This in turn may contribute to edema (abnormal accumulation of fluid) in the nervous system. One symptom of edema is increased nervous tension and stress reactivity.

EATING DISORDERS.   Tens of millions of Americans are overweight or obese. Generally, people are classified as overweight if they are 10 to 20 percent overweight, and obese if they are more than 20 percent overweight (Suitor & Hunter, 1980). There are far too many causes of overeating to consider here, but stress may well play a role. Obese people may confuse nonhunger physiological cues with hunger cues, and eat in response to anxiety, fatigue, or tension (Hodgson & Miller, 1982). Overeating can be a form of emotion-focused coping and a way to maintain social support. And people with eating problems often experience more stressful life events, have lower self-esteem, possess more irrational beliefs, use avoidance coping, and are less likely to use cognitive and behavioral coping strategies (Mayhew & Edelmann, 1989; Soukup, Beiler & Terrell, 1990).

Some people who suffer from extreme malnutrition and weight loss simply do not consume enough food. Patients with anorexia nervosa have an abnormally intense concern about body image and seek an extremely thin appearance. Claiming to "feel fat" when they are actually thin, anorexics limit their food intake so that their body weight is at least 15 percent below their ideal. Bulimia is a related disorder that involves binge eating followed by induced vomiting. Both anorexics and bulimics experience considerable personal stress and depression.

A few researchers suspect that anorexic and bulimic eating may contribute to, or be caused by, a malfunctioning of the hypothalamus, the body's stress trigger (Halmi, Owen, Lasky & Stokes, 1983). Changes in the hypothalamus may alter the body's regulation of fat metabolism, water balance, endocrine gland, secretion and possibly dopamine production (associated with depression).

At the very least, episodes of binge eating or severe eating restraint can be brought on by anxiety, depression, and interpersonal stress (Carrol & Leon, 1981), and most bulimics feel relief from anxiety and depression as a result of eating. However, the relationship among anorexia, bulimia, and stress is complex. Both disorders are associated with poor overall adjustment (Johnson & Berndt, 1983), suggesting a general deficiency in coping skills.

Addiction and Substance Abuse

In considering substance abuse, it is useful to differentiate among addiction, dependence, and abuse. In *addiction*, a person can become physically or psychologically dependent on an addicting substance. In *physical dependence*, the body adapts to a substance so that larger and and larger doses are required to achieve an effect. When the substance is no longer ingested, a person experiences withdrawal, or a set of unpleasant physical and psychological symptoms, including anxiety, craving, nausea, and tremors. Substances differ considerably in their addictive potential. *Psychological dependence* occurs when a person feels driven to use a substance to produce a pleasant effect, even without physical addiction. The substance is used to help adjust to stress. Finally, *substance abuse* is the overuse of a substance. Generally, abuse is defined as at least a month of a clear pattern of pathological heavy use that is difficult to stop or reduce, and problems at work or home resulting from use of the substance.

Substance abuse is a complex process, promoted in part by social pressure and modeling, and maintained by avoidance of physical withdrawal symptoms. We are interested in the relationship between stress and addiction, and will consider substance abuse as a form of *emotion-focused coping* (Lazarus & Folkman, 1984), directed toward reducing distress rather than solving a stressful problem.

It is useful to consider the involvement of stress at three stages of the addictive process: initiation, or the start of the addictive process; continuation of addictive behavior; and relapse, or the return to addictive behavior after an attempt has been made to stop (Wills, 1990). Although much is understood about the general effects of such drugs as depressants, stimulants, narcotics, opiates, psychedelics, hallucinogens, and tranquilizers, (see Table 8.1), most stress research has focused on tobacco and alcohol, and, to a lesser extent, the opiates. These are also the drugs we shall consider in detail.

Tobacco

Smoking has a wide range of negative effects on physical health. Not only does it contribute to lung and other forms of cancer, but it is a risk factor for hypertension, heart disease, lung disorders, impaired immune system functioning, impaired healing, and even premature wrinkling of the skin.

Research has focused on two major by-products of smoking: carbon monoxide and nicotine. (A third by-product, tars, or minute particles of burnt residue, have attracted less attention.) Carbon monoxide is readily absorbed in the blood and quickly affects its oxygen-carrying capacity. Too much carbon monoxide can impair performance.

Nicotine is a very powerful and addicting poison. Indeed, the amount found in a single cigarette would be a fatal dose if extracted and injected into a person. When a cigarette is smoked, nonfatal doses enter the bloodstream through the mouth, nose, and lungs, travel to the brain, and cause the release of catecholamines. As we have seen, this activates the central and sympathetic nervous systems, increasing heart rate and blood pressure. In short, the body is aroused. Also, in a way that is not completely understood, nicotine alters the absorption of certain neurotransmitter substances in the brain. Together, the physiological changes produce a smoker's "fix" or "lift." But there is a cost: nicotine reduces the lung's capacity to process air and take in oxygen. In addition, it is powerfully addicting, with such withdrawal symptoms as headache, nausea, fatigue, and difficulty concentrating.

Smoking behavior can become closely tied to stress regulation in general. People smoke for *positive affect*, that is, pleasurable stimulation and reduced tension (Tomkins, 1968). People who show strong physiological reactions to their first attempts at smoking are more likely to continue, suggesting that greater physiological reactivity increases susceptibility to smoking and relapse (Abrams et al., 1987).

People usually begin smoking between the ages of twelve and sixteen. Most of the research on who starts smoking has been conducted on school-age children. A handful of studies, conducted on large samples of between several hundred and several thousand subjects, shows a clear link between stress and smoking initiation. Recent negative events, school change, schoolwork stress (for males), concerns about appearance (for females), feelings of helplessness, Type A behavior, and anger all emerge as predictors of smoking (Wills, 1990). If we examine their coping skills, nonsmokers use problem-solving, cognitive reappraisal, and a search for social support from adults; smokers are more likely to rely on aggression, distraction, and peer group activity (Wills, 1986).

TABLE 8.1 Psychoactive Drugs and Their Effects

Classification	Drug	Effects	Tolerance	Psychological Dependence	Physiological Dependence
Depressants	Alcohol	Reduced tension and anxiety	Yes	Yes	Yes
	Barbituates	Reduced tension, sleep	Yes	Yes	Yes
	Tranquilizers		Yes	Yes	Yes
Stimulants	Nicotine	Alertness, reduced fatigue, increased endurance, euphoria	Yes	Yes	Yes
	Caffeine		Yes	Yes	Yes
	Amphetamines		Yes	Yes	No?
	Cocaine		Some	Yes	No?
Narcotics (opioids)	Opium	Pain relief, relaxation, euphoria, reduced tension	Yes	Yes	Yes
	Morphine		Yes	Yes	Yes
	Heroin		Yes	Yes	Yes
	Codeine		Yes	Yes	Yes
Psychedelics and hallucinogens	Marijuana	Distortions in perception, changes in mood and behavior, loss of contact with reality	No	Yes	No
	Hashish		No	Yes	No
	Mescaline		No	Yes	No
	Psilocybin		No	Yes	No
	LCD		No	Yes	No
	PCP		No	Yes	No
Minor tranquilizers	Librium	Reduced tension, sleep	Yes	Yes	Yes
	Miltown		Yes	Yes	Yes
	Valium		Yes	Yes	Yes

Research on the continuation of smoking behavior has focused primarily on adults. Heavy smokers report more job and family stress (Wills, 1990). Subjects are more likely to smoke on high-stress days than on low-stress days (Conway, Vickers, Ward & Rahe, 1981). In one study, smokers were presented with stressful social situations while they smoked or did not smoke (Gilbert & Spielberger, 1987). Those who smoked claimed they felt less anxiety and greater effectiveness in expressing their opinions.

Most of those who quit smoking experience at least one relapse. As with most forms of substance abuse, a relapse occurs in a discrete episode rather than as a slow process. Negative life events, personal conflict, and "negative affect smoking," that is, smoking done when one feels frustrated, tense, or anxious (Pomerleau, Adkins, & Pertschuck, 1978), predict the likelihood of relapse. Relapsers also have low expectation of success and low personal adjustment.

A growing body of research has examined the coping strategies of relapsers. Successful quitters combine both cognitive modification of self-statements (self-reward, positive self-statements, thought of consequences, intention to delay possible relapse) and behavioral coping (distracting activity, relaxation) to deal with relapse. A combination appears to be more effective than either strategy alone for dealing with crises situations in which relapse is imminent. Either approach of coping was more effective than no coping attempt. (Curry & Marlatt, 1985; Glasgow, Klesges, Mizes, & Pechacek, 1985; Shiffman, 1982, 1984a, 1984b). Indeed, virtually every subject who makes no attempt to cope with relapse continues smoking. Interestingly, relapsers appear to be deficient in relaxation skills as well as social skills specifically related to dealing with smoking-specific situations (such as resisting social pressure to smoke), rather than social skills in general.

Alcohol

Experts disagree on the definition of alcoholism and problem drinking. However, most would agree that an alcoholic is one with a serious drinking problem that impairs health and functioning at work and home.

Alcohol has a powerful impact on just about every organ in the body, including the brain. The more highly specialized the tissue, such as the brain, liver, pancreas, and endocrine glands, the greater the impact. Alcohol abuse is related to several clear organic brain syndromes, including alcohol dementia and alcohol amnesia (memory) syndromes, or Korsakoff's psychosis. Physical disorders include cirrhosis of the liver, gastritis, and even heart disorders. Most people are aware of the potentially serious consequences of alcohol abuse. Psychological dependence can also be destructive to overall life adjustment, contributing to deterioration in coping at home and work.

Just how alcohol affects stress is not entirely known. At low to moderate doses, alcohol reduces tension and anxiety, and produces euphoria. Its reinforcing quality may rise from its impact on neurotransmitters (Livezey, Balbkins, & Vogel, 1987). In addition, alcohol may reduce stress by facilitating the diversion of attention from stressful thoughts to ongoing activity (Josephs & Steele, 1990). Alcoholics may metabolize alcohol differently, which contributes to their dependency. At the very least, the cell metabolism of the person who has developed an alcohol dependency has adapted to alcohol and requires its continued presence to avoid withdrawal.

The pattern for the initiation of alcohol abuse is at times similar to that of smoking. Generally, alcohol immediately reduces tension and anxiety, while also increasing euphoria. This combination provides powerful pressure to continue drinking in spite of its maladaptive long-term consequences (Bandura, 1969; Levenson, Sher, Grossman, Newman, & Newlin, 1980). In addition, the amount of alcohol that drinkers consume a day is related to the amount of stress on that day. Generally, economic stress, feelings of vulnerability, job and marital stress, and poor physical condition all relate to alcohol use. Those who have little social support and who use avoidance coping strategies are more likely to use alcohol for coping (Cronkite & Moos, 1984).

Once a drinking pattern has developed, alcoholics show low stress tolerance, negative self-image, feelings of inadequacy, isolation, and depression. More severe impairment includes lack of responsibility, difficulty in controlling impulses, and a tendency toward deceitfulness and manipulation. It is often observed that serious alcoholics make frequent use of denial, rationalization, and projection as defense mechanisms. Alcoholics who try but fail to quit show a pattern similar to that of smokers and opiate users: negative emotional states, increased stress, poorer coping skills, lower levels of assertiveness, and lower learned resourcefulness. Use of active cognitive and behavioral coping predicts the likelihood of staying off alcohol, where as relapsers use more avoidance and aggressive coping, such as taking their emotions out on others.

Opiates

Opiates are derived from the opium poppy, and include morphine and heroin. Opiates have both analgesic (pain-reducing) and positive mood effects resulting from the secretion of catecholamines and endogenous opiates. As we have seen, the nerves of the brain and spine have special receptor sites for special neurotransmitters. Morphine and similar drugs block pain and evoke pleasure because they fit these sites.

The opiate user experiences an immediate euphoric spasm lasting about a minute, followed by a "high" in which one is lethargic, withdrawn, relaxed, and contented. This can last for four to six hours. Eventually there is a craving for more drug.

Opiate addictions have serious consequences. Not only are the drugs illegal, but the costs of addiction escalates. One becomes able to tolerate ever-increasing doses, requiring higher amounts of the drug. This can lead to the ruinous expense of maintaining a habit. Withdrawal symptoms can be severe and include sweating, pain, nausea, vomiting, and diarrhea. Finally, unsanitary conditions associated with opiate use, such as dirty needles, can lead to serious health consequences.

Predictors of more serious drug use are complex and include subjective stress, as well as rejection by family and school, and depression. How stress contributes to addiction is open to debate. According to the theory of *exposure orientation*, endorphins are released under stress and produce stress-induced analgesia. The use of opiates may lead to a breakdown of the body system that synthesizes endorphins

(Jaffee, 1985). The addict then continues to use opiates because of the breakdown in the body's normal ability to block pain. Similarly, since withdrawal is a source of serious pain, there is additional incentive for opiate use.

In contrast, the *adaptive orientation* perspective (Alexander & Hadaway, 1982) states that addiction is not automatic; both the person and the situation must be considered. For example, drug use may increase under conditions of extreme stress, feelings of helplessness and low self-efficacy, and low support for refraining from drug use.

Much addiction research has focused on who stays in and who quits treatment programs for opiate dependence. Predictors of relapse include life events stress, loss of social support, pain, depression, and low efficacy expectations for the ability to resist the relapse temptation (Wills, 1990). In addition, relapsers are more likely to lack coping skills for such unexpected stressors of the nondrug world as low-status work, unemployment, and the recreational drug use of nonaddict co-workers (Platt & Metzger, 1987).

Stress and Substance Abuse

In general, three models help explain the relationship between stress and substance abuse. The *affect regulation mode* assumes that tobacco, alcohol, or opiate use reduces pain and stress while providing pleasure. This then contributes to continued use (Wills, 1990). In addition, the physiological impact of such substances may distract attention from stressors or interfere with the processing of potentially upsetting information. Such an impact is in turn reinforced by the positive affect evoked by drugs.

The *self-control model* derives from the cognitive fatigue model of stress aftereffects (Cohen, 1980; see also Chapter 10). Stressful tasks (especially those that are uncertain and unpredictable) call for increased vigilance and coping. This mental effort contributes to cognitive fatigue that can persist as a stress aftereffect. Fatigue can impair performance on a variety of tasks, including resisting the temptation to smoke, drink, or use drugs. In other words, when compromised by the debilitating effects of stress, one is more likely to resort to substance use as a coping mechanism and have fewer coping resources to resist substance use.

Marlatt's relapse model (Marlatt, 1985; Marlatt & George, 1984; Marlatt & Gordon, 1985) focuses more on the effect of stress on those who are attempting to quit substance use. According to this theory, the first episode of postcessation drug use is a "lapse," and a full return to drug use is a "relapse." A lapse is most likely when a person encounters a stressful situation involving interpersonal conflict and social pressure and experiences negative affect. Those who have effective coping responses should have greater feelings of self-efficacy and a greater likelihood of actually changing a stressful situation. As a result, they should be less likely to resume substance use.

In contrast, those more likely to experience relapse and continue with substance use display an *abstinence violation effect*, a cognitive-affective reaction that has two components: (1) an attribution of the cause of the lapses to internal, stable, and global factors (see Chapter 6) that are uncontrollable (for example, lack of will power and an addictive personality); and (2) negative emotions of self-blame and guilt.

Presumably, increasing a person's repertoire of coping skills should reduce the abstinence violation effect and contribute to maintained abstinence.

However, in fact relatively little is understood about the dynamics of stress and
substance abuse as well as the relationship among stress, eating, and exercise. Who
is more likely to use one particular substance for emotion-focused coping? Under
what conditions is this more likely to occur? What are the short- and long-term physiological, psychological, and environmental consequences of substance abuse? How
do these consequences in turn help maintain substance abuse? Table 8.2 illustrates
how the array of such variables can be considered in terms of the transactional
matrix for quitting smoking. Clearly, researchers have just begun to understand the
complex interactions of stress and substance abuse.

TABLE 8.2 The Transactional Matrix for Quitting Smoking

Variable	Long-Term Antecedents	Immediate Antecedents	Stressful Event (Quitting)	Immediate Consequences	Long-Term Consequences
Personal		Physiological reactivity, concerns about appearance (women), feelings of helplessness, type A behavior, anger, low personal adjustment, general absence of coping and relaxation skills		*Physiological:* Reduced blood oxygen levels, increased arousal *Emotional:* Smoker's "lifts" reduced tension *Performance:* Poorer performance	Heart disease, cancer, immune system impairment, addiction
Situational			Low expectation of success; failure to use problem-solving, cognitive reappraisal, and social support from adults; rely more on distraction, aggression, and peer support; smoking used to reduce stress ("negative affect smoking")		
External		Recent negative events, school change, schoolwork (males)			

APPLICATION BOX 8.1

Risky Behaviors

Are any of the health-risk behaviors discussed in this chapter a problem for you? If so, describe how you understand the link between this behavior and stress. Use the transactional matrix to help you come up with ideas. Specifically, see if you can answer the following questions.

· How have external antecedents (life events, lack of social support, etc.) contributed to your problem?
· How have personal antecedents, such as the personality traits discussed in Chapter 6, contributed?
· How has an absence of coping skills contributed to your problem? Think of a stress situation in which you engaged in your risk behavior because you did not know how to cope.
· How has irrational or biased thinking contributed to your problem?
· How have you used your health-risk behavior as a form of emotion-focused coping or defense?

Here is how Christine, a problem cigarette smoker, answered these questions:

· I seem to smoke when I am confronted with an overwhelming bunch of negative life events. School . . . home . . . work—everything seems to be going wrong. No one is around to help. I start smoking.
· I guess you might say I have a "pessimistic explanatory style." When over-whelmed by stress, I blame myself, think the problem will last forever, and exaggerate the seriousness of the problem. Feeling fatalistic, I think, "Oh, what's the use!" and light up a cigarette.
· Last week my boss criticized me unfairly. I simply didn't know what to say. So I lit up a cigarette.
· When I start smoking, I find myself thinking irrationally about my smoking habit. I say to myself, "This is my last cigarette. I'll be satisfied when I finish it and won't need to smoke any more." That's a joke!
· I smoke to soothe my nerves. That's emotion-focused coping. And I guess I smoke sometimes to avoid facing a troublesome problem. I say to myself, "This is too difficult. I need a smoke." That's avoidance.

References

ABRAMS, D. B., MONTI, P. M., PINTO, R. P., ELDER, J. P., BROWN, R. A., JACOBUS, S. I. (1987). Psychosocial stress and coping in smokers who relapse or quit. *Health Psychology, 6,* 289–303.

ALEXANDER, B. K., & HADAWAY, P. F. (1982). Opiate addiction: The case for an adaptive orientation. *Psychological Bulletin, 92,* 367–381.

BAHRKE, M. S., & MORGAN, W. P. (1978). Anxiety reduction following exercise and meditation. *Cognitive Therapy and Research, 2,* 323–333.

BANDURA, A. (1969). *Principles of behavior modification.* New York: Holt, Rinehart & Winston.

BELLOC, N. B., & BRESLOW, L. (1972). Relationship of physical health status and health practices. *Preventive Medicine, 1,* 409–421.

BROWN, J. D. (1991). Staying fit and staying well: Physical fitness as a moderator of life stress. *Journal of Personality and Social Psychology, 60,* 555–561.

BROWNELL, K. D. (1980). Obesity: Understanding and treating a serious, prevalent, and refractory disorder. *Psychological Bulletin, 88,* 370–405.

CARROL, K., & LEON, G. R. (1981). *The bulimia-vomiting disorder within a generalized substance abuse pattern.* Paper presented at the 15th annual convention of the Association for the Advancement of Behavior Therapy, Toronto.

COHEN, S. (1980). Aftereffects of stress on human performance and social behavior: A review of research and theory. *Psychological Bulletin, 88,* 82–108.

CONWAY, T. L., VICKERS, R. R., JR., WARD, H. W., & RAHE, R. H. (1981). Occupational stress and variation in cigarette, coffee, and alcohol consumption. *Journal of Health and Social Behavior, 22,* 155–165.

CREWS, D. J., & LANDERS, D. M. (1987). A meta-analytic review of aerobic fitness and reactivity to psychosocial stressors. *Medicine and Science in Sports and Exercise, 19,* S114–S120.

CRONKITE, R. C., & MOOS, R. H. (1984). The role of predisposing and moderating factors in the stress-illness relationship. *Journal of Health and Social Behavior, 25,* 372–393.

CURRY, S. G., & MARLATT, G. A. (1985). Unaided quitters' strategies for coping with temptations to smoke. In S. Shiffman & T. A. Wills (Eds.), *Coping and substance use* (pp. 243–265). Orlando, FL: Academic Press.

CZAJKOWSKI, S. M., HINDELANG, R. D., DEMBROSKI, T. M., MAYERSON, S. E., PARKS, E. B., & HOLLAND, J.C. (1990). Aerobic fitness, psychological characteristics, and cardiovascular reactivity to stress. *Health Psychology, 9,* 676–692.

FOLKINS, C. H., LYNCH, S., & GARDNER. M. M. (1972). Psychological fitness as a function of physical fitness. *Archives of Physical Medicine and Rehabilitation, 53,* 503–508.

FOLKINS, C. H., & SIME, W. E. (1981). Physical fitness training and mental health. *American Psychologist, 36,* 373–389.

GILBERT, D. G., & SPIELBERGER, C. D. (1987). Effects of smoking on heart rate, anxiety, and feelings of success during social interaction. *Journal of Behavioral Medicine, 10,* 629–638.

GLASGOW, R. E., KLESGES, R. C., MIZES, J. S., & PECHACEK, T. F. (1985). Quitting smoking: Strategies used and variables associated with success in a stop-smoking contest. *Journal of Consulting and Clinical Psychology, 53,* 905–912.

GOLDWATER, B. C., & COLLIS, M. L. (1985). Psychologic effects of cardiovascular conditioning: A controlled experiment. *Psychosomatic Medicine, 47,* 174–181.

HALMI, K. A., OWEN, W., LASKY, E., & STOKES, P. (1983). Dopaminergic regulation in anorexia nervosa. *International Journal of Eating Disorders, 22,* 129–134.

HODGSON, R., & MILLER, P. (1982). *Self-watching addictions, habits, and compulsions: What to do about them*. New York: Facts on File Publications.

HOLMES, D. S., & ROTH, D. L. (1985). Association of aerobic fitness with pulse rate and subjective responses to psychological stress. *Psychophysiology, 22*, 525–529.

HUGHES, C. A., (1974). A comparison of the effects of teaching techniques of body conditioning on physical fitness and self-concept. *Dissertation Abstracts International, 34*, 3957A–3958A. (University Microfilms No. 73–31, 255)

JAFFEE, J. H. (1985). Opioid dependence. In H. I. Kaplan & B. J. Sadock (Eds.), *Comprehensive textbook of psychiatry* (4th ed., vol. 1, pp. 987–1003). Baltimore: Williams & Wilkins.

JOHNSON, C. T., & BERNDT, D. J. (1983). Preliminary investigation of bulimia and life adjustment. *American Journal of Psychiatry, 140*, 774–777.

JOSEPHS, R. A., & STEELE, C. M. (1990). The two faces of alcohol myopia: Attentional mediation of psychological stress. *Journal of Abnormal Psychology, 99*, 115–126.

KING, A. C., TAYLOR, G. B., HASKELL, W. L., & DeBUSK, R. F. (1989). Influence of regular aerobic exercise on psychological health: A randomized, controlled trial of healthy middle-aged adults. *Health Psychology, 8*, 305–324.

KOBASA, S. C., MADDI, S. R., & PUCCETTI, M. C., (1982). Personality and exercise as buffers in the stress-illness relationship. *Journal of Behavioral Medicine, 5*, 391–404.

KOSTRUBALA, T. (1977). Jogging and personality change. *Today's Jogger, 1*, 14–15.

LAZARUS, R. S., & FOLKMAN, S. (1984). *Stress, appraisal, and coping*. New York: Springer.

LEVENSON, R. W., SHER, K. J., GROSSMAN, L. M., NEWMAN, J., & NEWLIN, D. B. (1980). Alcohol and stress response dampening: Pharmacological effects, expectancy, and tension reduction. *Journal of Abnormal Psychology, 89*, 529–538.

LIVEZEY, G. T., BALBKINS, N., & VOGEL, W. H. (1987). The effect of ethanol (alcohol) and stress on plasma catecholamine levels in individual female and male rats. *Neuropsychobiology, 17*, 193–198.

LOVALLO, W. R., PINCOMB, G. A., SUNG, B. H., EVERSON, S. A., PASSEY, R. B. & WILSON, M. F. (1991). Hypertension risk and caffeine's effect on cardiovascular activity during mental stress in young men. *Health Psychology, 10*, 236–243.

MARLATT, G. A. (1985). Relapse prevention: Theoretical rationale and overview of the model. In G.A. Marlatt & J.R. Gordon (Eds.), *Relapse prevention: Maintenance strategies in the treatment of addictive behaviors*, pp. 3–70. New York: Guilford.

MARLATT, G. A., & GEORGE, W. H. (1984). Relapse prevention: Introduction and overview of the model. *British Journal of Addictions, 79*, 261–273.

MAYHEW, R., & EDELMANN, R. J. (1989). Self-esteem, irrational beliefs, and coping strategies in relation to eating problems in a non-clinical population. *Personality and Individual Differences, 10*, 581–584.

PINCOMB, G. A., LOVALLO, W. R., PASSEY, R. B., BRACKETT, D. J., & WILSON, M.F. (1987). Caffeine enhances the physiological response to occupational stress in medical students. *Health Psychology, 6*, 101–112.

PLATT, J. J., & METZGER, D. S. (1987). Cognitive interpersonal problem-solving skills and the maintenance of treatment success in heroin addicts. *Journal of Addictive Behaviors, 1*, 5–13.

POMERLEAU, O. F., ADKINS, D., & PERTSCHUCK, M. (1978). Predictors of outcome and recidivism in smoking cessation treatment. *Addictive Behavior, 3*, 65–70.

ROBERTSON, D., FROLICH, J. C., CARR, R.K., WATSON, J. T., HOLLIFIELD, J. W., SHAND, D. G., & OATES, J. A. (1978). Effects of caffeine on plasma renin activity, catecholamines, and blood pressures. *New England Journal of Medicine, 298*, 181–186.

RODIN, J. (1986). Aging and health: Effects of the sense of control. *Science, 233*, 1271–1276.

ROTH, D. L., & HOLMES, D. S. (1985). Influence of physical fitness in determining the impact of stressful life events on physical and psychologic health. *Psychosomatic medicine, 47*, 164–173.

SHIFFMAN, S. (1982). Relapse following smoking cessation: A situational analysis. *Journal of Consulting and Clinical Psychology, 50*, 71–86.

SHIFFMAN, S. (1984a.) Cognitive antecedents and sequelae of smoking relapse crises. *Journal of Applied Social Psychology, 14*, 296–309.

SHIFFMAN, S. (1984b). Coping with temptations to smoke. *Journal of Consulting and Clinical Psychology, 52*, 261–267.

SINYOR, D., SCHWARTZ, S. G., PERONNET, F., BRISSON, G., & SERAGANIAN, P. (1983). Aerobic fitness level and reactivity to psychosocial stress: Physiological, biochemical, and subjective measures. *Psychosomatic Medicine, 45*, 205–216.

SOUKUP, V. M., BEILER, M. E., & TERRELL F. (1990). Stress, coping style, and problem-solving ability among eating-disorders inpatients. *Journal of Clinical Psychology, 46*, 592–599.

SUITOR, C. W., & HUNTER M.F. (1980). *Nutrition: Principles and application in health promotion.* Philadelphia: Lippincott.

TOMKINS, S. (1968). A modified model of smoking behavior. E. F. Borgatta & R. R. Evans (Eds.), *Smoking, health, and behavior.* Chicago: Aldine.

WILLS, T. A. (1986). Stress and coping in early adolescence: Relationships to smoking and alcohol use in urban school samples. *Health Psychology, 5*, 503–529.

WILLS, T. A. (1990). Stress and coping factors in the epidemiology of substance use. In L. T. Kozlowski, H. M. Annis, H. D. Cappell, F. B. Glaser, M.S. Goodstadt, Y. Israel, H. Kalant, E. M. Sellers, & E. R. Vingilis (Eds.), *Research advances in alcohol and drug problems* (Vol. 10, pp. 215–250). New York: Plenum.

PART **III**

Application of Concepts

In Part III we examine specific areas of stress research. We begin in Chapter 9 with crises, catastrophes, and disasters and consider crisis theory, stage models of coping, and the link between crises and psychopathology. We continue in Chapter 10 with crises associated with human life span and the family, focusing on developmental stages from infancy to old age as well as divorce and dual-career families. In Chapter 11, we move from the family to work and examine the various causes and consequences of occupational stress. We conclude in Chapter 12 with stress associated with the environment and society, including crowding, commuting, noise, air pollution, and prejudice and discrimination.

CHAPTER 9

Crises, Catastrophes, and Disasters

It is a sad fact that the most dramatic stressors in recent decades have involved the massive traumas and dislocations associated with war. Actual combat has always produced psychological casualties. Soldiers can experience prolonged fear and anxiety when placed in situations of extreme unpredictability and uncontrollability in which killing (and perhaps being killed) are expectations. During World War I, Mott (1919) coined the term "shell shock" to describe traumatic reactions to combat and proposed that it was caused by minute hemorrhages in the brain. Combat traumas were successively called "operational fatigue" and "war neuroses" during World War II, and eventually "combat fatigue" or "combat exhaustion" in the Korean and Vietnam wars. Whatever it was called, combat exhaustion proved to be a serious problem. During World War II, it was the single greatest cause of the loss of personnel (Bloch, 1969).

Similar problems are encountered by survivors of prison and concentration camps. Prisoners in Nazi concentration camps were subjected to the most inhumane of conditions. In the Korean and Vietnam wars, prisoners of war received treatment only slightly better. A common syndrome in response to such conditions is denial (the feeling that "this isn't really happening to me"), as well as debility induced by starvation, disease, and fatigue; dependency produced by solitary confinement and removal of social support; and dread of possible death, pain, and deformity (Farber, Harlow, & West, 1956).

The extremes of war are not the only catastrophes and disasters of modern life. On the nightly news we see volcanoes, earthquakes, hurricanes, mud slides, floods, tornadoes, droughts, nuclear accidents, plagues, fires, and toxic spills. Unlike war, relatively little is known about catastrophes and disasters in general. Such events are often unexpected and short-lived, which has limited the amount of extensive research that can be organized. They are also singular, which restricts the possibility of meaningful replication or comparison. (A person can easily compare a divorced parent with a nondivorced parent, but what is the appropriate comparison for the victim of a volcanic eruption?) Finally, there is the basic issue of how to define a disaster or catastrophe.

War has created many disasters and catastrophes studied by stress researchers.   *(Photo by Reuters/Bettmann.)*

Catastrophes and Disasters

Catastrophes and disasters are different from everyday stressors and hassles. Generally, they are distinguished by eight stimulus characteristics (Berren, Beigel, & Stuart, 1980; Bolin, 1988; Quarantelli, 1985): (1) the type (a natural event versus one perpetrated by humans); (2) the duration (a fire versus a famine); (3) the degree of personal impact (losing one's family and home versus losing time at work); (4) the breadth of impact (localized versus widespread property damage); (5) the potential for recurrence (a one-time lightning strike versus the annual spring flood); (6) the degree of warning; (7) the presence of a low point at which the worst is over, and (8) the possibility of preventing a recurrence. An understanding of these dimensions can help us determine the severity of a catastrophe or disaster and the type of assistance that may be required. For example, a victim of a long and brutal kidnapping may require considerable psychological assistance. Problems may be severe because the pain was inflicted by another person over an extended period and had a personal impact. The difficulty in predicting or controlling a recurrence might make the problems worse.

Part of the impact of a disaster may result from how people respond to it. For example, Bolin (1988) suggests that evacuations can be a source of stress, especially if they separate families, are not based on a consensus, are poorly managed, and expose victims to danger. Temporary or emergency shelter can be a source of stress if it is used for protracted periods, becomes a center of interpersonal conflict, isolates victims from their former communities and neighborhoods, and is dangerous, inadequate, socially heterogeneous, unstable, or unreliable.

Researchers often distinguish natural from human-made disaster (Baum, 1991; Smith, North, & Price, 1989; see Table 9.1). Natural disasters (earthquakes, floods, etc.) are often sudden, powerful, damaging, somewhat predictable, and uncontrollable, and their effects tend to be relatively short-lived. In contrast, many human-made disasters (nuclear accident, toxic dumping, oil spill, etc.) may be sudden or drawn out, are less predictable, have an unclear low point, and may have uncertain, chronic consequences. The full implications of these differences have yet to be fully studied. Given the increased complexity of society, with the greater possibility of human-made disasters, this is a dimension worthy of further study.

What do we know about catastrophes and disasters? They cause substantial disruption of people's lives, society, and the environment. But then, this is true by definition: would a disaster be a disaster if it were not disruptive? Beyond this, it is important to emphasize how little is known. In response to the Three Mile Island accident in which a nuclear power station suffered near meltdown and released considerable radiation, the Nuclear Regulatory Commission sponsored a symposium of stress experts to make predictions about the psychological effects of the disaster. Their predictions, based on the best research available, did not match what actually happened (Warheit, 1988).

TABLE 9.1   Characteristics of Natural and Human-Made Disasters

Characteristic	Natural Disasters	Human-Made Disasters
Suddenness	Often sudden, some warning	May be sudden or drawn out
Powerful impact	Usually powerful	Usually powerful
Visible damage	Usually causes damage and loss	May not cause damage and loss
Predictability	Some predictability	Low predictability
Low point	Clear low point	Unclear low point
Perceptions of control	Uncontrollable, lack of control	Uncontrollable but potentially controllable; the result of loss of control
Extent of effects	Usually limited to victims	Victims' and public's loss of confidence and credibility in perceived human agents
Persistence of effects	Up to a year, mostly acute	May be chronic, long-term uncertainty

SOURCE   From Baum, A. (1991). Toxins, technology, and natural disasters. In A. Monat & R. S. Lazarus (Eds.), *Stress and coping* (3rd ed., p. 135.) New York: Columbia University Press. Reprinted by permission.

The conclusions that can be made about the effects of catastrophes and disasters are rather general, and include the following (Warheit, 1988):

1. There is no evidence that large-scale, community-wide disasters produce panic or mass hysteria. People often respond to disasters in a purposeful and highly organized way.
2. Disasters do not produce an increase in psychotic reactions.
3. Disasters appear to increase the prevalence of relatively minor symptoms of anxiety, depression, and psychological complaints. These symptoms appear to be relatively short-lived and may be self-limiting.
4. Disasters seem not to increase problems among the elderly or those with a history of mental health problems.
5. Disasters often lead to a sense of personal and social cohesiveness.

In a more general sense, work on catastrophes and disasters reveals in harsh light some of the very basics of stress and coping. In terms of the transactional perspective, those who survive appear to have coping beliefs, values, and commitments as well as coping skills. Defense can become a survival tool; social support becomes a necessity.

So far we have taken a stimulus approach to exploring catastrophes and disasters; the event has defined our domain of study. What are the *effects* of war, the *consequences* of earthquake, the *costs* of a nuclear accident? A more fruitful investigation would be an *individual focus* not on the content of catastrophe and disaster but on the response to what people perceive to be crises. Here, using the transactional lens, we can examine the complex processes of coping.

Coping with Crises

The modern study of crises can be traced to a single domestic tragedy. It was evening, November 28, 1942. The American nation had experienced the largest single building fire in its history. As Boston's Coconut Grove nightclub went up in flames, 493 people perished. In addition to the usual inquiries probing possible building code violations, arson, and so on, something unusual happened. Lindemann and others at the Massachusetts General Hospital organized a massive effort to help survivors with their psychological trauma, especially the loss of loved ones. The resulting report (Lindemann, 1944) became the cornerstone of work on the grieving process, and signaled the onset of current studies on crises.

Crisis Theory

The very semantics of the word *crisis* suggest its current meaning. The Chinese terms for crisis, *weiji*, means both danger and opportunity (Wilhelm, 1967). According to Slaikeu (1990, p. 15), a crisis is "a temporary state of upset and disorganization, characterized chiefly by an individual's inability to cope with a particular situation using customary methods of problem solving, and by the potential for a radically positive or negative outcome."

A University of California student sits in stunned crisis after a fire destroys over 600 homes in Oakland, California. *(Photo by UPI/Bettmann.)*

Many crisis theories focus on the breakdown of coping strategies. For example, Caplan (1964) has suggested four crises stages:

1. A crisis generally has a clear beginning. Some events (such as rape, death, or serious illness) are so devastating that they are almost always traumatic. Other events must be seen in context. For example, retirement may be additionally traumatic if forced upon a person at an early age.
2. Once a crisis occurs, tension increases, and habitual coping strategies are attempted. If these strategies fail, the crisis event is not resolved and feelings of upset increase.
3. Other coping strategies are attempted. The crisis may be resolved, the problem redefined, or tightly held goals relinquished.
4. If the crisis is not resolved, and problem-focused or emotion-focused coping strategies break down, tension increases, resulting in emotional disorganization, disequilibrium, and suggestibility. One may feel helpless, confused, and anxious. Functioning at work, home, and in social relationships may suffer. Partly as a result of the breakdown in coping, a person in crisis is suggestible and vulnerable. An openness to new ways of appraising and coping may well prove to be desirable, providing that helpful suggestions are offered.

Finally, crises are usually acute, with a sudden onset and short duration. Frequently, the severe disorganization and disruption lasts four to six weeks, although lingering problems may persist for years.

Horowitz (1982) has suggested a different model of crises that emphasizes the cognitive and emotional changes that occur and that eventually lead to acceptance and a decision to go on living. The first reaction is *outcry*, an emotional reaction such as weeping, panic, screaming, or fainting. Next comes either *denial* or *intru-*

siveness. We have already considered denial as a defensive coping strategy. Here, denial refers to an emotional and intellectual movement away from the crisis event. A person may feel dazed and unable to attend to or recognize the significance of stimuli related to the crisis event. Emotionally, a person may feel a sense of numbness "clouding," or a loss of the real vividness of the world. In extreme cases, a person may even experience amnesia and forget aspects of the event. All these symptoms have in common a shielding or avoiding of a variety of aspects of the crisis.

Intrusion is in some sense the opposite of denial. Here, a person emotionally and intellectually moves toward a reliving of the event. He may become extremely vigilant and easily startled. A wide range of outside stimuli can serve as painful reminders of the crisis. He may be disturbed by nightmares related to the event, preoccupied with pent-up memories and emotions, and have an inability to attend to other topics. In extreme cases, he may experience hallucinations and illusions related to the event. (For example, mistaking someone in the distance as a dead relative.)

Denial and intrusiveness are part of a natural process of working through a crisis. In intrusive phases, one is "dosed" with thoughts and feelings concerning the crises in order to learn to cope with them. Others have called this the "work of worry" (Janis, 1958) or "grief work" (Lindemann, 1944). However, any one crisis contains far too many issues to be worked through at any one time. For example, in dealing with the death of a spouse, a person may have to consider such ramifications as learning to live alone, not having a trusted companion, and having to support a family. When a crisis victim has reached a limit of how much can be worked through, intrusion is followed by a denial. Denial offers a needed break from the working-through process—an opportunity to recover from experienced pain and to regroup resources. In time, the victim may be ready for another intrusive phase. Thus, denial and intrusiveness do not occur as lock-step stages. Instead, a person moves from denial, to intrusion, and back to denial, again and again. The process of working through a crisis is a zigzag pattern of assimilating its full implications.

What is the outcome of working through? Put simply and eloquently, Horowitz (1982) describes it as learning to face and accept the reality of the crisis—"Yes, my wife has died and will no longer be with me"—and choosing to go on living—"I can now go on. I have a life to live." This process involves integrating the facts of a crisis into the rest of life, leaving a person open to the future, and developing new coping strategies and new resources. Others (Moos & Schaefer, 1986) have differentiated five goals of the working-through process:

1. Establishing and understanding the personal significance of the situation.
2. Confronting reality and responding to the requirements of the external situation.
3. Sustaining relationships with family members and friends as well as with others who may be helpful in resolving the crisis and its aftermath.
4. Maintaining a reasonable emotional balance by managing upsetting feelings aroused by the situation.
5. Preserving a satisfactory self-image, and maintaining a sense of competence and mastery.

Just what *is* worked through in a crisis? We have considered the most abstract answer: intrusive thoughts and feelings. However, more specifically, a variety of themes have to be considered. Horowitz (1982) has identified the following:

FEAR OF REPETITION.   For a person who has survived a crisis or catastrophe, one painful possibility is that it may happen again. The fire, flood, or attack may recur. Victims can also fear intrusive feelings of pain and panic associated with a crisis.

SHAME OVER HELPLESSNESS OR EMPTINESS.   Our society praises those who appear to be in total control, no matter how illusory this control may be. A crisis or catastrophe can challenge such beliefs. An illness can demonstrate personal vulnerability, as can a rape or accident. A person can experience upset over not having prevented or controlled the crisis, even though it was quite uncontrollable. People who have had a heart attack may well apologize profusely because they can no longer do ordinary chores. After being burned out of a home, parents may feel deflated in the eyes of their children.

RAGE AT "THE SOURCE."   People in crisis often experience anger toward any person who, however irrationally, may be seen as actually or symbolically responsible. People wish to believe they understand or can control events. They seek answers to the question, "Why did it happen?" The fact that there may be no clear answer can be a painful fact. Seeking someone, or something, to blame at least provides a false sense of understanding—"I know who did it"—or control—"I can deal with the person responsible."

GUILT, SHAME, AND FEAR CONCERNING ANGER.   Feelings of rage often lead to destructive fantasies toward perceived sources of a crisis, especially when it involved violence. However, such vengeful fantasies may conflict with one's conscience, resulting in guilt or shame. A common variation of this theme is anger toward someone who has died, followed by intense guilt or shame over such feelings. In addition, a person may become preoccupied with fear that the anger will be expressed or provoke retaliation. For example, a soldier traumatized by war may fear physically attacking others in civilian life.

SURVIVAL GUILT.   When others have been killed by a fire, flood, or accident, the survivors often ask the painful question, "Why did I survive?" Of course, such a question often has no answer. However, survivors often become preoccupied with feeling that they do not deserve their good fortune, or for "selfishly" rejoicing in their good fortune when others may have perished.

BARGAINING.   After a crisis, some people experience an irrational urge to bargain for a better outcome. The cancer patient may plead with his doctor, "I'll live a healthy lifestyle if you just make me healthy"; an accident victim might pray, "God, I'll go to church if you let me live." Although such bargaining usually doesn't change a problem, it does provide the victim with feelings of control.

SADNESS.   Most crises and catastrophes involve a serious loss. A friend or loved one may die. Cherished possessions may be stolen or destroyed. Personal capacities may be limited through illness or accident. Cherished hopes may no longer be possible. An important theme to be worked through is accepting that which can no longer be.

Stage Models of Coping with Crises

Many writers have proposed that coping with a crisis progresses through specific stages. Although different models have been suggested for various situations, Shontz's (1975) model for dealing with illness or disability contains features characteristic of most. The first stage, in which the crisis occurs, is *shock*. A person may well feel a sense of detachment and continue functioning with little disruption. In the ensuing *encounter* phase, she may experience extreme helplessness, panic, and disorganization. This is followed by *retreat*, which is a psychological numbing similar to what Horowitz (1982) terms denial. The coping process involves shifting back and forth between retreat and confrontation of the facts of a crisis. Other models often include these basic features, occasionally adding a stage reflecting one of Horowitz's crisis themes such as sadness or rage at the source.

There is considerable controversy concerning these stage models of coping with crises. Often they are based on little information. People in fact tend to progress through stages in different orders, making the notion of one "typical" sequence problematic. Often stages are skipped and other stages unidentified by a model are experienced. More seriously, any stage model creates expectations in the victim and those who wish to help concerning appropriate feelings and actions. For example, patients experiencing depression may be encouraged to "feel your anger" because that is perceived as the next stage. Perhaps it is more useful to examine the processes and themes involved in coping with crises and ask which are productive and counterproductive (Lazarus & Folkman, 1984).

Friends and relatives help a child cope with the crisis of illness and hospitalization.   *(Photo by Patrick James Watson,* The Image Works.*)*

Coping with Illness

We conclude our section on coping with crisis with a type of crisis that is perhaps encountered most often: serious illness. Millon (1982, pp. 11 to 13) has suggested eight coping styles that can influence a person's susceptibility to illness, compliance with prevention and treatment regiments, and prospects for recovery.

1. *Introversive style.* These individuals are rather colorless and emotionally flat and tend to be quiet and untalkative. They are often concerned with their problems, but are vague concerning specific symptoms. In addition, they may passively avoid taking care of themselves. They also tend to minimize, ignore, deny, or rationalize the personal significance of illness or stressful information. Generally, they are "oblivious to the implications of their illness and indifferent to medical procedures that normally arouse anxiety."

2. *Inhibited style.* Such people tend to be "shy and ill at ease; they expect to be hurt, are disposed to feel rejected, and are overly concerned about whether others will think well or ill of them." They tend to keep their problems to themselves, suspecting that others may take advantage of them. Indeed, they may see illness as punishment and fatalistically accept the "inevitable."

3. *Cooperative style.* These people eagerly attach themselves to sources of support and follow advice religiously, as long as they can assume little responsibility. Illness may be experienced with a sense of relief as a respite from the demands of living. Such people are often dependent and demanding, seeking reassurance and nurturing from others.

4. *Sociable style.* Although outgoing and charming, these individuals have highly changeable likes and dislikes, are often undependable, and appear more concerned with appearance than with substance. When confronted with serious problems, they would rather not deal with them. Indeed, illness is often seen as little more than a strategy for obtaining attention and compliance from others. At times, such people appear to be dramatic and emotional, seeking to be attractive and desirable.

5. *Confident style.* These individuals display a calm, narcissistic air of superiority. They may fear illness and disease and once ill, strive hard to regain a state of health. Characteristically, they expect special treatment and may well take unjust advantage of others. Being sick can signify a severe threat to their self-image. "They are snobbish, self-confident, even grandiose at times. Often displaying arrogance and a disdain of others, they occasionally precipitate competitive struggles for status, even with medical personnel who are in a position to treat them well or badly."

6. *Forceful style.* These individuals are more aggressive and hostile than those who exhibit the confident style. Indeed, they are often domineering and tough-minded. They may be unwilling to accept a sick role, and instead "go on the attack" in dealing with illness or disability. The may apply this style so forcefully as to insist that an injured body part were still intact.

7. *Respectful style.* Many cope with illness by becoming over responsible and conforming, trying to impress others with the discipline and seriousness. They tend

to see illness as a sign of weakness, failure, or shameful loss of control. Understandably, they often tend to try to deny or conceal problems they feel might be humiliating or, when denial is impossible, become model patients.

8. *Sensitive style*. Those who display a sensitive style are moody individuals who are often dissatisfied with much of their life. They often act as if they were born to suffer and even complain that treatment and reassurance has produced more harm than good.

Crises and Psychopathology

What happens when coping fails? The popular notion of a "nervous breakdown" reflects a simplified view that people experience extreme disruption and upset. Of course, the actual picture is much more complex.

First, most forms of psychopathology are at least partially associated with stress. The *diathesis-stress model* states that psychopathology occurs when a person has a predisposition, or a diathesis, for a type of disorder and then encounters stress. In addition, stress is a part of the most widely used classification system for disorders in the United States, the *Diagnostic and Statistical Manual of Mental Disorders* (third edition, revised) (DSM-III-R), published by the American Psychiatric Association (1987).

At one level, the DSM-III-R conceptualizes psychopathology along five dimensions called *axes*. The first three assess standard psychiatric and medical conditions:

I. Clinical syndrome, such as schizophrenia, mood disorders, and anxiety disorders.
II. Long-lasting personality problems in adults or specific developmental problems in children and adolescents.
III. Medical or physical disorders that may be associated with psychopathology, such as ulcers and anxiety.

Therapists often make multiple diagnoses on several axes, since patients may display a variety of mental and physical symptoms.

The final two axes reflect stress:

IV. Severity of psychosocial stressors.
V. Level of adaptive functioning.

Axis IV presents a six-point scale for rating stressor severity from "none" to "catastrophic" (see Tables 9.2 and 9.3). Stressors can be either acute or chronic situations. A clinician must judge the stressfulness of a situation on the basis of what an "average" person would experience under similar circumstances, and not what the patient, with her specific vulnerabilities, may actually undergo. Taken into account are the amount of change created by the stressor, the undesirability of the stressor, the degree to which the stressor is under the person's control, and the number of stressors.

163

TABLE 9.2   DSM-III-R Severity of Psychosocial Stressors Scale: Adults

	Examples of Stressors	
Level of Stress	Acute Events	Enduring Circumstances
None	No acute events that may be relevant to any psychiatric disorder under consideration	No enduring circumstances that may be relevant to the disorder
Mild	Broke up with boyfriend or girl-friend; started or graduated from school; child left home	Family arguments; job dissatisfaction; residence in high-crime neighborhood
Moderate	Marriage; marital separation; loss of job; retirement; miscarriage	Marital discord; serious financial problems; trouble with boss; being a single parent
Severe	Divorce: birth of first child	Unemployment; poverty
Extreme	Death of spouse; serious physical illness diagnosed; victim of rape	Serious chronic illness in self or child; ongoing physical or sexual abuse
Catastrophic	Death of child; suicide of spouse; devastating natural disaster	Captivity as hostage; concentration camp experience

SOURCE   From American Psychiatric Association, *Diagnostic and Statistical Manual of Mental Disorders, Third Edition, Revised*, Washington, DC, American Psychiatric Association, 1987, p. 11. Reprinted by permission.

TABLE 9.3   DSM-III-R Severity of Psychosocial Stressors Scale: Children and Adolescents

	Examples of Stressors	
Level of Stress	Acute Events	Enduring Circumstances
None	No acute events that may be relevant to any psychiatric disorder under consideration	No enduring circumstances that may be relevant to the disorder
Mild	Broke up with boyfriend or girlfriend; change of school	Overcrowded living quarters; family arguments
Moderate	Expelled from school; birth of sibling	Chronic disabling illness in parent; chronic parental discord
Severe	Divorce of parents; unwanted pregnancy; arrest	Harsh or rejecting parents; chronic life-threatening illness in parent; multiple foster home placements
Extreme	Sexual or physical abuse; death of a parent	Recurrent sexual or physical abuse
Catastrophic	Death of both parents	Chronic life-threatening illness

SOURCE   From American Psychiatric Association, *Diagnostic and Statistical Manual of Mental Disorders, Third Edition, Revised*, Washington, DC, American Psychiatric Association, 1987, p. 11. Reprinted by permission.

Stressors are also rated as acute (duration of less than six months) or enduring and chronic (duration of greater than six months). Axis IV enables a clinician to evaluate the role of stress in contributing to the development, recurrence, or exacerbation of psychopathology. Stress may also be a consequence of pathology.

Axis V contains an overall evaluation of psychological functioning, social relationships, and occupational activities (see Table 9.4). Ratings are made for current functioning and highest level of functioning in the previous year. Axis V can be viewed as a stress-related dimension since it essentially asks for an assessment of how well a person is coping as well as symptoms that can be stress related.

At another level, the DSM-III-R identifies two specific disorders that are stress related: the adjustment disorder and post-traumatic stress disorder. An *adjustment disorder* occurs within three months of a common stressor (such as divorce or job loss) and involves impairment beyond what would normally be expected. Impairment is defined in terms of predominant symptoms, such as depressed mood, anxious mood, disturbed conduct, disorders at work and school, withdrawal, or physical complaints. Typically, these symptoms lessen once the stressor has subsided or the person learns to cope. For adjustment disorders, the predisposition of the individual is not considered relevant.

For a *posttraumatic stress disorder*, the stressor is traumatic and uncommon (although this point is debated), that is, outside the realm of typical human experience. Examples include war, kidnapping, and physical violence. In addition, victims experience a pattern of symptoms lasting at least a month:

1 Intrusive reexperiencing of the traumatic event.
2. Denial symptoms involving avoiding or blocking stimuli associated with the trauma.
3. Symptoms of stress arousal.

These symptoms can emerge six months after the stressor was experienced, in which case the posttraumatic stress disorder is considered delayed. In addition, the symptoms can be chronic, lasting six months or more. Note the similarities between the symptoms of the posttraumatic stress disorder and the stress reactions described by Horowitz (1982).

The posttraumatic stress disorder has received considerable attention in the press. Frequent accounts are presented (and often are made) of Vietnam War veterans, victims of concentration camps, and prisoners of war who experience dramatic flashback memories of their trauma (intrusion), reduced emotional involvement with their spouses (denial), nightmares (intrusion), and night sweats and irritability (stress arousal).

Examples of Coping

We close with two examples of individuals dealing with crises and catastrophes. See if you can determine which of the coping styles we have discussed are illustrated.

TABLE 9.4   DSM-III-R Global Assessment of Functioning Scale[*]

Level of Adjustment	Examples
81–90	Absent or minimal symptoms (e.g., mild anxiety before an exam), good functioning in all areas, interested and involved in a wide range of activities, socially effective, generally satisfied with life, no more than everyday problems or concerns (e.g., an occasional argument with family members).
71–80	If symptoms are present, they are transient and expectable reactions to psychosocial stressors (e.g., difficulty concentrating after family argument); no more than slight impairment in social, occupational, or school functioning (e.g., temporarily falling behind in school work).
61–70	Some mild symptoms (e.g., depressed mood and mild insomnia) OR some difficulty in social, occupational, or school functioning (e.g., occasional truancy, or theft within the household), but generally functioning pretty well, has some meaningful interpersonal relationships.
51–60	Moderate symptoms (e.g., flat affect and circumstantial speech, occasional panic attacks) OR moderate difficulty in social, occupational, or school functioning (e.g., few friends, conflicts with co-workers).
41–50	Serious symptoms (e.g., suicidal ideation, severe obsessional rituals, frequent shoplifting) OR any serious impairment in social, occupational, or school functioning (e.g., no friends, unable to keep a job).
31–40	Some impairment in reality testing or communication (e.g., speech is at times illogical, obscure, or irrelevant) OR major impairment in several areas, such as work or school, family relationships, judgment, thinking, or mood (e.g., depressed man avoids friends, neglects family, and is unable to work; child frequently beats up younger children, is defiant at home, and is failing at school).
21–30	Behavior is considerably influenced by delusions or hallucinations OR serious impairment in communication or judgment (e.g., sometimes incoherent, acts grossly inappropriately, suicidal preoccupation) OR inability to function in almost all areas (e.g., stays in bed all day; no job, home, or friends).
11–20	Some danger of hurting self or others (e.g., suicide attempts without clear expectation of death, frequently violent, manic excitement) OR occasionally fails to maintain minimal personal hygiene (e.g., smears feces) OR gross impairment in communication (e.g., largely incoherent or mute).
1–10	Persistent danger of severely hurting self or others (e.g., recurrent violence) OR persistent inability to maintain minimal personal hygiene OR serious suicidal act with clear expectation of death.

[*] Consider psychological, social, and occupational functioning on a hypothetical continuum of mental health-illness. Do not include impairment in functioning due to physical (or environmental) limitations.

SOURCE   From American Psychiatric Association, *Diagnostic and Statistical Manual of Mental Disorders, Third Edition, Revised*, Washington, DC, American Psychiatric Association, 1987, p. 12. Reprinted by permission.

Mary is a student at a local community college. She is renting a room from an older couple. One evening she returned from the library and discovered that a major fire had destroyed the entire house. At first she didn't believe it. "This can't be," she thought. Then, the reality began to sink in. She started blaming herself for the fire. "Did I leave the heater on? I *knew* I should have unplugged the TV." Some days she simply seemed to be depressed. Her friends noted that she displayed a lack of enthusiasm in her schoolwork. Other days she seemed irritable, warning her friends about potential fire hazards in their rooms. Four months later, Mary continued to be upset. Eventually she dropped out of college for a term and took a vacation. The following year she enrolled in a different college and was much less disturbed by the tragedy that had long since passed.

George was recently attacked by a group of gang members in his neighborhood. Although not badly injured, he did suffer a few broken bones and lost his wallet. But the psychological harm was more serious. He kept saying, "There was nothing I could do! They pinned me down and kept hitting me! I can't believe I didn't do a thing!" At first, George tried to put the event out of his mind. Then he tried making his room more secure by installing extra locks. However, no matter what he did, he found himself feeling more and more fearful of a repeat attack. He avoided his friends and even stayed home several days from work.

Eventually a therapist helped him cope with his problems more effectively. In some sessions, he talked with some urgency about his feelings of terror, pain, and embarrassment. In other sessions, he felt "blank", and nothing seemed to come to mind. Although from time to time George wondered why he showed such "flip-flops" in counseling, his therapist did not seem overly concerned. Eventually, George began to feel a greater sense of calm and could easily talk about his attack with others. It was now behind him, and he could go back to his life.

APPLICATION BOX 9.1

The Disaster

Here is clipping from a fictitious newspaper article:

Tornado Smashes Local Town

A powerful tornado roared through the streets of Bowling Green village. Four buildings were completely destroyed, including the new county library and much of the local college. Miraculously, no lives were lost. Mrs. Cordelia, a 90-year old resident, recalled, "This tornado is nothing. Sure, my lovely little pet cat blew away, but I'll get over that. We knew it was coming. We knew when the worst was over. If you want to hear about a disaster, let me tell you about the time the gas pipes started exploding. Nobody knew when the next pipe would blow up. Houses caught on fire unexpectedly. That was a disaster!"

Can you interpret this account using concepts introduced in this chapter? Notice the difference between the natural (tornado) and man-made (pipes bursting) disaster. Notice that the predictability of the tornado reduced its severity, whereas the unpredictability of the gas pipe problem made it worse.

Find an example of a crisis, catastrophe, or disaster in your local newspaper. Try to find an example that describes how people reacted. Interpret these reactions in terms of concepts introduced in this chapter.

References

AMERICAN PSYCHIATRIC ASSOCIATION (1987). *Diagnostic and statistical manual of mental disorders*, (3rd ed., rev.). Washington, DC: Author.

BAUM, A. (1991). Toxins, technology, and natural disasters. In A. Monat, & R. S. Lazarus (Eds.), *Stress and coping* (3rd ed., pp. 97–139). New York: Columbia University Press.

BERREN, M. R., BEIGEL, A., & STUART, G. (1980). A typology for the classification of disasters. In R. H. Moos (Ed.), *Coping with life crises* (pp. 295–305). New York: Plenum.

BLOCH, H. S. (1969). Army clinical psychiatry in the combat zone 1967–1968. *American Journal of Psychiatry, 126,* 289.

BOLIN, R. (1988). Response to natural disasters. In M. Lystad (Ed.), *Mental health response to mass emergencies* (pp. 22–51). New York: Brunner-Mazel.

CAPLAN, G. (1964). *Principles of preventative psychiatry.* New York: Basic Books.

FARBER, I. E., HARLOW, H. F., & WEST, L. J. (1956). Brainwashing, conditioning, and DDD (debility, dependency, and dread). *Sociometry, 19,* 271–285.

HOROWITZ, M. J. (1982). Psychological processes induced by illness, injury, and loss. In T. Millon, C. Green, & R. Meagher (Eds.), *Handbook of clinical health psychology* pp. 53–67). New York: Plenum.

JANIS, I. L. (1958). *Psychological stress: Psychoanalytic and behavioral studies of surgical patients.* New York: Wiley.

LAZARUS, R. S., & FOLKMAN, S. (1984). *Stress, appraisal, and coping.* New York: Springer.

LINDEMANN, E. (1944). Symptomatology and management of acute grief. *American Journal of Psychiatry, 101,* 141–148.

MILLON, T. (1982). On the nature of clinical health psychology. In T. Millon, C. Green, & R. Meagher (Eds.), *Handbook of Clinical health psychology* (pp. 1–27). New York: Plenum.

MOOS, R. H., & SCHAEFER, J. A. (1986). Life transitions and crises. In R. H. Moos (Ed.), *Coping with life crises* (p. 3–33). New York: Plenum.

MOTT, F. W. (1919). *War neuroses and shell shock.* Oxford: Oxford Medical Publications.

QUARANTELLI, E. L. (1985). What is disaster? The need for clarification in definition and conceptualization in research. In B. J. Sowder (Ed.), *Disasters and mental health: Selected contemporary perspectives* (pp. 41–73). Rockville, MD: U.S. Department of Health and Human Services.

SHONTZ, F. C. (1975). *The psychological aspects of physical illness and disability.* New York: Macmillan.

SLAIKEU, K. A. (1990). *Crisis intervention: A handbook for practice and research* (2nd ed). Boston: Allyn and Bacon.

SMITH, E. M., NORTH, C. S., & PRICE, P. C. (1988). Response to technological accidents. In M. Lystad (Ed.), *Mental health response to mass emergencies* (pp. 52–95). New York: Brunner-Mazel.

WARHEIT, G. J. (1988). Disasters and their mental health consequences: Issues, findings, and future trends. In M. Lystad (Ed.), *Mental health response to mass emergencies* (pp. 3–21). New York: Brunner-Mazel.

WILHELM, R. (1967). *The book of changes, or The I Ching.* Princeton: Princeton University Press.

CHAPTER 10

Stress, the Life Span, and the Family

There are two general types of stress everyone experiences: growing up and being part of a family. We are all products of some type of family unit, whether it be a traditional nuclear family or one of the many alternatives. The family provides the defining context for much of the stress of development. In addition, the family itself can be seen as an entity that can be subject to stress.

The Stress of the Life Span

Human growth and development can be viewed in terms of transitions, phases, and even preoccupations (Erikson, 1963; Havighurst, 1952; Neugarten, 1979). Erikson's stage theory is the most widely cited in the stress literature. Each stage presents its own crisis. However, the resolution of a crisis involves not putting it aside but incorporating both its negative and positive aspects into a person's personality. Put differently, each stage presents a type of threat or challenge, the resolution of which can lead to adaptive forms of primary and secondary appraisal as well as adaptive coping skills. Each stage presents a wide variety of tasks, as shown in Table 10.1. We shall consider some of the highlights.

Infancy

In the first year of life, the infant's main contact with reality is mediated by the mother. It is the mother who provides life's chief reinforcers: food, warmth, physical contact, and so on. From this an infant learns the lesson that the world and himself are generally trustworthy or not trustworthy. If reinforcers are generally predictable, the infant learns, for example, whether the mother is a reliable source of food. Erikson (1963, 1964) describes such general learnings as a sense of *basic trust* and *basic mistrust*. One must acquire appraisals and skills related to both.

Some trust and hope are necessary throughout life. As seen in Chapter 5, such general coping beliefs, values, and commitments as optimism can indeed be adaptive. However, it would be maladaptive and unrealistic to go through life trusting

169

TABLE 10.1   Development Throughout the Life Span*

Stage	Transition Theme	Tasks/Preoccupations	Possible Crisis Events[†]
Infancy (0–1)	Trust versus mistrust	Feeding	Disruption in feeding
		Developing Sensory discrimination and motor skills	Physical illness, injury
		Gaining emotional stability	Rejection by primary caretaker
Toddlerhood (1–2)	Autonomy versus shame and doubt	Walking, talking	Physical injury
		Developing sense of independence	Conflict with primary caretaker over increased assertiveness, toilet training, etc.
		Adjusting to socialization demands	
Early childhood (2–6)	Initiative versus guilt	Learning skills and muscle control	Physical injury
		Developing body concepts and learning about sex differences	Conflict with teachers/ parents re: early sex play
		Learning cultural values and sense of "right and wrong"	Conflict with teachers, peers
		Developing concepts of social and physical reality	Entering school (preschool or kindergarten)
		Developing interpersonal skills (family, peers)	Loss of friends through moving/migration
Middle childhood (6–12)	Industry versus inferiority	Mastering school subjects (three Rs, science, humanities)	Learning difficulties in school
		Developing learning and problem-solving skills	Peer conflicts
		Relating to peers, teachers, and unfamiliar adults	Conflict with teachers
		Developing sense of independence within family context	Conflict with parents

(continues)

TABLE 10.1 *Continued*

Stage	*Transition Theme*	*Tasks/Preoccupations*	*Possible Crisis Events*[†]
		Developing- self-control and frustration tolerance	Change in schools
Adolescence (12–18)	Identity versus role confusion	Adjusting to bodily changes and new emotions	Menstruation Sexual intercourse Unwanted pregnancy
		Achieving gradual independence from parents/caretakers	Graduation from high school Going to college
		Questioning values/ developing life philosophy	Conflict with parents over personal habits and life style
		Exploring intimate personal relationships	Breakup with girlfriend/ boyfriend; broken engagement
		Exploring vocational options	Career indecision Difficulty on first job Success/failure in: academics, athletics
Young Adulthood (18–34)	Intimacy versus isolation	Selecting and learning to live with a mate/ partner	Rejection by potential partner; extramarital affairs; separation, divorce
		Starting a family (or, not . . .)	Unwanted pregnancy; inability to bear children; birth of a child
		Developing parenting skills	Discipline problems with children; illness of son or daughter; inability to manage the various demands of parental role
		Deciding about military service	Entering military service; being drafted; avoiding service
		Getting started in an occupation	Academic difficulties; failure to graduate from high school/

(continues)

TABLE 10.1   *Continued*

Stage	*Transition Theme*	*Tasks/Preoccupations*	*Possible Crisis Events[†]*
			college; inability to find satisfactory career; poor performance in chosen career
		Overall development of personal life style in social context	Purchase of home; financial difficulties; conflict between career and family goals; age 30 transition
Middle adulthood (35–50)	Generativity versus stagnation	Adjusting to physiological changes of middle age	Awareness of physical decline
			Chronic illness (self or spouse)
			Climacteric
		Adjusting to changes in children (e.g., to young adults)	Rejection by rebellious adolescent children
			Divorce of child
		Dealing with new responsibilities regarding aging parents	Decision about care of aging parents
			Death or prolonged illness of parents
		Increasing productivity and developing socio-economic consolidation	Setback in career; conflict at work
			Financial concerns
			Moving associated with career advancement
			Unemployment
		Re-examination of earlier life choices (mate, career, children) - and reworking of earlier themes (identity, intimacy)	Awareness of discrepancy between life goals and achievements
			Regret over earlier decisions to not

(continues)

TABLE 10.1   *Continued*

Stage	Transition Theme	Tasks/Preoccupations	Possible Crisis Events[†]
			marry, not to have children, or vice versa
			Dissatisfaction with goals achieved
		Shift in life structure in light of changes in family and work responsibilities	Promotion
			Break/conflict with mentor
			Marital problems/ extramarital affairs
			Return to work (female) post child–rearing
			Death of friends
Maturity (50–65)	Generativity versus stagnation	Adjusting to physiological aging (e.g., changes in health, decreased strength)	Health problems
		Preparing for retirement	Decisions re: retire-ment (leisure time, new career)
			Change in physical living arrangements (farmhouse to city apartment)
		Developing mutually rewarding relation-ships with grown children	Conflict with grown children
		Re-evaluating, consolida-ing relationship with spouse/significant other, or adjusting to his/her loss (death, divorce)	"Empty nest" (last child leaves home)
			Death of spouse, divorce
		Assisting aging parents	Conflict with parents
		Making productive use of increased leisure time	Resistance to retirement (separation or letting go of work roles/ responsibilities

(continues)

TABLE 10.1   *Continued*

Stage	Transition Theme	Tasks/Preoccupations	Possible Crisis Events[†]
Old age (65-death)	Ego integrity versus despair	Pursuing second/third career, and/or leisure interest	Financial difficulties
		Sharing wisdom from life's experience with others	Interpersonal conflict with children
			Interpersonal conflict with peers (e.g., in new living quarters)
			Neglect by adult children
		Evaluating past and achieving sense of satisfaction with one's life	Death of friends
			Awareness of loneliness
		Enjoying reasonable amount of physical and emotional comfort	Illness or disability
		Maintaining sufficient mobility for variety in environment	Difficulty in adjustment to retirement

*Stages, themes, and tasks represent summaries from J. E. Brophy, *Child Development and socialization*. Chicago: Science Research Associates, 1977; C. E. Kennedy, *Human development: The adult years and aging*. New York: Macmillan, 1978; R. J. Havighurst, *Developmental tasks and education*. New York: Longmans, Green & Company, 1952; S. Stevenson, *Issues and Crises during middlescence*. New York: Appleton-Century-Crofts 1977; E. H. Erikson, *Childhood and society*. New York: W. W. Norton, 1963; J. Conger, *Adolescence: Generation under pressure*. New York: Harper & Row, 1979; M. Fiske, *Middle age: The prime of life?* New York: Harper & Row, 1979; R. Kastenbaum, *Growing old: Years of fulfillment*. New York: Harper & Row, 1979.

†Whether or not these events present "crises" or not depends upon a number of variables, including timing of the event, as well as financial, personal and social resources.

SOURCE   From Karl A. Slaikeu, *Crisis intervention: A handbook for practice and research*, second edition, Copyright © 1990 by Allyn and Bacon. Reprinted with permission.

everyone and everything; a bit of mistrust can be useful. A generalized sense of mistrust, experienced in adulthood as generalized pessimism, also maladaptive. Erikson (1963, 1964) emphasizes that a person acquires a balance of trust and mistrust or, in behavioral terms, useful and rational appraisals and skills related to both trust and mistrust. One result of managing the crisis of any stage of life is the acquisition of global appraisals, or what cognitive behaviorists would call abstract schemas (Beck, 1963), basic beliefs or assumptions (Ellis, 1962), personal philosophies (Smith 1990), and the like. The infant who finds the world and herself trustworthy, develops a sense of virtue or *hope*. She has learned to risk in the face of possible disappointment, trusting that disappointment will not be overwhelming. Of course, such global appraisals are not acquired fully in infancy; instead, the threats and challenges of infancy set the stage for the development of more general cognitive appraisals.

Toddlerhood

Somewhere between the first and second year of life, the infant begins to acquire voluntary muscle control. He learns to hold on to and let go of objects (which can be tenaciously grabbed or tossed), and begins the troublesome task of toilet training, of holding on to and letting go of bodily wastes at the appropriate time. The crisis of toddlerhood revolves around acquiring a sense of independence or willful *autonomy* over one's body: of being able to grab and toss items and perform the basic bodily functions of elimination at appropriate times. The threat is one of having exposed, or *"shamed,"* himself by having grabbed, tossed, or eliminated at the wrong time in front of others. At this stage begins the development of global appraisals of *will*, or "the unbroken determination to exercise free choice as well as self-restraint, in spite of the unavoidable experience of shame and doubt in infancy" (Erikson, 1964, p. 119).

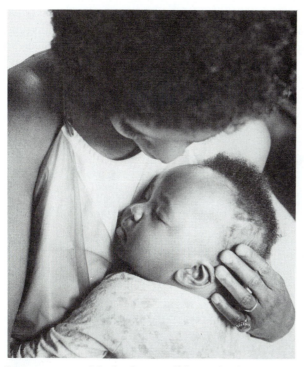

Basic trust is one of the first lessons of life an infant learns.
(*Photo by Suzanne Szasz,* Photo Researchers, Inc.)

Early Childhood

At around age two to six the child acquires new capacities of movement, speech, and thought that enable the child to initiate and plan actions and anticipate their consequences. Such abilities present a new set of threats: others who trespass or intrude upon plans, and guilt over having planned and initiated the wrong thing. Self-initiated activities can lead to rivalries with other children, frustrations, and profound frustrations when directed toward a parent. Erikson focuses on *initiative* and *guilt* as the central crisis themes of this age. Their resolution contributes to the development of global appraisals of *purpose*, or "the courage to envisage and pursue valued goals uninhibited by the defeat of infantile fantasies, by guilt and by the foiling fear of punishment" (Erikson, 1964, p. 122). An important part of the acquisition of purpose is the internalization of conscience, which is the taking on of moral and ethical guidelines presented and modeled by others; such guidelines give purpose, structure, and direction.

Middle Childhood

During middle childhood, from ages six to twelve, the child begins school and the process of learning the knowledge and skills needed for dealing with the world at large. Tasks include mastering basic school subjects, learning problem-solving skills, and relating to peers, teachers, and adults. These tasks must not only be initiated but industriously pursued to completion. The threat becomes one of inferiority, of failing in the child's own pursuits. A successful resolution of *industry* and *inferiority* is the global appraisal of *competence*, or "the free exercise of dexterity and intelligence in the completion of tasks, unimpaired by infantile inferiority" (Erikson, 1964, p. 124).

These young school children develop computer skills and begin to acquire a sense of basic competence.   (*Photo by Elizabeth Crews.*)

These young adults enjoy new capacities for love and intimacy.   (*Photo by Susan Lapides*, Design Conceptions.)

Adolescence

From ages twelve to eighteen mark the stage of adolescence, which is one of consol-
idating hope, will, purpose, and competence into a broader appraisal of self-identity.
Adolescence provides an important moratorium from making final decisions, during which a variety of roles can be experimented with and explored. Such explorations must confront a potentially confusing array of tasks: experiencing rapid
bodily growth and changes, dealing with increased sexual urges, achieving independence from caretakers, exploring intimate relationships, considering vocational
options, questioning values, and developing a personal philosophy. In most general
terms, the threat is one of *role confusion,* and the outcome, a sense of *identity.* Erikson
describes the global appraisal associated with this stage as *fidelity*, or "the ability to
sustain loyalties freely pledged in spite of the inevitable contradictions of value systems" (Erikson, 1964, p. 125).

Young Adulthood

As young adulthood begins (ages eighteen to thirty-four), the individual can begin to
share the identity developed in adolescence. By knowing who she is, she can com-
mit herself *intimately* to others. The threat is one of *isolation,* of not succeeding in, or
not being ready to, share. The global appraisal is *love,* or "mutuality of devotion forever subduing the antagonisms inherent in divided function" (Erikson, 1964, p. 129).
With intimacy comes a variety of specific challenges, for example, selecting a part-

ner, starting (or not starting) a family, parenting, dealing with military service, and beginning a career.

Middle Adulthood and Maturity

With middle adulthood and maturity (ages thirty-five to sixty-five), Erikson's description of life themes and challenges becomes a bit more abstract. He sees the task of these stages as one of transcending the self-related interests developed in young adulthood, and focusing more on helping others and generations to come. From this comes a sense of *generativity* and *care*. Without it comes *stagnation* and *boredom*, a sense that a person is living an empty and unsatisfying life. More concretely, middle adulthood and maturity present a variety of challenges, including the physiological deficits of aging, the climacteric, possible rejection of children, possible career changes, and preparation for retirement.

Old Age

Old age (age sixty-five to death) represents a period of standing back and taking stock. Neugarten has described this time as one of increased *interiority*, a shifting from involvement with the external challenges of work and family to an accommodation to the constraints of the outside. For Erikson (1964), the development of *ego integrity* and *wisdom* offers a more philosophical perspective of the whole of life in the context of history, "a detached concern with life itself in the face of death itself" (p. 133). In contrast, *despair* is the appraisal that life has been futile and in vain.

Evaluation of the Stage Theories

An important question concerning the stage theories is whether each stage has specific boundaries (Levinson, Darrow, Klein, Levinson, McKee, 1976), or whether the tasks and challenges of various stages can occur at all ages. To an extent, Erikson (1964) acknowledged that tasks associated with earlier ages may be repeated later; however, he tended to emphasize that for stage issues to reemerge, they must not be resolved at an earlier age.

Neugarten (1979) has noted that themes from earlier crises are often revisited or reworked later in life. People have a certain concept of what a normal life cycle is, something of a timetable of when events should occur. Many events become stressful because of when they occur in this timetable. Finishing school, marrying, having a child, starting a job, advancing in a job, becoming a grandparent, and retiring can occur either "on time" or "off time" in the life cycle. Off-time events are much more likely to be stressors. Such events can mean that a person is deprived of the support of peers who are confronting similar stressors. He can miss the pride and satisfaction that come from accomplishing a task on time, or the chance of preparing for a new role (Lazarus & Folkman, 1984).

Developmental challenges and tasks may be different for males, females, and various minorities. Gilligan (1979) has noted that some criteria for development

Life transitions, such as graduation from college, can be particularly stress-ful if they occur late or early. (*Photo by Fredrik D. Bodin,* Stock Boston.)

are more appropriate for women (such as concern for others and the ability to develop attachment) and others for men (such as separation from family and first jobs). One can extend this line of thinking even further. Children who live in a dangerous inner city or family environment may need to develop a healthy sense of mistrust (rather than Erikson's trust) in order to survive. In some communal societies, cooperation may be more important than industry for middle childhood.

The Family

Another way of looking at the stages of development is in terms of the family unit. Separate families are joined in marriage, have children, and cope with children growing and leaving. Carter and McGoldrick (1980) have outlined more specifically some of the stages of the family life cycle:

- *The unattached young adult*: The single person learns to accept separation from the family. Career and friendships are developed.

- *Marriage*: The married person commits to a new marital system. New relationships and friendships are made from the spouse's family system.
- *Children*: The married couple that decides to have children learns to take on parenting roles. Grandparents and other relatives acquire new roles in relation to children.
- *Adolescents*: As children mature into adolescents, the family becomes increasingly flexible to include children's independence. In midlife parents begin to refocus marital and career issues, and to shift their concerns toward the older generation.
- *Children leaving*: As children become adults and leave the home, the family adjusts to accept a multitude of exits and entries into the family system. New relationships are developed between grandchildren and in-laws. In addition, grandparents' disabilities and deaths become issues.
- *Later life*: The family accepts shifting generational roles. Members face physical decline and possibly new family responsibilities. The middle generation plays a more central role, and increasing support is provided for the elderly. Death and loss become issues to be dealt with.

Divorce

Divorce may well present the most common, complex, and traumatic constellation of stressors to the family and the developing child. Roughly two million people divorce each year. Many reasons are cited, and they are often different for husbands and wives. Levinger (1966) found that husbands cite mental cruelty, neglect of home and children, infidelity, and sexual incompatibility. Wives emphasize mental and physical cruelty, financial difficulties, and drinking. As might be expected, middle class husbands and wives are more concerned with psychological frustrations, and lower class couples with finances and physical violence.

Although divorce is weighted with 73 life change units in the Social Readjustment Rating Scale (see Chapter 2), which is 10 more than the death of a family member, people may in fact appraise divorce quite differently. Some see divorce as a failure and experience depression. Others may have to cope with loss of security. For still others, divorce is an overdue release from burden and frustration. As Kraus (1979) has observed:

> Emotional pain is related to both the commitment one had to one's marriage, but also to the belief in marriage itself as the best form of adult life. . . . [I]f one holds the irrational belief that a divorce is a catastrophe, one can easily make oneself miserable. An individual whose value system says that a divorced person is a failure, and a person without a mate is worthless, will most certainly experience a great deal of distress, if he finds himself in that position. (p. 115)

The process of divorce itself is complex, consisting of at least six phases, each with its own threats and challenges (Bohannan, 1972). *The emotional divorce* occurs when partners simply withhold feelings from either other and grow apart emotionally. This significant separation often calls for important grief work to be done, with phases of denial, anger, guilt, blame, and depression (Kraus, 1979). With the *legal divorce*, the actual separation is formalized. The legal process itself can be long and frustrating, and contribute to feelings of stress. When partners begin dividing property and assets, *economic divorce* occurs. With the potential loss of property and support, stress may increase. Eventually, the couple must decide what to do with the children, and determine who has custody and visitation rights. Such *co-parental divorce* can mean either significant loss of relationship or additional child-rearing burdens. The *community divorce* occurs when spouses lose friends and community ties sustained by the marriage. Finally, when all issues of the divorce have been resolved, and when the separate parties have coped with and resolved outstanding problems, *psychic divorce* has occurred.

Children of Divorce

For children, divorce presents its own coping tasks, often as severe as losing a parent through death. One might expect that such coping tasks have an immediate disruptive impact on children and a long-term effect in adulthood. Wallerstein (1986) has observed that the child must first acknowledge the reality of a marital rupture. Often intense feelings must be coped with, including distorted and terrifying fantasies of parental abandonment and disaster. Eventually a child must learn to resume everyday activities and disengage from parental conflict and distress, accept the losses of personal and material comforts provided by the original family, resolve anger and self-blame, and finally accept the permanence of divorce. For children, one important task is learning that a divorce of parents does not mean that all relationships will have the same fate, and that real possibilities exist for successful relationships and marriage.

There are three reasons to postulate that divorce may have disruptive effects on a child. The *parental absence perspective* states that through divorce a child loses a parental role model, a source of emotional support, and parental practical help and supervision. The *economic disadvantage perspective* states that single-parent divorced families are more likely to experience economic hardship, which in itself can be disruptive to the child. Finally, the *family conflict perspective* states that the interpersonal conflicts often associated with divorce are most likely to have a harmful effect on a child. Research suggests that the overall impact of divorce on the well-being of children is generally weak. Although there is modest evidence for each of the three perspectives discussed, the strongest evidence is that family conflict is disruptive to a child's well-being (Amato & Keith, 1991a).

One cannot assume that all children will react to divorce similarly. Younger children may be particularly vulnerable to feelings of insecurity; school-age children may react by displaying poor study habits; teens may fear a repetition of separation traumas in their own friendships. Tables 10.2 and 10.3 show some of the complexities involved (Arnold & Carnahan, 1990).

What happens to children of divorce when they become adults? Such adults indeed often have problems; however, the effect is modest (Amato & Keith, 1991). Divorced family adults are at risk for lower psychological well being (depression, low

TABLE 10.2   Possible Stressors for Children from Parental Separation / Divorce

Stressor	Age and Sex Risk Groups	Likely Effects and Mechanisms
Preceding marital strife	Younger children at first; older children and adolescents for long term	Insecurity. Fearfulness. Distorted view of male-female relations. Long-term painful, vivid memories of marital violence (except if below age 5 at divorce).
Break-up of home; loss of familiar; losss of ideal family life	Younger children and adolescents; boys; families where divorce decision impulsive	Disorientation; anger at parents; loss of stability; confusion about concept of "family; regression. Aggression and other antisocial behavior. Reconciliation fantasies. Self-blame.
Need to move	School-age and adolescents	Loss of friends, disruption of peer relations. Change of school, disruption of education.
Psychological demand of having two homes.	School-age; joint custody children	Instability. Need to juggle two sets of friends or periodically leave them. Concerns about fairness.
Lowered standard of living (perhaps poverty)	School-age (younger children if severe poverty); girls slightly more	Varies from social embarrassment and peer-relation impairment to cultural deprivation, possible malnutrition. General adjustment and school affected. Lower SES, results in lower social and academic competence.
Loss of noncustodial parent in general	Younger children	Grieving, depression, denial, regression, fantasy of reunion, anger, separa- tion anxiety. Fear of abandonment by both parents. Single-parents families linked with lower social and academic competence on school entry.
Loss of father in particular	Young boys (preschool and elementary); adolescent girls; possibly toddler girls	Boys: poor grades and work habits; nonassertiveness; poor impulse control; cognitive stunting; gender identity problems. Girls (adolescent): Aggression; seeking of male attention; sexual precocity; wide variance in heterosexual trust; lowered self-esteem; identification with mother who is perceived as rejected by father.
Change in frequency of grandparent	Younger children	Possible loss of noncustodial grand- parents takes away support at time

(continues)

TABLE 10.2   *Continued*

Stressor	Age and Sex Risk Groups	Likely Effects and Mechanisms
contact (more or less)		most needed. If custodial parent moves in with own parents, constant contact with grandparent could sour relationship or make strong attachment. If latter, then loss when eventually move out.
Parent divorce stress (litigation, economic hardship, emotional loss, need to move)	Younger children	Attachment problems (insecure or anxious). Parent preoccupation. Child perception of neglect or rejection. Guilt from blaming self for parent distress.
Custody/visitation battles and other post-divorce hostilities:		Psychological, sometimes physical, danger in crossfire. Ambivalence. Duplicity. Affect constriction. Pseudomaturity. Anxiety, tension, depression, somatization. Identity problems if side with opposite-sex parent; heterosexual trust problems if side with same-sex parent. Self-blame. Distortion of reality; confusion; possible "brain-washing." Witnessing parental fights leads to avoidance, attempts to control, submissive distress, some aggression. Abuse allegation leads to high risk whether true or false. Loss of contact with one parent.
Witnessing parental fights	Early school age	
Pressure to take sides	Late school (preadolescents)	
Loyalty conflict	Early school age	
Court testimony	School age and adolescent	
Abuse allegation	Younger children	
Child stealing	Younger children	
Decreased parental availability (parents preoccupied with own problems, single parent spread thin)	Younger children; resurgence of risk in adolescence	Feeling of rejection/neglect. Insecurity, fear of abandonment. Angry acting out of frustration/disappointment or attempt to seduce more attention by good behavior. Tension. Somatic complaints.
Chronic "after-shock" (knowledge that parents had divorced)	Age 8 and below	Sense of loss and vulnerability. Longing for ideal, intact family. At ten-year follow-up, divorce was central life experience for half of those 6–8 years at divorce.

(continues)

TABLE 10.2   *Continued*

Stressor	Age and Sex Risk Groups	Likely Effects and Mechanisms
Remarriage	Girls	Further changes in home. Both sexes at first externalizing problems, continuing beyond two years for girls. Interferes with reconciliation fantasies and with close mother-daughter bond. Further dilution of parental attention. Intrusion of step-parent, step-siblings, and half-siblings. In some cases positive, especially for boys (reestablish two-adult home; dampen parent hostility or grief).

Table taken from *Childhood stress*, L. E. Arnold & J. A. Carnahan, in L. E. Arnold (Ed.), © 1990 by John Wiley & Sons, Inc. Reprinted by permission of John Wiley & Sons, Inc. Sources include Fergusson, Dimond, & Horwood, 1986; Gamble & Zigler, 1986; Guibudaldi & Perry, 1984, 1985; Hetherington, 1972; Hetherington, Cox, & Cox, 1985; Johnston, Campbell, & Mayes, 1985; Kalter, 1987; Kalter, Reimer, Brickman, & Chen, 1985; Kalter & Rembar, 1981; Radin, 1981; Soldano, 1990; Southworth & Schwartz, 1987; Wallerstein, 1985, 1987; and Wallerstein & Kelly, 1984.

satisfaction); problems in family relationships (low quality of relationships, divorce); lower socioeconomic status (low education and income, welfare, having children out of wedlock, heading single-parent families); and poorer physical health. However, it is important to note that many factors can mitigate the long-term impact of divorce. Both parents can maintain a good relationship with their children, parental conflicts can be resolved after a divorce, and children can be provided for economically.

Dual-Career Families

Nearly 45 percent of all married women now work outside of the home. Even in families with children under the age of six, 37 per cent of the wives are working (Cooper, 1983). The phrase *dual career family* was coined by Rapoport and Rapoport (1971), and these researchers are responsible for much of the work in this area (Rapoport & Rapoport, 1971, 1976, 1978).

The dual-career family experiences a variety of sources of internal and external strain (Skinner, 1986). Work and role overload is a common source of such stress. With both partners working outside the home, household tasks are generally viewed as overload. Overload can be exaggerated by a commitment to have children and a high standard of living, and a failure to allocate family chores reasonably. In our society, male and female gender roles are closely tied to the family; the male is the traditional breadwinner, and the female the tender of home responsibilities. Often it

TABLE 10.3 Age and Time Considerations in Children's Responses to Stress of Parental Divorce

Age at Divorce	Early Response (First 2 Years)	Chronic or Delayed Response (4–10 Years after Divorce)
Preschool	Unable to understand finality; some deny divorce. Feeling of causing divorce, guilt feelings. Fear, bewilderment, repression. Preoccupation with replaceability. Separation anxiety, frustration, violent fantasies. Changes in aggression (increased or decreased). Loss of play and enjoyment. Fear of abandonment. Deterioration through first 18 months of divorce, especially boys. Impairment of social and academic competence on school entry.	Repression of divorce memories; lowered cognitive competence. Longing for ideal, intact family. Aggressive/antisocial and withdrawing behavior. Boys aggressive, antisocial. Girls anxious, depressed, lower social competence. One-third depressed at five-year follow-up. Better overall adjustment at 10-year follow-up than 10-year follow-up of children older at divorce. Reconciliation fantasies, continued awareness of father with renewed need in adolescence. If below 1½ years at divorce: Girls: Increased peer aggression. Boys: Academic problems and peer non-aggression in adolescence. Both sexes: Non-aggression to parents in school age. If age 3–5¼ at divorce: Boys: School behavior problems and subjective symptoms in school age. Girls: Academic problems in adolescence. Both sexes: Increased adolescent aggression (family and peers).
Elementary school age	Girls communicate more with mothers, boys less. Worry about not being able to visit enough. Boys nonaggressive with peers but aggressive to objects. If age 6–8: Frightened, disorganized. Grieving. Reconciliation fantasies. Anger to mother; inhibited aggression to father. Loyalty conflicts.	Worse adjustment than those younger at divorce. Dependency; irrelevance, withdrawal, blaming. School refusal, truancy. Inattentiveness, decrease in school work, aggression, misbehavior, mainly in boys. Girls much better adjustment unless remarriage. If remarriage, both sexes initial externalizing problems, but boys adjust in two years. In adolescence, girls increase hostility, power struggles, antisocial rebellion, seeking male attention. Both sexes: Adolescent regression to school-age dress, manner, and interests, or pseudo-maturity.

(continues)

TABLE 10.3 *Continued*

Age at Divorce	Early Response (First 2 Years)	Chronic or Delayed Response (4–10 Years after Divorce)
Elementary school age (*continued*)	If age 9–12: Loyalty conflicts: likely to choose sides with ambivalence to other. Attempt to master through activity and play. Identity problems. Anger. Somatization. Half incur severe drop in schoolwork. Boys more troubled.	If age 6–8 at divorce: At 10-year follow-up: Fear of disappointment in love. Low expectations for career and relationships. Sense of powerlessness. Muted anger. Anxiety about independence. Concerns about father loss, renewed adolescent need for father, and perceived rejection by father. Poor grades. Longing for ideal, intact family. Half experience vivid, painful memories of marital violence. Girls episodic recklessness, early sexual activity (one-fourth undergo abortions at age 13–16); depression, suicide. If age 9–12 at divorce: At 10-year follow-up: Memories of divorce worse than younger groups. Adolescent delinquincy. Sadness, resentment, sense of deprivation. Conservative morality.
Adolescence	Concern about parents' motives. Withdrawal from parents. Mourning of parents' marriage and family stability. Concern about own ability for lasting marriage. Depression, angry outbursts. Vacillating loyalties. Regression or maturational spurt. Less sex differences than younger.	If early pubertal at divorce: Midadolescent regression to school-age dress, interests, and interpersonal style, or pseudo-maturity. At 5 year follow up: Adjustment depended on quality of parenting, lowered divorce conflict, and continuity of visits. Girls: low self-esteem and more variance in heterosexual relations at college age. In adulthood 10-year post-divorce: Vivid, troubling memories of divorce; sadness, resentment, sense of deprivation, worry about repeating parents' unhappy marriage, especially in women. High unemployment. Low rate of college. Conservative morality.

Table taken from *Childhood Stress*, L. E. Arnold and J. A. Carnahan, in L. E. Arnold (Ed.), © 1990 by John Wiley & Sons, Inc. Reprinted by permission of John Wiley & Sons, Inc. Sources include Fergusson, Dimond, & Horwood, 1986; Guidubaldi & Perry, 1984, 1985; Hetherington, 1972; Hetherington,Cox, & Cox, 1985; Kalter,1987; Kalter, Reimer, Brickman, & Chen,1985; Kalter & Rembar, 1981; Soldano, 1990; Southworth & Schwartz, 1987; Wallerstein, 1985, 1987; and Wallerstein & Kelly, 1984.

A working couple must often juggle stress at home and at work.
(*Photo by Carl Glassman,* The Image Works.)

the female who bears the greatest strain of integrating work and home roles. Additional strain can came from *role cycling,* or the meshing of career and family cycles so that periods of stress do not coincide. For example, dual-career families may choose to have children after establishing themselves at work. However, such cycling can be a complex source of stress, especially when husband, wife, and family have potentially conflicting cycles (husband starting college, wife starting college, both seeking promotions, both desiring children). Some general family characteristics can contribute further to stress, especially the presence of children and the absence of potentially helpful relatives. Similarly, certain job characteristics can pose a problem, including pressures for geographic mobility, full-time work (with little time for home), and a wife's availability to entertain guests of her husband.

One model helps organize the many variables involved in dual-career stress. Guelzow, Bird, and Koball (1991) suggest that the combined pressures of work and home contribute to dual career-role strain (see Chapter 2), which can lead to stress at work, in the marriage, and in the parenting role. However, the research indicates that role strain can be reduced by three major coping resources. *Role reduction* involves reducing responsibilities in major life roles, including career duties, avocational activities, and household chores. This can also be achieved by permitting legitimate excuses to avoid some responsibilities and lower standards of performance for certain tasks, cutting back on leisure activities, and limiting involvement on the job. *Cognitive restructuring* involves reappraising potential threats as benign, for example, by believing that there are more advantages than disadvantages to one's life style, by overlooking difficulties, and by focusing on the good things about one's family. Finally, coping efforts can be directed toward maintaining *marital relationship equity*, whereby members of the family perceive that rewards and demands are fairly allocated. Such fairness is more likely to occur when flexibility, open communication, willingness to negotiate, empathy, and nurturing are emphasized.

A number of coping strategies mentioned in the dual-career family literature combine role reduction, cognitive restructuring, and equity. Dual-career families must often take care to establish their priorities for work and home, and to determine which family needs come first when in conflict with work. This strategy can involve deciding when work or home aspirations must be compromised. In addition, it is often useful to compartmentalize work and family problems, and not to take family concerns to work and work concerns to the home (Poloma, 1972). When possible, control over scheduling can be a valuable coping strategy, enabling the husband or wife who can shift work assignments to different times to accommodate family problems. Additional work strategies include the sharing of job responsibilities with others, who can take over during family emergencies, and split-location employment.

Finally, working families often need to be especially aware of the possibility of stress and what they can do to reduce it. Open communication, empathy, emotional reassurance, and other interpersonal skills also reduce stress. In addition, couples often establish "tension lines," or points beyond which each partner cannot be pushed. A partner may make it clear that when that person has to work on Saturday, Sunday is to be a day of rest.

Other Stressors

A single chapter cannot hope to cover the many types of stress associated with development and the family. We have not examined such topics as having (or not having) children, menopause, midlife crisis, retirement, living with relatives, family violence, childhood illness, gay and lesbian couples, and being single. However, the sample of issues we have considered does illustrate that stage models often conveniently summarize complex sources of stress and coping modalities.

APPLICATION BOX 10.1

Stress and Growing Up

One important idea of stage theories of development is that stages can be revisited. Can you think of times in your life when issues important at an earlier age seemed important again? For example, when you felt a deep concern about trusting or mistrusting others?

Imagine a person who has problems trusting others. She constantly suspects others will abandon her or do her wrong. How might you interpret this behavior in terms of:

- Ellis (What irrational thoughts might lead to such mistrust?)
- Beck (How might such distrust reflect biased thinking?)
- Lazarus (How is such distrust primary or secondary appraisal?)
- Personality traits (How does such distrust reflect any of the personality traits discussed in Chapter 6?)
- Erikson (What developmental stage is such distrust most associated with?)

References

AMATO, P. R., & KEITH, B. (1991). Parental divorce and adult well-being: A meta-analysis. *Journal of Marriage and the Family, 53,* 43–58.

AMATO, P. R., & KEITH, B. (1991a). Parental divorce and the well-being of children: A meta-analysis. *Psychological Bulletin, 110,* 26–46.

ARNOLD, L. E., & CARNAHAN, J. A. (1990). Child divorce stress. In L. E. Arnold (Ed.), *Childhood stress*, (pp. 373–403). New York: Wiley.

BECK, A. T. (1963). Thinking and depression: I. Idiosyncratic content and cognitive distortions. *Archives of General Psychiatry, 9,* 324–333.

BOHANNAN, P. (1972). The six stations of divorce. In J. Bardwick (Ed.), *Readings on the psychology of women* (pp. 156–163). New York: Harper & Row.

CARTER, E. A., & McGOLDRICK, M. (Eds.). (1980). *The family life cycle: A framework for family therapy.* Boston: Allyn and Bacon.

COOPER, C. L. (1983). Identifying stressors at work: Recent research developments. *Journal of Psychosomatic Research, 27,* 369–376.

ELLIS, A. (1962). *Reason and emotion in psychotherapy.* New York: Lyle Stuart.

ERIKSON, E. (1963). *The challenge of youth.* New York: Doubleday.

ERIKSON, E. (1964). *Insight and responsibility.* New York: Norton.

FERGUSSON, D. M., DIMOND, M. E., & HORWOOD, L. J. (1986). Childhood family placement history and behavior problems in six-year-old children. *Journal of Child Psychology and Psychiatry, 27,* 213–226.

GAMBLE, T. J., & ZIGLER, E. (1986). Effects of infant day care: Another look at the evidence. *American Journal of Orthopsychiatry, 56,* 26–42.

GILLIGAN, C. (1979). Woman's place in a man's life cycle. *Harvard Educational Review, 49,* 431–446.

GUELZOW, M. G., GIRD, G. W., & KOBALL, E. H. (1991). An exploratory path analysis of the stress process for dual-career men and women. *Journal of Marriage and the Family, 53,* 151–164.

GUIDUBALDI, J., & PERRY, J. D. (1984). Divorce, socioeconomic status, and children's cognitive-social competence at school entry. *American Journal of Orthopsychiatry, 54,* 459–468.

GUIDUBALDI, J., & PERRY, J. D. (1985). Divorce and mental health sequelae for children: A two-year follow-up of a nationwide sample. *Journal of the American Academy of Child and Adolescent Psychiatry, 24,* 531–537.

HAVIGHURST, R. J. (1952). *Developmental tasks and education.* New York: Longmans, Green.

HETHERINGTON, E. M. (1972). Effects of father absence on personality development in adolescent daughters. *Developmental Psychology, 7,* 313–326.

HETHERINGTON, E. M., COX, M., & COX, R. (1985). Long-term effects of divorce and remarriage on the adjustment of children. *Journal of the American Academy of Child and Adolescent Psychiatry, 24,* 518–530.

JOHNSTON, J. R., CAMPBELL, L. E. G., & MAYES, S. S. (1985). Latency children in post-separation and divorce disputes. *Journal of the American Academy of Child and Adolescent Psychiatry, 24,* 563–574.

KALTER, N. (1987). Long-term effects of divorce on children: A developmental vulnerability model. *American Journal of Orthopsychiatry, 57,* 587–599.

KALTER, N. REIMER, B., BRICKMAN, & A. CHEN, J. W. (1985). Implications of parental divorce for female development. *Journal of the American Academy of Child Psychiatry, 24,* 538–544.

KALTER, N. & REMBAR, J. (1981). The significance of a child's age at the time of parental divorce. *American Journal of Orthopsychiatry, 51,* 85–100.

KRAUS, W. S. (1979). The crisis of divorce: Growth promoting or pathogenic? *Journal of Divorce, 3,* 107–119.

LAZARUS, R. S., & FOLKMAN, S. (1984). *Stress, appraisal, and coping.* New York: Springer.

LEVINGER, G. (1966). Sources of marital dissatisfaction among applicants for divorce. *American Journal of Orthopsychiatry, 36,* 803–807.

LEVINSON, D. J., DARROW, C. M., KLEIN, E. B., LEVINSON, M. H., & MCKEE, B. (1976). Periods in the adult development of men: Ages 18–45. *The Counseling Psychologist, 6,* 21–25.

NEUGARTEN, B. L. (1979). Time, age, and the life cycle. *American Journal of Psychiatry, 136,* 887–894.

POLOMA, M. M. (1972). Role conflict and the married professional woman. In C. Safilios-Rothschild (Ed.), *Toward a sociology of women.* Lexington, MA: Xerox.

RADIN, R. (1981). The role of the father in cognitive, academic, and intellectual development. In M. Lamb (Ed.), *The role of the father in child development* (pp. 378–427). New York: John Wiley.

RAPOPORT, R., & RAPOPORT, R. N. (1971). *Dual-career families.* Harmondsworth, England: Penguin.

RAPOPORT, R., & RAPOPORT, R. N. (1976). *Dual-career families reexamined.* New York: Harper & Row.

RAPOPORT, R., & RAPOPORT, R. N. (Eds.), (1978). *Working couples.* New York: Harper & Row.

SKINNER, D. A. (1986). Dual-career family stress and coping. In R. H. Moos (Ed.), *Coping with life crises* (pp. 103–113). New York: Plenum.

SLAIKEU, K. A. (1990). *Crisis intervention* (2nd ed.). New York: Allyn and Bacon.

SMITH, J. C. (1990). *Stress scripting: A guide to stress management.* New York: Praeger.

SOLDANO, K.W. (1990). Divorce: Clinical implications for treatment of children. In B. D. Garfinkel, G. A. Carlson, & E. B. Weller (Eds.), *Psychiatric disorders in children and adolescents* (pp. 392–409). Philadelphia: W. B. Saunders.

SOUTHWORTH, S., & SCHWARTZ, J. C. (1987). Post-divorce contact, relationship with father, and heterosexual trust in female college students. *American Journal of Orthopsychiatry, 57,* 371–382.

WALLERSTEIN, J. S. (1985). Children of divorce: Preliminary report of a ten-year follow-up of older children and adolescents. *Journal of the American Academy of Child and Adolescent Psychiatry, 24,* 545–553.

WALLERSTEIN, J. S. (1986). Children of divorce. In R. H. Moos (Ed.), *Coping with life crises* (pp. 35–58). New York: Plenum.

WALLERSTEIN, J. S. (1987). Children of divorce: Report of a ten-year follow-up of early latency-age children. *American Journal of Orthopsychiatry, 57,* 199–211.

WALLERSTEIN, J. S., & KELLY, J. (1984). Children of divorce: Preliminary report of a ten-year follow-up of young children. *American Journal of Orthopsychiatry, 54,* 444–450.

CHAPTER 11

Work Stress

Occupational stress is one of the hottest topics in business today. The reasons are clear: About 14 percent of worker's compensation illness claims appear to be stress related, and insurance benefits for stress average $15,000, twice the amount for physical injury (McCarthy, 1988). An average of one million workers are absent on any given day primarily because of stress disorders (Rosch & Pelletier, 1987). In sum, in what is perhaps one of the most widely cited stress statistics, stress may well cost business over $150 billion a year in lowered productivity, absenteeism, and disability (Pelletier & Lutz, 1988; see also Table 11.1).

TABLE 11.1   Organizational Consequences of Mismanaged Stress

Direct Costs	*Indirect Costs*
Participation and membership	Loss of vitality
Absenteeism	Low morale
Tardiness	Low motivation
Strikes and work stoppages	Dissatisfaction
Turnover	
	Communication breakdowns
Performance on the job	Decline in frequency of contact
Quality of productivity	Distortions of messages
Quantity of productivity	
Grievances	Faulty decision-making
Accidents	
Unscheduled machine	Quality of work relations
downtime and repair	Distrust
Material and supply	Disrespect
overutilization	Animosity
Inventory shrinkages	
	Opportunity costs
Compensation awards	

SOURCE   Reprinted from Quick, J. C., & Quick, J. D. (1984). *Organizational stress and preventive management.* New York: McGraw Hill. Reprinted with permission of McGraw Hill.

Furthermore, evidence is mounting that stress management is a good investment. The Kenecott Copper Corporation reduced sickness and accident costs by 75 percent when they introduced a stress management program (Egdahl & Walsh, 1980). The PA Medical Corporation reduced absenteeism by 14 percent by instituting a stress reduction program (Everly & Girdano, 1980). A number of other companies, including General Electric, Minnesota Mining and Manufacturing, IBM, New York Telephone, Xerox, and Kimberly-Clark, have also begun stress management and "wellness programs" that have a successful stress management component.

However, stress statistics can seem a bit removed from reality. They acquire meaning when the individual costs of stress are considered. For example, Xerox has estimated that one executive with heart disease will probably cost a corporation $600,000, whereas the cost of effective stress reduction is considerably less. It is not surprising that up to twelve thousand companies already offer stress-coping programs (Hays, 1987). In sum, Carol Schneider (1987), past president of the American Biofeedback Society, has estimated that businesses can save an average of five dollars for every dollar spent on stress management.

It is useful to think of work stress in broad terms. The very factors that contribute to stress on the job can contribute to stress in other parts of life, including attending school, volunteering, vacationing, managing leisure and recreation, doing household chores, participating in sports, running a family, and even something as simple as setting up a car pool. In each of these areas, stress-related decrements in performance, as well as absenteeism, tardiness, accidents, illness, substance abuse, and reduced morale, can be important concerns. What is traditionally termed "occupational stress" can perhaps more appropriately be called the "stress of managing the tasks of living." It must be emphasized that each of the concepts we shall consider in this chapter apply equally well to performance in school, work, the arts, and sport.

Sources of Work Stress

We have already considered many factors important for understanding work stress, including life-change events, social support, arousal, cognitive appraisal, coping, and defense. However, in this chapter we shall examine factors related to the type of work one does (whether it be on the job, in volunteer activity, at school, or so on). In terms of the transactional matrix, these include such stimuli as work load, specific work responsibilities, and the work environment.

Work Load

How often have you complained about being overworked? Overload is one of the most important sources of work stress. When a person feels he has too much work to do in too little time, he is suffering from *quantitative overload*. This is especially serious when there is little control over the rate at which the work must be completed (Hurrell, 1987). However, if the problem is not time but a lack of training or ability to do the job, the person is experiencing *qualitative overload*. We can see the difference between quantitative and qualitative overload with an example. Imagine having to wash fifty cars in one day. Clearly this is quantitative overload simply because of the sheer amount of work to be done. If the task is to study a textbook on an unfamiliar subject, qualitative overload might be experienced. How work load is scheduled can create additional stress. For example *shift work*, which involves rotating night and day schedules, can disrupt biological rhythms and thus contribute to stress.

Finally, sometimes work *underload*, or too little work, is stressful. Factors that can aggravate underload are a mechanically controlled pace of work, repetitiveness, few demands on worker skills or attention, use of predetermined tools and techniques, and highly specialized tasks (Walker & Guest, 1952).

Work Responsibilities

Even when there is adequate time, skill, and ability to do a job, the specific nature of defined work responsibilities can be a source of stress, as this example illustrates:

> Marge has started to work as a social worker in a local community clinic. At first, her job involved counseling clients. This is an enjoyable task, and one that she had expected to do at the clinic. However, over the months state funding for the clinic was cut back, and a number of staff members had to be laid off. Marge found herself doing such secretarial work as typing reports, filing papers, and answering the phone. At times, unexpected emergencies would get in the way of her counseling duties; for example, he might have to answer the phone for her supervisor when a client is waiting. From time to time, staff members from other departments would call on her to help. In addition to such hassles, Marge found her job less secure and the possibilities for career advancement less likely.

It is easy to see that Marge is under considerable stress. At first she knew what was expected of her. However, as funding was cut back, she found that her duties were less clear. Such a problem is called *role ambiguity*. It arises when a person's work role or responsibilities are poorly defined. A similar problem, *role conflict*, occurs when one job duty conflicts with or is incompatible with another, or with a worker's personal standards. Such role stressors are often related to psychological problems and reduced performance (Jackson & Schuler, 1985). Role ambiguity and conflict both result from *boundary-spanning activities* in which individuals are required to work with people in other departments or organizations, thus crossing organizational boundaries.

Too much or too little *responsibility for others* can be another important source of job stress. Such stress can come from having to evaluate others for pay raises, promotions, or dismissal; offer incentives; and manage employee problems and shortcomings. However, not having responsibility or authority can also be stressful, especially in very demanding jobs. For example, a worker may have complex work to complete and yet have to clear every action with her supervisors. Or someone may be in a position to see how things go wrong but could be improved, and yet have little authority to make changes or even express an opinion. A survey of 1,500 workers has found lack of participation in decision-making to be related to low self-esteem, job dissatisfaction, illness, drinking, depression, and absenteeism (Margolis,

A department head, confused about her job responsibilities, illustrates the stressfulness of role ambiguity.   (*Photo by Alan Carey*, The Image Works.)

Kroes, & Quinn, 1974). It should be noted that responsibility in and of itself need not be a source of stress, provided that a person has *job decision latitude*, or the freedom to make decisions without clearing them with others.

Work reviews and assessments are rarely pleasant. However, the manner in which such evaluations are completed can do much to create needless stress. Particularly destructive are unfair and arbitrary reviews in which expectations are not clearly or openly defined. In addition, the criteria for evaluation may be clear but insufficient feedback may be given, leaving workers in the dark as to how well they are doing. Finally, evaluators often tend to focus on negative criticism and ignore the positive. This may not be deliberate or malicious, but a simple consequence of the way we deal with problems in our society. If something is going wrong, it has to be corrected, or the problem may continue; negative feedback is often an absolute requirement to set things right. However, when things are going well, there is no urgent need to make changes or give feedback. Unfortunately, people learn best when they receive positive feedback, and can find excessive negative feedback frustrating and demoralizing.

Work Environment

A large number of environmental factors can make even the best job stressful, including lack of physical or financial resources, problems with co-workers, and uncomfortable work settings (too much or too little light, heat, or cold, noise, odors, pollution, crowding, lack of privacy, and even poor desk layout). To these can be added more abstract aspects of the work environment, such as job insecurity, low pay, and lack of opportunities for career advancement. To some extent, people differ in what types of environment they expect and can tolerate. For example, a person would not expect the same degree of quiet in an automobile factory as in an executive office. And obviously, people differ in their preferences for the amount of sound, light, privacy, and so on. However, most of us *habituate* or become insensitive to constant environmental assaults. After a few months, a person may get used to living next to an airport or in a polluted city. Ominously, the environment can still contribute to stress-related illness, even when we are not aware of it.

Organizational Retrenchment and Decline

In a highly competitive world, organizations must often cut back to survive. Even then, not every organization succeeds. Retrenchment and decline, particularly in business organizations, can be an important source of stress. Jick (1983), summarizing the research in this area, concludes that ten factors related to cutbacks can contribute to experienced stress and uncertainty:

1. The greater the size of budget cuts;
2. the greater the extent to which cuts affect changes in goals, programs, or organizational survival;
3. the higher the frequency of cuts;
4. the less organizational slack and the fewer the opportunities for alternate funding;
5. the fewer the management assurances regarding job security or departmental survival;
6. the more the cuts are selective rather than uniform;
7. the less warning about impending cuts;
8. the lower the information clarity regarding impending cuts;
9. the less response time available between the mandate to cut and the actual cuts; and
10. the longer the mandated duration of cuts.

The stresses associated with retrenchment and decline can contribute to possible dysfunctional organizational coping strategies, including inappropriate centralization, absence of long-range planning, curtailment of innovation, scapegoating, resistance to change, turnover, decreased morale, loss of slack, emergence of special interest groups (politics), loss of credibility of top management, conflict and infighting, and across-the-board rather than prioritized cuts (Cameron, Whetten, & Kim, 1987).

Work Stress and Performance

One of the most important consequences of work stress is impaired performance. Such costs can be seen in a variety of contexts, such as completing everyday job responsibilities, interviewing for new positions, taking tests at school, and performing at sports and in the arts. In each of these areas of performance, similar basic mechanisms may be operating.

Arousal and Performance

One early theory, known as the Yerkes-Dodson Law (Yerkes & Dodson, 1908), suggests an "inverted-U relationship" between arousal and performance (see Figure 11.1). When arousal is low, as it is in sleep, drowsiness, and deep relaxation, performance should be poor. Obviously, one has to be awake to do one's best. As arousal increases, so does performance, until an ideal level is reached. This level may be different for different tasks. For complex tasks, the optimal range of arousal may be narrow and low, whereas for simple tasks, the level may be higher and broader (Easterbrook, 1959; Farber & Spence, 1953; Fiske & Maddi, 1961). That is, people who play the flute or perform surgery (complex tasks) may do best at a relatively low level of arousal, and may experience performance decrements if the level deviates even slightly from their ideal. In contrast, those who run races or lift heavy objects

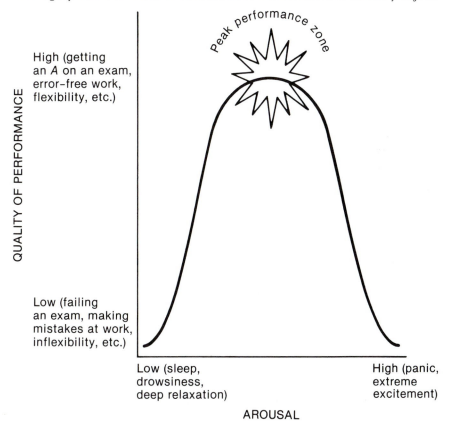

FIGURE 11-1   The Yerkes-Dodson Law: The inverted-U relationship between arousal and performance.

Overload is one of the most common forms of work stress.

(simple tasks) may do better at higher levels of arousal and may tolerate considerable deviations from their ideal.

For any task there is a point of too much arousal. At high arousal, a number of potential problems may emerge. Attention is narrowed to simple, obvious cues (Easterbrook, 1959), and short-term memory for immediate facts is impaired. Under stress, you may be so focused on reading this book that you fail to note the ringing phone, boiling coffeepot, and so on. In addition, highly aroused people may tend to think in rigid, oversimplified ways and consider only immediately available or obvious solutions. Put differently, people under stress may find themselves in "thinking ruts" at the very time they most need to look for new options. Narrow, rigid, and oversimplified thinking may, of course, not be a problem, if stressful situations are simple with clear-cut solutions (such as running away from an attacking dog). However, for complex tasks, excessive arousal can be a problem.

Recently, the inverted-U hypothesis has come under considerable attack (Neiss, 1988, 1990). As we discussed earlier in Chapter 3, equal levels of arousal can be present in diverse psychological states, including anger, surprise, joy, sadness, and sexuality. Performance may either improve or deteriorate at the same arousal level. For example, the athlete or musician who is highly "psyched up" and performing at peak levels may be just as aroused as the performer who is "frozen with fear." The criticism continues that the inverted-U hypothesis may hold true in situations that are "true-but-trivial," for example, when "the motivated outperform the apathetic and the terrified" (Neiss, 1988, p.355). However, even at extreme levels of arousals, such as those that occur in life-threatening situations when most people are bewildered and psychologically incapacitated, 12 to 25 percent show efficient, organized coping responses (Tyhurst, 1951).

As seen in Chapter 3, specificity views of arousal bring into the question the validity of global, nonspecific physiological states. To determine whether a person is under stress, we need to know more than their level of arousal; similarly, to know if a person is going to perform at peak capacity, we need to examine their cognitive appraisals, coping skills, levels of emotion, and facilitative and debilitative emotional states. Perhaps an athlete at peak performance may appraise a game as a challenge, be well trained, and be enthusiastic about playing; physiologically, the muscle groups required for peak performance may thus be aroused and efficiently coordinated. An athlete doing poorly may perceive a game as a threat, be out of practice, and experience fear. For this athlete, various muscle groups may also be aroused, but work against one another (as when one is "choked up," or "paralyzed in fear").

Test Anxiety

Test anxiety occurs in situations in which a person's performance is publicly evaluated, for example, taking tests, interviewing, giving lectures, or performing in the arts or sports. Two components of test anxiety are frequently identified: *worry*, or negative thinking, and *emotionality*, or awareness of bodily stress symptoms (Sarason & Sarason, 1990). Worry appears to be the more serious symptom since it is not only unpleasant, but can interfere with performance.

Many studies find that as test anxiety increases, performance declines, particularly for complex and demanding tasks (Sarason, 1980). Wine (1982) has offered an attentional interpretation of what happens. Test anxiety evokes task-irrelevant thoughts likely to interfere with performance, as individuals become "self-absorbed" instead of "task-absorbed." Rather than efficiently focus on the task at hand, they are more likely to become preoccupied with blaming themselves for perceived poor performance and comparing their performance with that of others. Indeed, Schwartz and Garamoni (1986) have estimated that test-anxious people think twice as many negative thoughts as positive thoughts, whereas nonanxious people show the reverse ratio.

In addition, test-anxious individuals display maladaptive coping strategies. They are more cautious and less confident in making decisions, set lower levels of aspiration, and assume passive and avoidant coping strategies (Geen, 1987). For example, while taking a college exam, a test-anxious student may hesitate putting down an answer about which she is not absolutely certain. This is clearly an inefficient strategy that not only slows performance but reduces the likelihood of guessing at the right answer. When given the opportunity, a test-anxious student will simply avoid a question rather than trying to answer it correctly. Finally, test-anxious individuals appear to have difficulty organizing material efficiently (Naveh-Benjamin, McKeachie, & Lin, 1987). They may, for example, answer test questions haphazardly rather than systematically answering the easy ones first and returning to the more difficult ones.

However, the field of test anxiety is not without controversy. Subjects may be test anxious because they have not studied and know they will do poorly. In such cases, anxiety does not interfere with performance, but is part of an accurate prediction that one is going to do poorly (Benjamin, McKeachie, Lin, & Holinger, 1981; Culler & Holahan, 1980).

Negative and Positive Thinking

Recent research reveals an additional complexity to test-anxiety research. Goodhart (1986) examined which conditions facilitated and which impaired performance on anagram puzzles (described as a test of verbal ability). Specifically, he looked at negative and positive thinking, and whether subjects were asked before the task to estimate how well they thought they might perform relative to other students. Negative thoughts in an area unrelated to the test, such as, social relations actually improved task performance. ("Everyone seems to have friends here but me. . . . I always seem to say the wrong things.") Perhaps subjects tried to compensate for their perceived social deficits by doing well on the test. Also, when subjects were not asked to predict how well they would do on the test, general negative thinking about achievement also improved performance. ("Whenever I'm sure I know something, I find out I'm wrong. . . . I know deep down that I'm not as capable as I'd like to be.") Perhaps negative thinkers who were asked to give an estimate of their performance did poorly to meet their own negative expectations. On the other hand, positive thinking improved performance when subjects had positive thoughts related to the task ("Deep down I think I'm a pretty competent person.") rather than positive thoughts unrelated to the task ("Most people seem to enjoy my company."), and had to give a prediction about how well they would perform. It would seem that positive thinkers strive to achieve goals they set for themselves.

Stress Aftereffects

So far we have described the kinds of problems that can occur during a stressful situation. However, once stress is over, performance can still be affected. This lingering problem is called the *stress aftereffect*. Most people can recall times when this phenomenon has impaired their performance. For example, after a harrowing drive to work in rush-hour traffic, a person may make more mistakes, even if the work environment is not particularly stressful. After an argument with a roommate, someone may do poorly on a relatively simple exam. What is particularly interesting is that stress aftereffects appear to persist even after arousal levels have returned to normal (Cohen, 1980). The individual may feel more or less physically relaxed, and the stressful encounter may well be over, but performance may still suffer.

A number of hypotheses have been offered to explain stress aftereffects. Perhaps, through learned helplessness, stressed individuals simply give up trying. Stressful frustrations may evoke anger and irritation, resulting in reduced motivation to do well. During stress, attention may be narrowed to essential information, a coping strategy that may persist even when stress has passed.

In addition to these learned helplessness, frustration-aggression, and persistent coping hypotheses, another explanation for stress aftereffects has received considerable attention. Cohen (1980) has argued that stressors, particularly those that are unpredictable and uncontrollable, place increased demands on attentional capacity, which eventually result in *cognitive fatigue*. It is fatigue that shrinks attentional capacity and leads to stress aftereffects. It is easy to see how this can happen. When a stressful situation is unpredictable and uncontrollable, a person must spend additional time and effort at primary and secondary appraisal. A person must think about which stimuli are threatening, how they are threatening, and how to cope. This extra work is fatiguing, and fatigue can persist even when the stressful situation is over.

Burnout

The concept of *burnout* is a stress aftereffect that is similar to but more general than fatigue. It is typically defined in terms of three symptoms (Freudenberger, 1980; Jackson, Schwab & Schuler, 1986; Maslach & Jackson, 1981):

1. Emotional exhaustion, or feeling drained and empty because of excessive work demands:

   I no longer look forward to going to work each morning.

   As the end of each day, I feel totally drained and exhausted. I no longer have the energy and enthusiasm I once did.

   I just plod through each day's chores.

2. Depersonalization, or becoming insensitive, closed off, callous, cynical, or hostile toward others:

   Why can't my clients (students, customers, etc.) be more responsible?

   I find myself treating the people I work with as objects. I just can't get myself to care about their problems.

   My clients are just lazy and good for nothing. They'll never change.

3. Low feelings of accomplishment, or feeling frustrated and helpless because your efforts seem wasted and worthless:

   Boy, did I make a mistake getting into this line of work. Nothing I do makes any difference.

   I feel like my life is a waste.

   I'm really depressed about my job.

Burnout has been applied in a wide range of settings, including "burnt out relationships," "burnt out artists," and simple work "tedium" (Farber, 1983). Indeed, such broad usage has prompted a deserved skepticism in the popular press. The *New York Times* (Quinnett, 1981) has observed that:

> We have stumbled upon a worthy and thoroughly modern concept with which to label our discontent. . . . The word *burnout* covers our personal failures much better than ordinary forms of irresponsibility to ourselves and others. It give us, as I see it, the perfect out.

Similarly, *Time* magazine has editorialized that burnout is a particular "hypochondria of the spirit" (Morrow, 1981).

Careful researchers tend to reserve *burnout* to describe only those in the helping professions (such as physicians, nurses, counselors, teachers, social workers, and police). It is also prevalent among people who are highly invested in and committed to their work, or who seldom see success from their efforts. Such people may first experience a "honeymoon" of enthusiasm and optimism, only to discover that work often does not fit their initially high expectations.

Complex Models of Work Stress

We have considered a variety of simple models of work stress. Some focus on the sources of stress, and others on the impact of stress on work itself. Two other rather complex models have also received considerable attention.

Person-Environment Fit

One of the most elegant models of job stress starts with an idea that has considerable common sense appeal: stress occurs when people do not fit their jobs or their jobs do not fit them. This is more formally expressed as the *person-environment (P-E) fit model* (French, Rogers, & Cobb, 1974). There are two ways in which a person may not fit her job environment. First, a person's skills and abilities may not match the demands and requirements of the job. Second, the job itself may not meet the person's needs. A lack of fit in either direction can create stress.

Furthermore, P-E fit can be either objective or subjective. Someone may type fifty-five words a minute at a job that requires the ability to type fifty-five words a minute. This is an objective fit. If the person types only twenty words a minute at such a job, there is an objective lack of fit and a potential for stress (until the person learns to type faster or gets a new job). But fit and lack of fit can also be subjective. If someone *thinks* he can type fifty-five words a minute (regardless of whether he types twenty words a minute or seventy words a minute), there will be subjective fit and a false sense of security. Conversely, if that person *thinks* he types only twenty words a minute but really types fifty-five words a minute, he will create needless stress and worry. Similarly, if someone *thinks* she needs a great deal of social contact on a job, which the job does not supply, stress will result.

The P-E fit model goes beyond simple one-dimensional models we have considered. For example, does job complexity contribute to overload and stress? The P-E fit theory says not to look at complexity as a single job characteristic that may or may not be stressful, but rather at the degree of fit between a person's need for complexity and the extent to which a job satisfies this need. A worker who desires little complexity would find a complicated job stressful; someone who wants a complicated job would find a simple job stressful. Similar patterns have been observed for quantitative work load, responsibility for persons, and role ambiguity (Caplan, Cobb, French, Harrison, & Pinneau, 1980).

Job Enrichment

Hackman and Oldham (1980) have proposed a complex model of job enrichment that can also serve as a model of stress. High stress (and low enrichment) result from

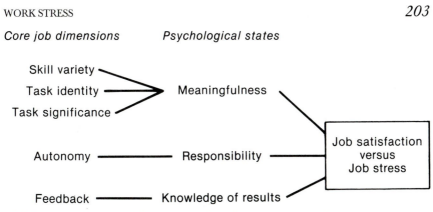

FIGURE 11.2   The core job dimensions of the job enrichment model of stress.

experiencing low levels of *meaningfulness, responsibility,* and *knowledge of results.* These psychological states are linked to five *core job dimensions: skill variety, task identity, task significance, autonomy,* and *feedback* (see Figure 11.2).

Meaningfulness is associated with skill variety, task identity, and task significance. Some jobs, such as managing a program, teaching, and nursing, tap a wide variety of skills. For example, a nurse must be able to counsel others, perform medical procedures, keep records, and persuade patients to keep up with treatment. In contrast, jobs such as cleaning streets and addressing envelopes require few skills. Task identity refers to the extent to which a worker can see a finished product. Assembly-line workers often have jobs with low task identity; they may install automobile engines and never see a finished car. A grade school teacher may spend hours counseling a child and never find out how that child developed as an adult. In contrast, jobs of high task identity include some forms of medical work and administration. A surgeon usually knows the consequences of her work. An administrator who sets up a program usually gets to see whether the program works. Finally, meaningfulness results from the significance of a job, that is, the extent to which it has an important impact on others.

Responsibility and knowledge of results are the products of the core job dimensions of autonomy and feedback. Autonomy refers to the extent to which a worker can make his own decisions concerning what to do and when to do it. Feedback, as noted, describes the extent to which others provide accurate and constructive information on what a person is doing well and what could be improved.

According to Hackman and Oldham (1980), the five core job dimensions are not always associated with stress. If one's primary motivation for work is simple survival, then meaningfulness, responsibility, and knowledge of results make little difference; just having a secure paycheck is enough to reduce stress. However, when survival is not a question (for example, when other jobs are available, or when self-expression and development are major goals), then the problems with core job dimensions can create stress.

Values and Work Stress

Locke and Taylor (1991) present an alternative view of stress on the job. Central to their theory is the extent to which work coincides with what people desire or consider to be good or beneficial: in other words, their *values*. They identify five general classes of values frequently studied in work stress research: (1) material well-being (comfortable life, money, family security); (2) achievement (sense of accomplishment, autonomy, success, challenge, freedom, wisdom); (3) sense of purpose (work offers significance, organizes a person's life, provides inner harmony); (4) social relationships (friendships, social recognition); and (5) maintenance of self-concept or self-respect. When work blocks these values, either externally or internally, stress can result. The following chart describes how each of the five values can be threatened:

1. Material well-being
    · Basing a person's entire self-concept and sense of personal worth on material success.
    · Deemphasizing other values that may offer satisfaction.
    · Being poor.
2. Achievement
    · Failing, which leads to lower self-esteem.
    · Performing boring, unchallenging work.
    · Losing control over work (role conflict, overload, boundary-spanning activities).
3. Sense of purpose
    · Losing a job or being demoted.
    · Sacrificing other, potentially enriching values for work.
    · Attaining a highly valued goal (and not replacing it with another).
4. Social relationships
    · Displaying increased sensitivity to interpersonal conflict and criticism (for those overly dependent on others).
    · Overemphasizing other values, which can lead to withdrawal from social relationships and feelings of alienation.
5. Self-concept
    · Performing poorly or failing.
    · Overemphasizing material goals.
    · Experiencing poor P-E fit between self-concept of abilities and skills and work requirements.

The New Look in Job Stress Research

Both the P-E fit and job enrichment models have transactional features. Both make it clear that it is not the job itself that creates stress but rather the job supplies and demands as specified in the P-E fit theory or the core job dimensions as outlined in the job enrichment theory. According to transactional theory, a job is a stimulus that can be appraised as beneficial, harmful, threatening, or challenging, depending on appraised fit or on whether a person's primary motivation for work is survival.

Recent work on job stress has become more transactional. Much builds on a model that integrates a life-stress emphasis (job demands, work load, deadlines, conflicts, and so on) with a focus on job satisfaction and decision latitude. One implication of this perspective is that stress and physical strain are seen as more likely to result from jobs that have high demands and low decision latitude. However, the transactional matrix would also have us go farther and examine the dimension of coping. Lack of fit, or an absence of core job dimensions or decision latitude, may not create stress for those who possess good coping resources.

Examples of Work Stress

As noted, it is important to remember that work stress is a very broad concept. It can apply to a variety of contexts outside the job, as the following examples demonstrate. In the first, we have identified some of the sources of stress. In the other two, see if you can identify what creates stress.

	Volunteering
	Roberta has volunteered to help out in a fund-raising drive for her singing group. After a few weeks, she finds herself doing more than she had expected.
Work overload	At first she answered phones, then stuffed envelopes, and then spent the weekend seeking donations from door to door.
Role ambiguity	She feels that she has little time left for her family and that this volunteer work has become a "bottomless pit."
Burnout	With all this work, Roberta is beginning to get cynical about volunteer work in general. As she has said, "Everyone wants to volunteer, but no one wants to do the work."

Vacationing

Burt and Julia have taken their family on a summer vacation, driving across the country to see the sights. Julia has been doing the driving and has made a few mistakes. Burt starts complaining, "Why didn't you check the map before getting on the turnpike? Now we have to turn off to see where we're going. And didn't you check the oil at the last gas station? Can't you do anything right?" Later, Burt and Julia get into an argument. Both want to drive in the morning. Burt complains, "We agreed that I would do the morning driving and you would drive in the afternoon." Julia disagrees.

Cleaning the Apartment

Bill and Bob have been college roommates for over a year. However, some problems have been brewing. Bob finally confronts Bill: "This year's lease is about up, and you still haven't let me know if we will be rooming together next year. This uncertainty isn't good. I need to know what's going to happen." Bill responds that he will continue rooming with Bob. However, there are a few issues he wants to clarify: "Let's make it clear just who is responsible for the dishes and who has to clean up. I'm feeling over-burdened by all the jobs that have to get done around here. This place is just too dusty for me to feel comfortable."

APPLICATION BOX 11.1

Burnout and Work Stress

Nearly everyone has experienced burnout, either at work, school, or home. Can you recall a recent burnout experience?

First, what stage of burnout did you experience? Emotional exhaustion? Depersonalization? Low feelings of accomplishment?

Second, during burnout, quality of work often deteriorates. We make mistakes, forget things, and display insensitive and inflexible behavior. Can you recall a time when your work deteriorated under stress? What concepts of this chapter seem to describe the cause of your lower performance?

- High arousal.
- Intrusive, "task irrelevant" thoughts.
- Negative thinking.
- Cognitive fatigue stress aftereffect.

References

BENJAMIN, M., MCKEACHIE, W. J., LIN, Y., & HOLINGER, D. P. (1981). Test anxiety: Deficits in information processing. *Journal of Educational Psychology, 73*, 816–824.

CAMERON, K. S., WHETTEN, D. A., & KIM, M. U. (1987). Organizational dysfunctions of decline, *Academy of Management Journal, 30*, 126–137.

CAPLAN, R. D., COBB, S. D., FRENCH, J. R. P., JR., HARRISON, R. V. & PINNEAU, S. R., JR. (1980). *Job demands and worker health.* Ann Arbor, MI: Survey Research Center Institute for Social Research.

COHEN, S. (1980). Aftereffects of stress on human performance and social behavior: A review of research and theory. *Psychological Bulletin, 88*, 82–108.

CULLER, R. E., & HOLAHAN, C. J. (1980). Test anxiety and academic performance: The effects of study-related behaviors. *Journal of Educational Psychology, 72*, 16–20.

EASTERBROOK, J. A. (1959). The effect of emotion on cue utilization and the organization of behavior. *Psychological Review, 66*, 183–201.

EGDAHL, R., & WALSH, D. (1980). *Mental wellness programs for employees.* New York: Springer-Verlag.

EVERLY, G. S., & GIRDANO, D. A. (1980). *The stress mess solution: The causes of stress on the job.* Bowie, MD: Robert J. Brady.

FARBER, B. A. (ED.) (1983). *Stress and burnout in the human service professions.* New York: Pergamon.

FARBER, I. E., & SPENCE, K. W. (1953). Complex learning and conditioning as a function of anxiety. *Journal of Experimental Psychology, 45*, 120–125.

FISKE, D. W. & MADDI, S. R. (1961). *Functions of varied experience.* Homewood, IL: Dorsey Press.

FRENCH, J. R. P., JR., ROGERS, W., & COBB, S. (1974). A model of person-environment fit. In G. V. Coelho, D. A. Hamburgh, & J. E. Adams (Eds.), *Coping and adaptation* (pp. 316–333). New York: Basic Books.

FREUDENBERGER, H. J. (1980). *Burnout: The high cost of achievement.* Garden City, NY: Doubleday.

GEEN, R G. (1987). Test anxiety and behavioral avoidance. *Journal of Research in Personality, 21*, 481–488.

GOODHART, D. E. (1986). The effects of positive and negative thinking on performance in an achievement situation. *Journal of Personality and Social Psychology, 51*, 117–124.

HACKMAN, J. R., & OLDHAM, G. R. (1980). *Work redesign.* Reading, MA: Addison-Wesley.

HAYS, L. (1987, April 24). But some firms try to help. *The Wall Street Journal*, p. 16D.

HURRELL, J. J., JR. (1987). An overview of organizational stress and health. In L.R. Murphy & T.F. Schoenborn (Eds.), *Stress management in work settings* (pp. 31–45). Washington, DC: National Institute for Occupational Safety and Health.

JACKSON, S .E. & SCHULER, R. S. (1985). A meta-analysis and conceptual critique of research on role ambiguity and role conflict in work settings. *Organizational Behavior and Human Decision Processes, 36*, 16–28.

JACKSON, S .E., SCHWAB, R. L., & SCHULER, R. S. (1986). Toward an understanding of the burnout phenomenon. *Journal of Applied Psychology, 71*, 630–640.

LOCKE, E. A., & TAYLOR, M. S. (1991). Stress, coping, and the meaning of work. In A. Monat & R. S. Lazarus (Eds.), *Stress and coping* (3rd ed., pp. 140–157). New York: Columbia University Press.

MARGOLIS, B., KROES, W. H., & QUINN, R. P. (1974). Job stress: An unlisted occupational hazard. *Journal of Occupational Medicine, 16*, 659–661.

MASLACH, C., & JACKSON, S. E. (1981). *The Maslach Burnout Inventory*. Palo Alto, CA: Consulting Psychologists Press.

McCARTHY, M. (1988, April 7). Stressed employees look for relief in worker's compensation claims. *The Wall Street Journal*, p. 34.

MORROW, L. (1981, September 21). The burnout of almost everyone. *Time*, p. 84.

NAVEH-BENJAMIN, M., McKEACHIE, W. J., & LIN, Y. G. (1987). Two types of test-anxious students: Support for an information processing model. *Journal of Educational Psychology, 79*, 131–136.

NEISS, R. (1988). Reconceptualizing arousal: Psychobiological states in motor performance. *Psychological Bulletin, 103*, 345–366.

NEISS, R. (1990). Ending arousal's reign of error: A reply to Anderson. *Psychological Bulletin, 107*, 101–105.

PELLETIER, K., & LUTZ, R. (1988). Healthy people, healthy business. *American Journal of Health Promotion, 2*, 5–12, 19.

QUICK, J. C., & QUICK, J. D. (1984). *Organizational stress and preventive management*. New York: McGraw Hill.

QUINNETT, P. (1981, August 26). The perfect out. *The New York Times*, p. A23.

ROSCH, P. J., & PELLETIER, K. R. (1987). Designing worksite stress management programs. In L. R. Murphy & T. F. Schoenborn (Eds.), *Stress management in work settings* (pp. 69–91). Washington DC: National Institute for Occupational Safety and Health.

SARASON, I. G. (Ed.). (1980). *Test anxiety: Theory, research, and applications*. Hillsdale, NJ: Lawrence Erlbaum.

SARASON, I. G., & SARASON, B. R. (1990). Test anxiety. In H. Leitenberg (Ed.), *Handbook of social and evaluation anxiety* (pp. 475–496). New York: Plenum.

SCHNEIDER, C. J. (1987). Cost effectiveness of biofeedback and behavioral medicine treatments: A review of the literature. *Biofeedback and Self-Regulation, 12*, 71–92.

SCHWARTZ, R. M., & GARAMONI, G .I. (1986). A structural model of positive and negative states of mind: Asymmetry and internal dialogue. In P.C. Kendall (Ed.), *Advances in cognitive-behavioral research and therapy* (Vol. 5, pp. 2–62). New York: Academic Press.

TYHURST, J. S. (1951). Individual reactions to community disaster. *American Journal of Psychiatry, 107*, 764–769.

WALKER, C. R., & GUEST, R. H. (1952). *The man on the assembly line*. Cambridge, MA: Harvard University Press.

WINE, J. D. (1982). Evaluation anxiety: A cognitive-attentional construct. In H.W. Krohne & L. Laux (Eds.), *Achievement, stress, and anxiety* (pp. 207–219). Washington, DC: Hemisphere.

YERKES, R., & DODSON, J. D. *(1908)*. The relation of strength of stimulus to rapidity of habit formation. *Journal of Comparative and Neurological Psychology, 18*, 459–482.

CHAPTER 12

The Environment and Society

It is, of course, a truism to say that we live in troubled times. Yet clearly every age has had its difficulties, and perhaps any special stress we experience reflects the clarity of present vision. Unlike times past, we have excellent tools for understanding and measuring stress and communicating what we know. The issue becomes more meaningful when we focus on specific aspects of stress in our environment and society.

Stress and the Environment

Crowding

Crowding has received considerable research attention. Most people have a fairly good concept of a crowd: the rush hour crush, too many tourists at a vacation spot, a long check-out line. However, before looking at crowding scientifically, it is important to make some distinctions. *Density* (Stokols, 1972) is the number of individuals per unit area. For example, the population density of New York is 8,500 people per square kilometer, whereas it is 40,000 people per square kilometer in Hong Kong. *Social density* is the result of increasing the number of people in a fixed space (doubling the number of students in a classroom), whereas *spacial density* is the result of reducing the amount of space for a fixed number of people (moving a class of thirty students to a smaller room). *Indoor density* is the ratio of people to space inside buildings, whereas *outdoor density* is the ratio outdoors.

In technical terms, *crowding* is a subjective experience that there are too many people in a certain place. This experience may or may not correspond to high density. Indeed, one study found that less than 10 percent of the experience of crowding is explained through density, with the rest related to factors such as job satisfaction and privacy (Gove & Hughes, 1980). However defined, crowding can be a source of stress, contributing to arousal, health problems, performance deficits, increased aggression, and reduced altruistic behavior.

When do people feel crowded? Two general psychological processes appear to be at work to create this feeling: loss of personal control and experiencing stimulus overload. Personal, social, and environmental factors can contribute to these processes. Those who feel less crowded often perceive that they are in control in crowded environments (internal locus of control), are more sociable, can more easily tolerate the presence of others, and are capable of screening stimuli, that is, they can focus on desired stimuli while tuning out unwanted stimuli. Finally, those who prefer or expect high densities, for example, at home, on the subway, or at work, often feel less crowded (Gifford, 1987).

A variety of social factors can contribute to a feeling of being crowded (Gifford, 1987). For example, some people may feel crowded if others watch or touch them, or engage in activities that they do not like or interfere with what they want to do. Forming coalitions (two of three roommates becoming close friends) can reduce the stressful impact of crowding, unless, of course, you are the one left out of the coalition. Likewise, when people get along well and see one another as similar, the feeling of crowding is reduced.

Obviously, a restricted physical setting increases density and can contribute to crowding. A number of other physical factors are also at work. Crowding on a small scale (a residence) is equally predicted by physical and psychological factors; however, crowding on a larger scale (a block or a city) is affected more by psychological factors. The architecture of a building can influence crowding. Long corridors appear to increase crowding by contributing to feelings of competitiveness, with-

A close examination of the faces in this picture reveals that not everyone finds crowds stressful.   (*Photo by Owen Franken,* Stock Boston.)

drawal, and reduced control. A higher floor in a high-rise, sunlight, high ceilings, and even desks that face away from each other are among the factors that can decrease crowding.

Some cultures (such as the Japanese or Chinese) cope with high density better than others. Gifford (1987) has suggested a variety of coping strategies that can be gleaned from such societies:

- Encouraging more psychological distance between individuals.
- Allowing times and places for escape.
- Developing stricter norms about what may be said to whom.
- Restricting who may go where within the home and how each space within the home is to be used.
- Discouraging social interaction with acquaintances inside the home but encouraging it in public places.
- Learning to appreciate higher levels of social stimulation (p. 186).

Commuting

Transportation plays an important role in our lives. As with crowding, commuting often becomes stressful when control is reduced and the danger of information overload increases (Singer & Baum, 1983). One source of such stress is the length and complexity of a commute. People who travel longer distances to work have higher blood pressure. The more interchanges one must negotiate on the way to work is related to the number of days off for illness (Stokols & Novaco, 1981). Driving on arterial and primary urban streets rather than freeways has been associated with increased arousal (Michaels, 1962). Other sources of commute complexity that contribute to stress include roadway curves, many passing cars, the need for braking (Altman, Wohlwill, & Everett, 1981), the presence of others who impede our progress, physical discomfort, noise, heat, and pollution.

Noise

Noise is another common and important source of stress. Indeed, much of the laboratory research on stress and performance has used a variety of sources of noise, including white noise, recordings of street traffic, and loud buzzers, to create stressful conditions. Often noise is made more stressful when there is a complex task to be completed in the presence of unpredictable or uncontrollable noise, such as trying to study a difficult text when a party is going in the next room (Cohen, 1980). Noise is particularly stressful if it changes in pitch or intensity, thus reducing the possibility of habituation (getting used to it). However, even though a person may tune noise out, it can still produce detrimental aftereffects (Cohen, 1981; Kryter, 1970).

Severe noise (over 90 decibels) can cause hearing loss, and high levels can increase blood pressure, heartbeat, muscle tension, and catecholamine secretion (Cohen, Evans, Krantz, & Stokols, 1980). By creating distractions and reducing the ability to think or attend to a task, noise can reduce learning in schoolchildren (more for girls than boys) and performance for adults (Bronzaft & McCarthy, 1975).

Noise pollution is one form of environmental stress that increases as our society grows more complex.   (*Photo by Robert V. Eckert, Jr.,* Stock Boston.)

Noise can even disrupt social behavior, contributing to more extreme likes and dislikes (Siegel & Steele, 1980). It also appears to increase aggression when a person is already angry (Konecni, Libuser, Morton, & Ebbeson, 1975). Finally, people are less likely to help others in noisy surroundings. In one interesting study, Mathews and Canon (1975) found that when an experimental confederate wearing an arm cast dropped an armload of books on the sidewalk, 80 percent of passers-by helped under low noise conditions, but only 15 percent helped in the presence of a loud (87 decibels) lawn mower.

Most of the explanations for the impact of noise are the same as those discussed earlier for stress aftereffects. Noise, particularly when it is unpredictable or uncontrollable, increases cognitive fatigue, frustration, hostility, and feelings of helplessness, and contributes to maladaptive perseverance of coping strategies. However, when examining the effects of noise, various moderating factors must be considered. Some noises, such as white noise (the roar of a waterfall), can mask or reduce the impact of other noise. And people differ considerably in what sounds they find disturbing. For a person who likes rock music, a neighbor's radio may cause no problem, whereas someone who hates rock music may find it an intolerable racket.

Air Pollution

Noise is not the only type of pollution that can lead to stress. Various foreign substances that befoul the air also contribute to stress. Contrary to what many believe, air pollution is a problem in both urban and rural areas, both indoors and outdoors, and is caused by factories and automobiles as well as by individuals (Gifford, 1987). Most people recognize air pollution as a nuisance and health hazard. But is it stressful? The research on this is difficult to conduct for ethical reasons. However, some findings are suggestive. For example, carbon monoxide, one of the major components of air pollution and cigarette smoke, impairs reaction time, arithmetic ability (Schulte, 1963), the ability to judge time (Beard & Wertheim, 1967), and the ability to detect changes in light intensity (Hovrath, Dahms, & O'Hanlon, 1971). Yet even though carbon monoxide can impair performance, people do not always feel different when exposed to this pollutant. As a result, it is often difficult to persuade them to take action against this invisible danger.

Air pollution may also affect social processes. People exposed to cigarette smoke are often more aggressive (Jones & Bogat, 1978). Correlational studies find a link between psychiatric emergency room visits and air pollution (Briere, Downes, & Pensley, 1983). Perhaps for those having trouble coping with stress, the subtle impairments brought on by air pollution can contribute to serious problems.

Given the real costs of air pollution, one might wonder why people rarely do something to remedy the problem. Two answers are suggested by research on adaptation and perceived costs. As we have seen, people often adapt to and tune out chronic stimuli, even those that are annoying. It is more difficult to detect a slight increase in a loud sound than a quiet sound. Similarly, Sommer (1972), has suggested that when pollution is slight, even a minor increase can be detected; however, when pollution is substantial, a major increase is required before it is noticed. Consistent with such a notion is the fact that when both long-term and new residents of Los Angeles were shown scenes of differing amounts of air pollution, the long-term residents had more difficulty deciding when smog was present (Evans, Jacobs, & Frager, 1982).

People also often do not take action against pollution because of the perceived costs. A person might speculate that if the cost of reducing pollution includes installing expensive equipment that may, for example, raise the cost of automobiles, some people may be less troubled by the problem of pollution.

Stress and Society: Prejudice and Discrimination

Research has found that in general stress impairs interpersonal behavior. Problems that may arise from stress include decreased sensitivity to others, a decrease in helping and recognition of individual differences, and increased aggression (Cohen, 1980). These same factors can in turn be sources of stress. Nowhere is this more evident than with what may be the most pervasive and intractable social problem of our planet: prejudice—negative attitudes toward a specific group of people, and discrimination—actions, that selectively exclude or harm a specific group.

Social intolerance has led to death and misery for untold millions of religious minorities, blacks, women, gays and lesbians, aged people, the disabled, and the list could go on. The causes of discrimination are far beyond the scope of this text; we can, however, begin to look at the issue in terms of coping and stress-related costs. Again, because it would be impossible to consider every group that has suffered discrimination, we shall discuss African-Americans, a visible minority that has received considerable research attention, and gays and lesbians, a relatively invisible minority that has, until recently, been the focus of little research.

African-Americans

By far, most stress-related research on African-Americans has focused on hypertension. The prevalence of essential hypertension (Chapter 7) in the African-American population is among the highest of any group in the world, and twice that of white Americans. As a result, African-Americans are also more likely to die from hypertension and most forms of heart disease (Anderson, 1989). Of course, many factors other than stress contribute to hypertension, including diet, exercise, and smoking.

The physical evidence is fairly clear: African-Americans display increased peripheral blood flow resistance and reduced sodium excretion, both factors that can contribute to hypertension (see Chapter 7). This can be aggravated by the high sodium diet characteristic of many African-Americans. Paradoxically, laboratory research suggests that African-Americans may respond to physical stressors with somewhat *decreased* cardiac reactivity (cardiac output and heart rate), which should lower blood pressure (Anderson, 1989).

However, not all African-Americans suffer from high blood pressure. Those with low-incomes are more vulnerable than low-income white Americans or high-income African-Americans. This group also reports more distress, perhaps because of poverty and racism, and is more likely to live in crowded and noisy conditions, which also contribute to stress. Even among low-income African-Americans, hypertension appears to be associated with perceptions of racial discrimination, marital status (unwed versus married), Type A behavior, occupational stress, feelings of cynicism and distrust, and lack of social support.

African-Americans, particularly in low-income areas, can be confronted with considerable anger and hostility. How they cope with anger may well effect the likelihood that they will have hypertension. In one study (Armsted, Lawler, Gorden, & Cross, 1989), twenty seven African-American college students viewed tapes of three interracial situations that were anger-provoking racist, anger-provoking nonracist, and neutral, respectively. Feelings of anger rose for both anger-provoking situations, but blood pressure rose only for the racist situation.

Society often disapproves of the expression of hostility, especially by disadvantaged minorities. If coping styles are examined, a person might expect an increased tendency among low-income African-Americans to suppress hostility when attacked and to feel guilty if they display anger when attacked. Consistent with this idea, Krieger (1990) found that African-Americans who claim they usually accept and keep quiet about unfair treatment are 4.4 times more likely to have hypertension than those who take action and talk to others. (This same study found no clear relationship for white Americans.)

The debate concerning the relative impact of stress and genetics continues. The issue is complicated because of the overlap of variables. It is possible that even peripheral resistance and sodium retention, which it can be argued, are inherited traits, are also affected by social factors. At the present, the least that can be said is that there is clear evidence that stress, particularly in low-income settings, does contribute to the higher rate of hypertension among African-Americans. However, the effect of stress may or may not be further affected by genetic differences.

Indeed, in other cultures the pattern may be quite different. In Brazil, the highest blood pressure occurs among mixed races and black Brazilians with low psychosocial resources; Afro-Brazilians with high psychosocial resources have lower blood pressure than white Brazilians (Dressler, dos-Santos, & Viteri, 1986).

Homosexuals

Gays and lesbians are subject to what may well be a uniquely hidden pattern of discrimination, one rarely mentioned in psychological texts. Unlike many conditions that determine minority status, a person's sexual preference can be kept silent, obscuring the presence of possible problems. But gays and lesbians exist at all levels of society and in all occupational groups. And, most importantly, severe and often violent anti-homosexual attitudes are still sanctioned by the church, military, and the Supreme Court, and anti-homosexual laws exist in half our states. All of this is aggravated by recent public fears concerning AIDS. In sum, gays and lesbians face substantial discrimination, harassment, and violence (National Gay and Lesbian Task Force, 1987).

STRESS AND THE "DIAGNOSIS" OF HOMOSEXUALITY.   Until recently, homosexuality was stigmatized as a disorder by psychiatrists and psychologists. Ironically, the very stigma-related stress experienced by some gays and lesbians was at first seen as a symptom indicating that homosexuality in itself is a disorder. The story of the "diagnosis" of homosexuality and stress is worth telling in its own right.

Until 1973, *American Psychiatric Association's Diagnostic and Statistical Manual of Mental Disorders* listed homosexuality as one of the "sexual deviations." In 1973, it substituted the category of homosexuality with "sexual orientation disturbance," a diagnosis applied to gay men and lesbians who are disturbed by, in conflict with, or wish to change their sexual orientation. Even this diagnosis was stigmatizing, since it ignored the possible role of prejudice in creating social stress. The official psychiatric position changed again with the third edition of the manual with the introduction of the category *ego-dystonic homosexuality*. This refers to a person who is distressed by homosexual feelings and wishes to become heterosexual. However, what is significant are those factors that contribute to ego-dystonic homosexuality including: negative societal attitudes toward homosexuality that have been internalized. In addition, features associated with heterosexuality, such as having children and socially sanctioned family life, may be viewed as desirable and incompatible with a homosexual arousal pattern. (American Psychiatric Association, 1980, p. 282)

However, this category was also stigmatizing. Discrepancies between values and behavior are common in our society (unfaithful marriage partners, clergy who gamble, former cigarette smokers who relapse), yet we do not ordinarily label such deviance as psychopathology.

In its most recent revision, the manual does not even include the category "Ego-Dystonic Homosexuality." Instead, anyone, homosexual or heterosexual, who experiences persistent and marked distress over one's sexual orientation fits in the catchall category of "Sexual Disorder Not Otherwise Specified." The fact is that psychological adjustment is not a factor differentiating homosexuals and heterosexuals.

WHERE ARE THE STRESS SYMPTOMS?   Given the severe and subtle discrimination that gays and lesbians encounter, it would be surprising not to find some evidence of stress among them. Gonsiorek (1982) has argued that stereotyping and prejudice can contribute to insecurity, self-hate, and neuroticism among any minority group. However, supporting evidence is difficult to find. Weinberg and Williams (1974) found no difference in psychopathology for homosexuals in three societies, the United States, the Netherlands, and Denmark, that might be thought to differ in the degree of antihomosexual stereotyping and prejudice. However, it may be more important to look at how homosexuals perceive the reactions of society rather than

Gay and lesbian lovers face considerable prejudice and discrimination from society. (*Photo by Joel Gordon.*)

what these reactions actually are. Indeed, Ross (1978) found that gays who perceive negative social reaction to their homosexuality show lower psychological adjustment. This becomes clear when we examine alcoholism among homosexuals.

ALCOHOLISM.   There is one symptom of stress that may well occur more frequently among gays and lesbians: alcoholism. Researchers frequently state that homosexuals are perhaps three times more likely to be alcoholic than heterosexuals (Schaefer, Evans, & Coleman, 1987). Such claims are most often based on a study of Los Angeles bargoers by Field (1975) entitled, "On My Way to Nowhere: Alienated, Isolated, Drunk." However, those who frequent bars may be at a higher risk for alcoholism regardless of sexual orientation. In a sample of 3,400 homosexuals, McKirnan and Peterson (1989) found that alcoholism may be a problem but is much less severe than previously assumed. Gays and lesbians are less likely to be abstainers and more likely to be moderate drinkers than the general population. They were just as likely to be heavy drinkers and somewhat more likely to report alcohol problems. However, even McKirnan and Peterson's sample was not representative, since 51 percent of the returns were from surveys included in a gay newspaper distributed primarily at gay bars.

If alcoholism is a problem among homosexuals, the cause may largely be discrimination and social prejudice (McKirnan and Peterson, 1989). Gay men who experience greater stress, display negative affectivity (see Chapter 6), and encounter discrimination are more likely to use alcohol and drugs (McKirnan and Peterson, 1988). Furthermore, acceptance of a person's homosexuality appears to be related to the successful maintenance of sobriety (Kus, 1988). Perhaps because of social discrimination, the bar is one of the few places available for homosexuals to socialize openly. Thus, discrimination may contribute to alcoholism in two ways: first, by increasing stress; and second, by driving homosexuals into social support settings where alcohol is readily available and its use is encouraged.

When considering stress among homosexuals, we return again and again to a core issue: social attitudes both overtly and covertly tell gays and lesbians to keep quiet about their sexual orientation, or, in other words, to stay in the closet. Such fear and loathing is often called *homophobia,* a source of stress to homosexuals and heterosexuals alike. Weinberg (1972) has hypothesized that homophobia can come from many sources, including rigid adherence to conservative Judeo-Christian teachings, repressed fear of being homosexual, and anxiety over threats to traditional values. Accepting homosexuality in the face of homophobia may well be the preeminent coping task for homosexuals. Here stress research has something to say.

STRESS, SUICIDE, AND COMING OUT.   Many postulate that the object of sexual attraction is part of one's gender identity at an early age (Money & Ehrhardt, 1972), if not genetically determined. The stress of facing sexual orientation is most clearly revealed in the dramatically high level of suicide among homosexual youth. Perhaps forty percent of homosexual men and women consider suicide, and thirty percent actually attempt it, a level two to three times higher than that of their heterosexual peers (Bell & Weinberg, 1978; Jay & Young, 1979; Remafedi, 1987; Remafedi,

Farrow, & Deisher, 1991; Roesler & Deisher, 1972; Saghir & Robins, 1973). Even more disturbing, more than half of the suicide attempts are serious, a level also greater than among heterosexuals (Kourany, 1987). A report commissioned by the U.S. Department of Health and Human Services (1989), found that 30 percent of the five thousand adolescents and young adults who take their lives each year are homosexual. Indicative of the discrimination that homosexuals face, this same report drew severe criticism from political conservatives; eventually the Bush administration responded that the findings concerning gay youth undermine the institution of the family (Maguen, 1991).

Suicide has many causes. Retrospective studies show that one-third of homosexuals' suicide attempts are personally attributed to their turmoil over their homosexuality, that one-third of first attempts occur within the same year that they identify themselves as bisexual or homosexual, and that most other attempts occur soon after (Remafedi et al., 1991).

As the statistics on suicide suggest, acceptance of a person's own sexual orientation can take some time. Three options are available. Homosexuals can deny to themselves and to others that they have strong attractions for members of their own sex. This concealment quite likely leads to serious consequences, as described by Fisher (1972):

> Every time a homosexual denies the validity of his feelings or restrains himself from expressing them, he does a small hurt to himself. He turns his energies inward and suppresses his own vitality. The effect may be scarcely noticeable: Joy may be a little less keen, happiness slightly subdued; he may simply feel a little run-down, a little less tall. Over the years, these tiny denials have a cumulative effect. (p. 249)

As we have seen, such costs are difficult to document for the simple reason that the homosexuals who are the most closeted, and presumably the most hurting, are also the least likely to participate in research.

The second option is to lead a double life by living a secret homosexual and a public heterosexual life. It is difficult to assess how many succeed at such duplicity because, once again, these individuals are unlikely to participate openly in research.

A third option is to deal realistically and honestly with homosexual feelings and come out of the closet. We have seen that stage theories can organize a variety of stress-related issues and coping options for disasters, catastrophes, illness (Chapter 9), and human development (Chapter 10). Such theories can be useful for understanding the continuing process of accepting sexual orientation if we recognize that they rarely present rigid steps, but rather themes that can emerge and reemerge. A surprising variety of models outline the process of "coming out" (Cass, 1979; Coleman, 1981-1982; Hanley-Hackenbruck, 1988; McDonald, 1982; Minton & McDonald, 1983-1984; Sophie, 1985-1986; Troiden, 1979). We shall consider the models offered by Cass and Coleman.

Cass (1979) has proposed the following six stages in the acceptance of a person's own homosexuality:

1. *Identity confusion:* One begins to feel same-sex feelings and label them as such. This can lead to feelings of "being different" and alienation, which are often

accompanied by denial, shame, anxiety, and ambivalence. As Lewis (1984) has described,

> This is a time of great dissonance and inner turmoil. A woman faces a conflict between the process of socialization, which teaches her that she will probably marry and have a family, and her feelings, which pull her toward wanting intimacy with other women (p. 465). Of course, a similar pattern could be described for gay men.

2. *Identity comparison:* The coping strategies of rationalization or bargaining predominate. A person thinks, "Maybe I'm gay, but then again, maybe I'm bisexual"; "Perhaps my feelings are temporary"; "I'll grow out of this"; and so on. In addition, a person experiences the stress of low social support, of feeling that "I don't belong anywhere," or that "I am the only person in the world like this."

3. *Identity tolerance:* A person begins to accept a different appraisal of herself and to tolerate the thought that "I am probably a homosexual." She also starts to associate with a few other homosexuals, primarily to counteract feelings of isolation and alienation. However, as Coleman (1981–1982) suggests, thoughts about her homosexuality are disclosed to only one or two trusted people, and often not to many close friends or family members.

4. *Identity acceptance:* A person increases contact with other homosexuals and begins to develop friendships with them, while starting to evaluate the homosexual life style more positively. Central to this stage is an acceptance, rather than a tolerance, of the knowledge that she is homosexual. Coleman (1981–1982) elaborates that this phase may be accompanied by more interpersonal and sexual experimentation, resulting in increased social skills.

5. *Identity pride:* As a homosexual orientation is increasingly accepted, one often becomes immersed in the gay and lesbian subculture. This can be accompanied by angry rejection of the heterosexual institutions (such as marriage and gender-role norms).

6. *Identity synthesis:* A homosexual identity becomes integrated with the rest of a person's identity. He is comfortable with himself, and less likely to react to heterosexual society with anger and rejection. Coleman (1981–1982) adds to this stage (and the preceding stage of identity pride) an important emphasis on increasingly mature and equal relationships.

It is crucial not to view these stages as rigid steps on a ladder. Instead, in terms of the transactional matrix, they summarize some of the important interpersonal pressures (society's demands to be heterosexual), costs (anxiety, confusion, anger, etc.), and coping strategies (denial, tentative acceptance, defiant pride, etc.) that characterize the process of dealing with prejudice and discrimination.

Stress and Our Times

The discussion of crowding, commuting, noise, air pollution, racism, and homophobia brings us again to the more general question: do we live in stressful times? This question is frequently asked by talk-show hosts and the popular press. In his 1970 classic *Future Shock,* Alvin Toffler argued that today's pace of technological change exceeds society's ability to cope. On the surface, it is hard to dispute that we do indeed live in rapidly changing times. More than seven thousand scientific articles are written each day. Scientific information increases by 13 percent each year (Naisbitt, 1982). Toffler has also argued (1980) that such changes have a direction. The *first wave* involved the development of agriculture and the establishment of cities. The *second wave* of civilization, he says, was founded on industrialism, religious idealism, and representative and centralized democracy. But these old structures of society are being dismantled to make way for a new society, the *third wave,* which, according to Toffler (1980), is

> based on diversified, renewable energy sources; on methods of production that make most factory assembly lines obsolete; on new, non-nuclear families; on a novel institution that might be called the "electronic cottage"; and on radically changed schools and corporations of the future. (p. 10)

The notion that our times are any more or less stressful than any others is an untestable proposition. Often such a statement is based on a simplistic application of stimulus models of stress (change = readjustment = stress). We have seen that the impact of change is mediated by a variety of factors, including cognitive appraisals of threat, coping resources, personality, and social support. There is no reason to doubt that the same is true for changes in society. Change is in the eye of the beholder.

APPLICATION BOX 12.1

Stress and Your Environment

What is the most stressful feature of your environment (crowding, noise, etc.)? Can you identify ways in which your coping attempts/cognitive appraisals might change the amount of stress you experienced? For example, if you find a crowded and noisy dorm room stressful, you might try the following:

Coping
    Spend more time outside.
    Study in the library.
    Negotiate with your roommate times when both can be alone.
    Establish quiet hours with roommate.
Cognitive Appraisals
    "Most students learn to put up with dormitory noise."
    "Noise will help me learn to concentrate."
    "I can always choose to be alone by going for a walk."

References

ALTMAN, I., WOHLWILL, J. F., & EVERETT, P. B. (Eds.). (1981). *Transportation and behavior.* New York: Plenum.

AMERICAN PSYCHIATRIC ASSOCIATION. (1980). *Diagnostic and statistical manual of mental disorders* (1st ed., 1952; 2nd ed., 1968; 3rd ed., 1980; rev. ed., 1983). Washington DC.

ANDERSON, N. B. (1989). Racial differences in stress-induced cardiovascular reactivity and hypertension: Current status and substantive issues. *Psychological Bulletin, 105,* 89–105.

ARMSTED, C. A., LAWLER, K. A., GORDEN, G., & CROSS, J. (1989). Relationship of racial stressors to blood pressure responses and anger expression in Black college students. *Health Psychology, 8,* 541–556.

BEARD, R. R., & WERTHEIM, G. A. (1967). Behavioral impairment associated with small doses of carbon monoxide. *American Journal of Public Health,* 57, 2012–2022.

BELL, A., & WEINBERG, M. (1978). *Homosexualities: A study of diversity among men and women.* New York: Simon and Schuster.

BRIERE, J., DOWNES, A., & SPENSLEY, J. (1983). Summer in the city: Weather conditions and psychiatric emergency-room visits. *Journal of Abnormal Psychology, 92,* 77–90.

BRONZAFT, A. L., & McCARTHY, D. P. (1975). The effects of elevated train noise on reading ability. *Environment and Behavior,* 7, 517–527.

CASS, V. C. (1979). Homosexual identity formation: A theoretical model. *Journal of Homosexuality, 4,* 219–235.

COHEN, S. (1980). Aftereffects of stress on human performance and social behavior: A review of research and theory. *Psychological Bulletin, 88,* 82–108.

COHEN, S. (1981, October). Sound effects on behavior. *Psychology Today,* pp. 38–49.

COHEN, S., EVANS, G. W., KRANTZ, D. S., & STOKOLS, D. (1980). Physiological, motivational, and cognitive effects of aircraft noise on children: Moving from the laboratory to the field. *American Psychologist, 35,* 231–242.

COLEMAN, E. (1981-1982). Developmental stages of the coming out process. *Journal of Homosexuality, 7,* 31–43.

DRESSLER, W. W., DOS-SANTOS, J. E., & VITERI, F. E. (1986). Blood pressure, ethnicity, and psychosocial resources. *Psychosomatic Medicine, 48,* 509–519.

EVANS, C. W., JACOBS, S. V., & FRAGER, N. B. (1982). Adaptation to air pollution. *Journal of Environmental Psychology, 2,* 99–108.

FIELD, L. (1975). *On my way to nowhere: Alienated, isolated, drunk.* Los Angeles: Gay Community Services Center.

FISHER, P. (1972). *The gay mystique: The myth and reality of male homosexuality.* New York: Stein and Day.

GIFFORD, R. (1987). *Environmental psychology.* Boston: Allyn and Bacon.

GONSIOREK, J. C. (1982). Social-psychological concepts in the understanding of homosexuality. *American Behavioral Scientist, 25,* 483–492.

GOVE, W. R., & HUGHES, M. (1980). In pursuit of preconceptions: A reply to the claim of Booth and his colleagues that household crowding is not an important variable. *American Sociological Review, 45,* 878–886.

HANLEY-HACKENBRUCK, P. (1988). "Coming out" and psychotherapy. *Psychiatric Annals, 18,* 29–32.

HOVRATH, S. M., DAHMS, T. E., & O'HANLON, J. F. (1971). Carbon monoxide and human vigilance: A deleterious effect of present urban concentrations. *Archives of Environmental Health, 23,* 343–347.

JAY, K., & YOUNG, A. (EDS.), (1979). *The gay report: Lesbians and gay men speak out about their sexual experiences and life-styles.* New York: Simon and Schuster.

JONES, J. W., & BOGAT, A. G. (1978). Air pollution and human aggression. *Psychological Reports, 43,* 721–722.

KONECNI, V. J., LIBUSER, L., MORTON, H., & EBBESON, E. B. (1975). Effects of a violation of personal space on escape and helping responses. *Journal of experimental Social Psychology, 11,* 288–299.

KOURANY, R. F. (1987). Suicide among homosexual adolescents. *Journal of Homosexuality, 13,* 111–117.

KRIEGER, N. (1990). Racial and gender discrimination: Risk factors for high blood pressure. *Social Science and Medicine, 30,* 1273–1281.

KRYTER, K. (1970). *The effects of noise on man.* New York: Academic Press.

KUS, R. J. (1988). Alcoholism and non-acceptance of gay self: The critical link. *Journal of Homosexuality, 15,* 25–41.

LEWIS, L. A. (1984). The coming-out process for lesbians: Integrating a stable identity. *Journal of the National Association of Social Workers, 29,* 464–469.

MAGUEN, S. (1991, September 24). Teen suicide. *The Advocate,* pp. 40–47.

MATHEWS, K. E., JR., & CANON, L. K. (1975). Environmental noise level as a determinant of helping behavior. *Journal of Personality and Social Psychology, 32,* 571–577.

MCDONALD, G. J. (1982). Individual differences in the coming-out process of gay men: Implications for theoretical models. *Journal of Homosexuality, 8,* 47–60.

MCKIRNAN, D. J., & PETERSON, P. L. (1988). Stress, expectancies, and vulnerability to substance abuse: A test of a model among homosexual men. *Journal of Abnormal Psychology, 97,* 461–466.

MCKIRNAN, D. J., & PETERSON, P. L. (1989). Alcohol and drug use among homosexual men and women: Epidemiology and population characteristics. *Addictive Behaviors, 14,* 545–553.

MICHAELS, R. M. (1962). The effect of expressway design on driver tension responses. *Public Roads, 32,* 107–112.

MINTON, H., & MCDONALD, G. (1983–1984). Homosexual identity formation as a developmental process. *Journal of Homosexuality, 9,* 91–104.

MONEY, J., & EHRHARDT, A. A. (1972). *Man and woman, boy and girl: Differentiation and dimorphism of gender identity from conception to maturity:* Baltimore: Johns Hopkins University Press.

NAISBITT, J. (1982). *Megatrends: Ten new directions transforming our lives.* New York: Warner Books.

NATIONAL GAY AND LESBIAN TASK FORCE. (1987). *Anti-gay violence, victimization, and defamation in 1986.* (Available from the National Gay and Lesbian Task Force Anti-Violence Project, 1517 U St. N. W., Washington, DC 20009)

REMAFEDI, G. (1987). Adolescent homosexuality: Psychosocial and medical implications. *Pediatrics, 79,* 331–337.

REMAFEDI, G., FARROW, J. A., & DEISHER, R. W. (1991). Risk factors for attempted suicide in gay and bisexual youth. *Pediatrics, 87,* 869–875.

ROESLER, T., & DEISHER, R. W. (1972). Youthful male homosexuality. *Journal of the American Medical Association, 219,* 1018–1023.

ROSS, M. W. (1978). The relationship between perceived societal hostility, conformity, and psychological adjustment in homosexual males. *Journal of Homosexuality, 4,* 157–168.

SAGHIR, M. T., & ROBINS, E. (1973). *Male and female homosexuality: A comprehensive investigation.* Baltimore: Williams & Wilkins.

SCHAEFER, S., EVANS, S., & COLEMAN, E. (1987). Sexual orientation concerns among chemically dependent individuals. *Journal of Chemical Dependency Treatment, 1,* 121–140.

SCHULTE, J. H. (1963). Effects of mild carbon monoxide intoxication. *Archives of Environmental Health, 7,* 524–530.

SIEGEL, J. M., & STEELE, C. M. (1980). Environmental distraction and interpersonal judgments. *British Journal of Social and Clinical Psychology, 19,* 23–32.

SINGER, J. E., & BAUM, A. (1983). Stress, environment, and environmental stress. In N. R. Feimer & E. S. Geller (Eds.), *Environmental psychology* (pp. 129–151). New York: Praeger.

SOMMER, R. (1972). *Design awareness.* New York: Holt, Rinehart and Winston.

SOPHIE, J. (1985–1986). A critical examination of stage theories of lesbian identity development. *Journal of Homosexuality, 12,* 39–51.

STOKOLS, D. (1972). On the distinction between density and crowding: Some implications for further research. *Psychological Review, 79,* 275–277.

TOFFLER, A. (1970). *Future Shock.* New York: Bantam Books.

TOFFLER, A. (1980). *The third wave.* New York: Bantam Books.

TROIDEN, R. R. (1979). Becoming homosexual: A model of gay identity acquisition. *Psychiatry, 42,* 362–373.

U.S. DEPARTMENT OF HEALTH AND HUMAN SERVICES. (1989). *Report of the Secretary's Task Force on Youth Suicide: Vol. 3. Prevention and interventions in youth suicide.* Rockville, MD: U.S. Department of Health and Human Services.

WEINBERG, G. (1972). Society and the healthy homosexual. New York: St. Martin's Press.

WEINBERG, M. S., & WILLIAMS, C. J. (1974). *Male homosexuals: Their problems and adaptations.* New York: Oxford University Press.

PART IV

Interventions

In this, the final part of our exploration of stress, we turn to stress management. The chapters that follow can be viewed as a summary of current options for prevention and treatment, and more generally as an exploration of the question, "What is coping?" as answered by clinicians.

We begin in Chapter 13 with relaxation, perhaps the most widely used approach to stress management. We examine eight different approaches, ranging from progressive muscle relaxation to meditation and biofeedback, and conclude with a discussion of the current controversy concerning the nature of relaxation. In chapters 14 and 15 we consider approaches to active coping. Primary behavioral approaches include problem-solving, negotiation training, assertiveness training, time management, and cognitive and complex approaches that include rational restructuring, crisis intervention, desensitization, and stress inoculation training. If you are interested in exploring these approaches, see Smith (1993).

CHAPTER **13**

Relaxation

Relaxation training is as old as civilization itself. Hundreds of techniques have evolved from the traditions of religion, magic, and science. Today, relaxation is the most widely used tool in stress management. In terms of the transactional model, it is a form of emotion-focused coping directed toward reducing distress rather than changing a problem situation. However, we shall see that relaxation can have much broader aims, including self-exploration, recovery, and creativity enhancement. Relaxation is even used as a source of insight for understanding the complexities of a stressful problem and a source of energy for solving a problem. We shall discuss the eight approaches to relaxation most often used in stress management: progressive relaxation, yoga stretching, breathing, nonauthoritarian hypnosis, autogenic training, imagery, meditation, and biofeedback.

Traditional Approaches to Relaxation

Progressive Relaxation

Progressive relaxation is perhaps the most widely used approach to relaxation in stress management. It was introduced by physician and psychologist Edmund Jacobson (1929) in the 1920s. He trained subjects to detect and recognize increasingly subtle levels of muscle tension and thus to remain relaxed throughout the day. In a session, a person would generate and let go of the smallest amount of tension possible. Care was taken to avoid suggestive patter, because of the (unfounded) fear of inducing hypnotic effects. Subjects would focus on two or three muscles a session, eventually covering over fifty muscle groups in a training period that could last up to a year.

Jacobson's method was cumbersome, although his gentle and minimal strategy of letting go of tension is still used. However, abbreviated versions of progressive relaxation are more popular, and most are similar to that introduced in 1958 by Joseph Wolpe. Wolpe and others placed greater emphasis on creating a considerable level

TABLE 13.1   Sample Abbreviated Progressive Relaxation Exercises

Hand Squeeze

While keeping the rest of your body relaxed, squeeze the fingers together by making a fist.
Do this *now*.
Squeeze the fingers together, making them tighter and tighter. Let the tension build completely.
Notice the tension . . . and *let go*.
PAUSE
Let yourself relax.
Let the tension go. You might want to think of a tight ball of string slowly unwinding.
Focus on your hand as it begins to relax more and more.
Attend to the good feelings as the momentum of relaxation begins to carry the tension away.

Right Arm Squeeze

While keeping the rest of your body relaxed, squeeze your lower and upper right arm
   together, bending at the elbow. You might want to imagine you are trying to touch your
   shoulder with your hand.
Do this *now*.
Let the tension build until the squeeze feels most satisfying and complete.
Squeeze them together more and more.
And *let go*.
Let your arms go limp like a floppy rag doll.
Enjoy the feelings of relaxation you create as your muscles smooth out.
Compare how your right arm feels with your left arm.
Just notice what it feels like as the muscles start to become more and more deeply relaxed.

Shoulder Squeeze

This time move your attention to your shoulders. Keep the rest of your body relaxed.
Squeeze them in whatever way feels best . . . by shrugging them up . . . by pulling them
   behind you . . . or by making a slow circling motion.
Squeeze them *now*.
Feel the good tension as it grows to a point where it is most satisfying and complete.
Squeeze every muscle fiber.
Notice how you can generate a complete squeeze.
And *let go*.
Let the momentum of relaxation begin to melt away tension.
Let your muscles go and think about the pleasant feelings of relaxation in your shoulders.
Give your shoulder muscles time to relax.
Let relaxation flow into every muscle.

Back of Neck Squeeze

This time move your attention up to your neck and gently tilt your head back. While keep-
   ing the rest of your body relaxed, gently press the back of your head against your neck *now*.
Let the tension grow, this time not too tightly.
Create a good, complete squeeze.
And *let go*.
PAUSE
Let the muscles of your neck relax like a floppy rag doll.
Let the tension unwind.

(continues)

TABLE 13.1   *Continued*

Enjoy the feelings of relaxation.
Let the momentum of relaxation carry the tension away.

SOURCE   Reprinted from Smith, J. C. (1989), *Relaxation dynamics*: pp. 69–75. *A cognitive-behavioral approach to relaxation*, Champaign, IL: Research Press. Reprinted by permission.

of relaxation in the first session by effortfully generating and releasing tension. Often up to sixteen muscle groups are targeted in a single session. As training progresses, muscle groups are combined, until one can essentially do what Jacobson taught: simply detect and let go of tension without first overtly creating tension. In the most abbreviated form of progressive relaxation, called *conditioned or cue-controlled relaxation*, a person thinks a relaxing cue word, such as *calm*, after practicing progressive relaxation. Eventually, the cue itself is enough to evoke relaxation.

Most explanations of progressive relaxation focus on the role of directing attention and creating a relaxation "rebound effect." Throughout training, the subject is directed toward attending to and differentiating subtle sources of tension and relaxation. The goal is to learn to detect tension that might ordinarily go unnoticed and to recognize when relaxation is occurring. Another goal, especially of the more contemporary, abbreviated approaches, is first to create considerable muscle tension by tightening up and then letting go. This permits a relaxation rebound in which the release of tension creates a greater level of relaxation than could be achieved by simply willing muscles to relax. For sample abbreviated progressive relaxation exercises, see Table 13.1.

Yoga Stretching

Traditional yoga began thousands of years ago in India as part of Hinduism. Hundreds of exercises have evolved, many with deep ties to religion and philosophy. The word *yoga* comes from a root that can mean to bind, join, attach, or yoke. It can also mean to direct and concentrate attention, to use and apply, or to unite or commune with God (Eliade, 1969). These meanings reflect the many goals of traditional yoga. There are exercises with many questionable claimed effects, including cleansing the body, activating the nervous system, increasing intelligence, improving sex life, developing paranormal powers, and healing virtually any organ system. Indeed, there is no such thing as a single yoga discipline; there are many yogas.

Contemporary practitioners of stress management have largely avoided that part of yoga that is religious, philosophical, pseudoscientific, and magical, and focused instead on the movement that is central to most yoga exercises: the focused stretch (Smith, 1989). Here one slowly, smoothly, and gently stretches and unstretches major muscle groups. This can be relaxing for many reasons. Stretching releases muscle tension; increases the flow of blood to the muscles, thus helping to cleanse the by-products of tension; stimulates the joints; diverts attention from stressful worry, and so on. For examples of yoga stretching, see Table 13.2.

TABLE 13.2   Sample Yoga Stretching Exercises

Arm and Side Stretch
Let both your arms fall limply to your sides.
PAUSE
Slowly, smoothly, and gently circle your right arm and hand up and away from you, like the hand of a clock or the wing of a bird.
PAUSE
Let your arm extend straight, and circle higher and higher.
PAUSE
Let it circle to the sky.
PAUSE
And then circle your arm over your head so your hand points to the other side . . . stretch and arch your body as you reach and point farther and farther, like a tree arching in the wind.
PAUSE
Now gently and easily
PAUSE
Like the hand of a clock or the wing of a bird
PAUSE
Circle your arm back over your head . . . to your side
PAUSE
Finally to the resting position.
PAUSE
And let your arm hang.

Back Stretch
Now, focus your attention on your back, below your shoulders.
Slowly, smoothly, and gently relax and bow over.
PAUSE
Let your arms hang limply.
PAUSE
Let your head fall forward, as you bow forward farther and farther in your chair.
PAUSE
Do not force yourself to bow over . . . let gravity pull your body toward your knees . . . farther and farther. It's OK to take a short breath if you need to.
PAUSE
Feel the stretch along the back.
PAUSE
Let gravity pull your body forward, as far as it will go.
PAUSE
Then gently and easily sit up.
PAUSE
Take your time.
PAUSE
Inch by inch, straighten up your body.
PAUSE
Until you are seated comfortably in an upright position.

Back of Neck Stretch
Now, while sitting erect, let your head tilt easily toward your chest.

(continues)

TABLE 13.2   *Continued*

PAUSE
Try not to force it down.
PAUSE
Simply let gravity pull your head down.
PAUSE
Farther and farther.
PAUSE
Feel the stretch in the back of your neck.
PAUSE
As the force of gravity easily and slowly pulls your head down
PAUSE
And when you are ready
PAUSE
Gently and easily lift your head.

SOURCE   Reprinted from Smith, J. C. (1989). *Relaxation dynamics: A cognitive-behavioral approach to relaxation*, pp. 89–102. Champaign, IL: Research Press. Reprinted by permission.

Breathing

Breathing exercises can be found in just about every relaxation technique. However, they are emphasized in many approaches to yoga as well as in a Western form of natural childbirth called Lamaze. Most breathing exercises have among their goals an emphasis on diaphragmatic (or "stomach") breathing, and increased control over breathing pace, volume, pauses, and rhythm. Specifically, the exercises usually require one to breathe more slowly, taking in more air with each inhalation,

Yoga stretching is one of the popular forms of relaxation.   *(Photo by Joel Gordon.)*

TABLE 13.3   Sample Breathing Exercises

Bowing and Stretching Breathing

As you inhale, reach and stretch. Arch your back and gently circle both arms up toward the
  sky, like the hands of a clock or the wings of a great bird. When you are ready to exhale,
  slowly circle your arms down so they are hanging heavily, and gently bow over, as before,
  squeezing out all the air. Let gravity pull your body down farther and farther. There is
  nothing for you to do.
Continue breathing this way for a while.

Inhaling Through Nose

As you breathe in, imagine you are sniffing a very delicate flower. Let the flow of breath into
  your nose be as smooth and gentle as possible, so you barely rustle a petal. Take a full
  breath.
PAUSE
And relax, letting yourself breathe out naturally, without effort.
PAUSE 5 SECONDS
Continue breathing this way, breathing in and out quietly and evenly at your own pace.

Exhaling Through Lips

Take a slow deep breath and pause.
And breathe out slowly through your lips, as if you were blowing at a candle flame just
  enough to make it flicker, but not go out. Continue breathing out, emptying all the air
  from your stomach and chest.
PAUSE
Then breathe in through your nose.
PAUSE
Continue breathing this way, making the stream of air that passes through your lips as you
  exhale as smooth and gentle as possible.
PAUSE 5 SECONDS
Let the tension flow out with every breath.

SOURCE   Reprinted from Smith, J. C. (1989). *Relaxation dynamics: A cognitive-behavioral approach to
relaxation*, pp. 87–101. Champaign, IL: Research Press. Reprinted by permission.

increasing the pauses between each breath, and breathing in an even, rather than
jerky, manner.

The important skill to master is breathing *control*. Some stress-related breathing
disorders, such as hyperventilation, involve taking in too much oxygen. Here,
breathing more deeply could be inappropriate. Under stress other people hold their
breath and breathe more slowly. For these individuals, learning to breathe even
more slowly would be inappropriate. Thus the overall goal is to increase control of
breathing, which usually (but not always) results in reduced pace, greater volume,
lengthened pauses, and more even rhythm. See Table 13.3 for sample breathing
exercises.

Nonauthoritarian Hypnosis

Hypnosis was popularized in the later 1800s, at about the time that Sigmund Freud
began his work. Early techniques were authoritarian and resemble the dramatic presentations often seen in the movies. A bearded, fatherlike hypnotist would state hyp-

notic commands while a passive client complied. Contemporary hypnosis is much less authoritarian, and is instead more of a collaborative effort between the hypnotist guide and the client.

Hypnotic suggestion has many uses, one of which is relaxation. In fact, relaxation is incorporated in the very hypnotic induction procedure. A typical contemporary induction (Wolberg, 1948) might begin with monotonous patter suggesting drowsiness and relaxation, while the client's attention is directed to a simple stimulus or sensation. As one begins to relax, certain physiological changes occur, some associated with relaxation (such as spontaneous muscle jerks) and others with the strain of maintaining attention (such as watery eyes). These may be interpreted or suggested as the initial signs of a hypnotic trance. After a set of suggestions intended to deepen drowsiness and relaxation, a graduated series of hypnotic tasks are presented, each requiring and contributing to a greater degree of hypnotic responsibility ("Your eyelids are so heavy they cannot be opened. . . Your arms and legs are so heavy they cannot be lifted. . . Your hands are clasped together so tightly they cannot be opened."). Eventually, the subject is ready for such standard hypnotic suggestions as hand numbness, age regression, hallucination, and posthypnotic suggestion (Smith, 1990).

Perhaps the two most influential contemporary hypnotists are Milton Erickson and Theodore Xeonphon Barber. Erickson's very popular approach, which is highly individualized and client focused, utilizes such techniques as confusion and double binds (suggesting the opposite of what is intended, presenting conflicting messages), indirect induction (making nonverbal communication, introducing suggestions by means of indirect metaphor), and naturalistic devices (weaving a client's existing symptoms, images, and experiences into the induction). Erickson directs suggestions to the presumed hidden or unconscious side of a patient; techniques such as confusion and diversion are designed to by-pass, exhaust, or divert goal-directed analytic thinking (Erickson, Rossi, & Rossi, 1976; Smith, 1990).

Barber comes from a behavioral tradition that views the words *hypnosis* and *trance* as unnecessary and potentially misleading terms. He prefers to focus on those conditions conducive to evoking "hypnotic" responses, specifically "task-motivational instructions" targeted at changing attitudes, motivations, and expectations (Barber, 1984; Smith, 1990). His approach includes inducing a state of deep relaxation, defining the situation as "hypnosis," noting that the suggestions are "easy" and can be "passed" by most subjects, reducing critical and analytic thinking, and vividly imagining what is described in suggestions.

Whatever the approach, the hypnotized subject is generally relaxed, and the hypnotist can choose to deepen relaxation through suggestion.

Autogenic Training

Autogenic training is perhaps the most widely used approach to relaxation in Europe. Developed by dermatologist Johannes Schultz (1932) and elaborated by Wolfgang Luthe (1969-1973), the contemporary technique is a sequence of exercises based on the idea that passively thinking suggestive images can bring about relaxation and changes in health. Autogenic training begins with six standard exercises that involve mentally repeating verbal formulas designed to suggest heaviness, warmth in the extremities, an easily beating heart, relaxed breathing, abdominal warmth, and a cool forehead. Emphasis is placed on the process of *passive volition*, that is, repeating suggestive phrases while maintaining complete indifference about their consequences.

In the United States, autogenic training usually stops with the six standard exercises. However, traditional training continues with a variety of special exercises. Organ-specific formulas tailor the standard suggestions to patient needs. For example, backache sufferers may think, "My back is warm," while a headache patient may say, " My forehead is cool." In addition, intentional formulas are targeted to behavioral changes ("I will study more and drink less.")

Finally, a series of seven "meditative," or imagery, exercises are presented. Patients begin by focusing on the color sensations that spontaneously occur with eyes closed in relaxation. Then, the colors that appear most frequently are attended to, until they can be produced and modulated on demand. The patients proceed to visualize simple concrete objects, abstract constructs (such as truth, justice, and friendship), emotional states, and other people. Eventually, exercises are directed toward seeking "answers from the unconscious," that is, asking questions ("What is the source of my rage?") and passively waiting for a spontaneous answer.

Imagery

Imagery has been diversely applied as an approach to relaxation, either alone or as part of another procedure. Images often form an important part of hypnotic induction, and the production of hallucinated images is a frequently suggested hypnotic response. Advanced autogenic training also involves a graduated series of both simple and complex images. As we shall see, many forms of meditation likewise incorporate the use of imagery. Finally, imagery exercises are frequently a part of psychotherapy and range from the association techniques of Freud and Jung to the desensitization and covert modeling techniques of behavior therapy.

Given its pervasiveness, perhaps the best way of understanding imagery is to catalog its diversity. All forms of imagery involve producing a covert or mental representation of external stimuli. As a relaxation tool, most imagery techniques include fantasy and daydream themes such as a nature setting, a childhood triumph, a rehearsal of coping with a future stressor, or a fantasy unconstrained by reality.

Imagery can also be classified according to the modality of its content: visual, verbal, auditory, olfactory, tactile, gustatory, or kinesthetic. Typically, the content is visual, with other sense modalities introduced as elaborations. Verbal imagery is somewhat less widely used, the most prominent example being autogenic formulas, or phrases that a person passively repeats.

Meditation

Meditation, like yoga, is one of the oldest approaches to relaxation. The instructions are very simple (Smith, 1986):

CALMLY ATTEND TO A SIMPLE STIMULUS
AFTER EVERY DISTRACTION
CALMLY RETURN YOUR ATTENTION
. . . again and again and again

Concentrative forms of meditation involve attending to a preselected stimulus, such as a meaningless sound or syllable called a *mantra*, the flow of breath, simple counting, a mental image, or an external image. More advanced forms of meditation, variously called Zen openness, *shikan-taza* (Japanese for "just sitting"), mindfulness or vipassana, involve attending to the flow of all stimuli (Smith, 1986). Finally, contemplation, an exercise very much like meditation, involves attending to a simple stimulus with the objective of stirring associations that enrich a person's appreciation of the stimulus (meditation has no such objective).

Biofeedback

Finally, biofeedback relaxation training is not so much a separate approach to relaxation as a way of letting people know when they are relaxed and tense. Specifically, it is the technique of

> using equipment (usually electronic) to reveal to human beings some of their internal physiological events, normal and abnormal, in the form of visual and auditory signals, in order to teach them to manipulate these otherwise involuntary or unfelt events by manipulating the displayed signals. (Basmajian, 1979)

Biofeedback equipment measures skin conductance (hand perspiration) and enables a client to view her level of physical stress.
(*Photo by* Biofeedback, NY 212-222-5665/SRS, Inc.–Redmond, WA.)

TABLE 13.4   Types of Biofeedback

Measures	*Physiological Activity Assessed*
Electrical	
Electrocardiogram (EKG)	Heartbeat
Electrodermal activity (EDA)	Perspiration; emotional sweating
Electroencephalogram (EEG)	Electrical activity of cerebral cortex
Electrogastrogram (EGG)	Stomach contractions
Electromyogram (EMG)	Muscle activity
Electro-oculogram (EOG)	Eye movement
Mechanical	
Plethysmograph	Volume of blood flow at a peripheral site; respiration; erectile response
Thermometer	Blood volume

SOURCE   Adapted from Reed, Katkin, and Goldband, 1986.

All biofeedback instruments essentially do the same thing: they enable us to hear or see body processes that are ordinarily silent. Once brought to our attention, we can learn to become more relaxed. We can see what relaxation works best at reducing tension. A thermometer or a stethoscope, for example, can be a biofeedback device.

Electromyographic (EMG) biofeedback is widely used in stress clinics to reduce skeletal muscle tension. Whenever a muscle contracts, it is accompanied by an electrical current, which can be measured by very sensitive electrodes placed on the skin over the muscle. This signal is then filtered, amplified, and transformed into a tone or light signal. When a person tenses, the signal immediately grows stronger, and when she relaxes, the signal grows weaker. Thus, she receives immediate feedback concerning level of tension and relaxation. This process can be very useful in teaching clients to relax. After first obtaining a base rate of resting tension, a clinician may introduce a few stressful tasks to determine what part of the body and what organ system are most likely to manifest tension (note how this is consistent with the specificity model described in Chapter 3). Then, relaxation techniques may be explored until one is found that successfully reduces tension. Of course, tension is often manifest in organ systems other than the skeletal muscles; for this, other forms of biofeedback, often in combination, are appropriate (see Table 13.4).

What Is Relaxation?

What is relaxation? This is a question rarely considered in stress management texts. Nearly everyone assumes they know the answer; relaxation is reduced tension, the opposite of stress arousal. However, something of a controversy over the definition now rages, with profound implications for how relaxation is studied and taught.

For decades, a single model dominated the study of relaxation (Smith, 1990). Benson (1975) most clearly stated this model as the *relaxation response,* a hypothalamically mediated wholesale response of lowered physiological arousal. The very organ systems energized and activated under stress come to rest in relaxation. Furthermore, this response is nonspecific and automatic; by simply practicing a relaxation technique, one triggers a wholesale reduction in physiological activity.

The most important impact of the relaxation response model centers on its argument that all forms of relaxation have the same effect: reduced arousal. Therefore there is little need to teach more than one technique, and the technique chosen is more or less arbitrary. This is in fact how relaxation is usually taught in hospitals and clinics.

However, this model has serious problems. Most people learn to reduce their physiological arousal in about a month or so, yet seasoned practitioners of some forms of relaxation, for example, imagery, yoga, and meditation, claim to still be learning even after years of practice. But how can this be, when some claim that relaxation is mastered so quickly? In addition, most major schools of relaxation, ranging from yoga in the East to autogenic training in the West, teach a combination of exercises, often starting with stretching and proceeding to breathing, imagery, and then meditation. If all techniques gave the same effect, why teach more than one? And why teach them in a specific order? Such problems led to the development of an alternative model of relaxation.

The cognitive-behavioral relaxation theory (Smith, 1990) argues that relaxation training has three general goals: (1) *reduced physiological arousal* (the relaxation response); (2) the acquisition of the *cognitive relaxation skills* of focusing, passivity, and receptivity; and (3) the development of *cognitive structures*, or enduring beliefs, values, and commitments conducive to deepened and more generalized relaxation. What is new to this model is the emphasis on skills and structures.

Focusing is the ability to put distraction aside and attend to a restricted stimulus, *passivity* is the ability to let go of needless goal-directed and analytic thought, and *receptivity* is the ability to tolerate and accept relaxation experiences that may be a bit unfamiliar. The importance of these skills can be seen in the following examples:

> One day I was doing my housework. Everything was happening at once—the TV was on, the kids were playing outside, the upstairs neighbors were playing loud music, and so on. I was getting very tense and decided I needed a rest. I went to my quiet den, closed the door, took the phone off the hook, and told myself "For the next few minutes I'm going to ignore all the distractions and attend to one thing—reading my favorite magazine.

> I was getting really tense over my job. Everything seemed like it had to be done at once. I was being pulled in a hundred directions at once, first to answer the phone, then work on a report, then answer a letter. Finally I said to myself, "Look, take it easy. Relax. Do one thing at a time and let everything else be."

> After studying a few hours I like to rest on my couch and close my eyes. I let a pleasant fantasy of some distant tropical island go through my mind. One day, I began to feel like I was floating. This was a new and strange sensation and I almost got up and called the doctor. However, I then decided that these feelings are OK, just a sign that I am relaxing. Now I even pretend that I am floating when I'm relaxing. (Smith, 1990, pp. 11–12)

As the examples above illustrate, the person who thinks "I'm going to ignore all the distractions" has, in a simple way, decided to focus. In the second example, the statement "Do one thing at a time" represents a decision to let go and take a more passive stance toward the world. Finally, the student who realizes that his sensations of floating are "OK, just a sign that I am relaxing" has learned to be more receptive and tolerate experiences that may at first seem uncertain, unfamiliar, or paradoxical. (Smith, 1990, p. 12)

The skills of focusing, passivity, and receptivity are needed at all levels of relaxation. For example, the practitioner of progressive relaxation must focus on muscles being tensed, let go of tension that is created, and accept the pleasurable feelings of relaxation (surprisingly, very tense individuals sometimes have difficulty tolerating the pleasant feelings of relaxation). Breathing relaxation requires that the subject attend to the flow of breath, let go and permit breathing to occur passively on its own, and, again, accept the pleasant feelings of relaxation. And meditation calls for attending to a simple stimulus, letting go of distraction, and accepting whatever changes may occur.

In addition, relaxation training involves the weakening of beliefs, values, and commitments that interfere with relaxation, and the development and strengthening of such structures that are conducive to relaxation. Incompatible beliefs include most of those suggested by Ellis (Ellis & Grieger, 1977) that were discussed in Chapter 4. For example, it is hard to see how someone who believed that a person should be perfect in all things at all times could be relaxed. Such thoughts must be replaced by beliefs more conducive to relaxation, such as "Live one day at a time," "First things first," "God's will be done," and "Keep things in perspective."

One of the most important implications of cognitive-behavioral relaxation theory is that different approaches to relaxation are not the same and are not interchangeable, but have quite different effects. Indeed, most approaches can be ranked on a nine-level hierarchy according to the amount of focusing, passivity, and receptivity involved, and the degree to which effective relaxation structures are fostered (Table 13.5).

Unlike Benson's (1975) relaxation response model, cognitive-behavioral relaxation theory has much to say about which techniques should be taught. For beginners, it is important to start with easy exercises low on the hierarchy. If several exercises are combined (which is usually the case), one should start low on the hierarchy and move up. Most importantly, different approaches to relaxation have different effects and work for different people and problems.

TABLE 13.5 A Hierarchy of Relaxation Techniques

1. Progressive relaxation
2. Yoga stretching
3. Breathing
4. Autogenic "warmth/heaviness" exercises
5. Autogenic suggestions targeted to internal organs (abdomen, heart, etc.)
6. Imagery (simple stimuli)
7. Imagery (unconscious answers)
8. Concentrative meditation (counting breaths, chanting a mantra, etc.)
9. Zen mindfulness meditation (openness to the flow of all stimuli)

Research on Relaxation

Most research on relaxation has been based on the relaxation response model. That is, the effects of one or two techniques might be assessed on the amount of physiological arousal or on a variety of physical symptoms that involve arousal. When so defined, there are few notable differences between relaxation and biofeedback techniques (Lichstein, 1988; Smith, 1990). Most techniques are modestly effective for a wide range of disorders.

Research is just beginning on cognitive-behavioral relaxation training. One study (Alexander & Smith, submitted for publication) asked subjects who use a wide range of relaxation techniques to indicate which of 230 words suggesting relaxation (calm, peaceful, serene, etc.) fit their experiences. Results indicated that most relaxation experiences were described by a few words (see application Box 13.1).

Interestingly, relatively few relaxation experiences seem to be manifestations of lowered physiological arousal. Instead, the largest relaxation category, *strengthened/aware*, seems to reflect feelings of self-efficacy (see Chapter 5) and focused attention. Future studies will have to determine if such a differentiated understanding of relaxation is useful.

APPLICATION BOX 13.1

Exploring Different Approaches to Relaxation

Try each relaxation exercise described in this chapter. Although the instructions given here are not sufficient to make you a master of relaxation, they can give you a taste of the different techniques. Spend about fifteen minutes with each one (no more than one a day).

What did you experience? Here is a list of the words people are most likely to use when describing what they experience when relaxing. Check which words fit each technique you practiced. Did you find that different techniques have different effects? If so, please describe. What were your favorite techniques? Why?

1. Absorbed	29. Free	57. Pleased
2. Accepted	30. Fun	58. Prayerful
3. Accepting	31. Glorious	59. Refreshed
4. Asleep	32. Glowing	60. Relaxed
5. Assured	33. Happy	61. Rested
6. At ease	34. Harmonious	62. Restored
7. Awake	35. Healing	63. Reverent
8. Aware	36. Heavy	64. Selfless
9. Beautiful	37. Hopeful	65. Sensuous
10. Blessed	38. Indifferent	66. Silent
11. Calm	39. Infinite	67. Simple
12. Carefree	40. Inspired	68. Sinking
13. Childlike	41. Joyful	69. Soothed
14. Clear	42. Knowing	70. Speechless
15. Complete	43. Laid back	71. Spiritual
16. Confident	44. Light	72. Spontaneous
17. Contented	45. Limp	73. Strengthened
18. Creative	46. Liquid	74. Thankful
19. Delighted	47. Loose	75. Timeless
20. Detached	48. Loved	76. Tingling
21. Dissolving	49. Loving	77. Trusting
22. Distant	50. Mysterious	78. Unafraid
23. Drowsy	51. Mystical	79. Untroubled
24. Energized	52. Optimistic	80. Warm
25. Fascinated	53. Passive	81. Whole
26. Floating	54. Patient	82. Wonderful
27. Focused	55. Peaceful	
28. Forgetting	56. Playful	

The Relaxation Wordlist © 1991, Jonathan C. Smith.

References

ALEXANDER, L., & SMITH, J. C. (1991). *The factor structure of relaxation experiences.* Manuscript submitted for publication.

BARBER, T. X. (1984). Hypnosis, deep relaxation, and active relaxation: Data, theory, and clinical applications. In R. L. Woolfolk & P. M. Leherer (Eds.), *Principles and practice of stress management* (pp. 142–187). New York: Guilford.

BASMAJIAN, H. V. (1979). *Biofeedback: Principles and practice for clinicians.* Baltimore: Williams and Wilkins.

BENSON, H (1975). *The relaxation response.* New York: Morrow.

ELIADE, M. (1969) *Pantanjali and yoga.* New York: Funk & Wagnalls.

ELLIS, A., & GRIEGER, R. (1977). *Handbook of rational-emotive therapy.* New York: Springer.

ERICKSON, M. H., ROSSI, E. L., & ROSSI, S. I. (1976). *Hypnotic realities.* New York: Irvington.

JACOBSON, E. (1929). *Progressive relaxation.* Chicago: University of Chicago Press.

LICHSTEIN, K. L. (1988). *Clinical relaxation strategies.* New York: Wiley.

LUTHE, W. (Ed.). (1969–1973). *Autogenic therapy* (Vols. 1–6). New York: Grune & Stratton.

REED, S. D., KATKIN, E. S., & GOLDBAND, S. (1986). Biofeedback and behavioral medicine. In F. H. Kanfer & A. P. Goldstein (Eds.), *Helping people change* (pp.381–436). New York: Pergamon.

SCHULTZ, J. H. (1932). *Das autogene training: Konzentratrative selbstent spannung (*12th ed.). Stuttgart: Georg Thieme.

SMITH, J. C. (1986). *Meditation: A sensible guide to a timeless discipline.* Champaign, IL: Research Press.

SMITH, J. C. (1989). *Relaxation dynamics: A cognitive-behavioral approach to relaxation.* Champaign, IL: Research Press.

SMITH, J. C. (1990). *Cognitive-behavioral relaxation training: A new system of strategies for treatment and assessment.* New York: Springer.

SMITH, J. C. (1993). *Creative stress management: The 1-2-3 COPE system.* Englewood Cliffs, N.J.: Prentice-Hall.

WOLBERG, L. R. (1948). *Medical hypnosis* (Vols. 1, 2). New York: Grune & Stratton.

WOLPE, J. (1958). *Reciprocal inhibition therapy.* Stanford, CA: Stanford University Press.

CHAPTER 14

Active Coping: Behavioral Approaches

Stress is a problem waiting to be solved (D'Zurilla, 1986). At times this involves changing behaviors, and at times, changing thoughts. All such approaches can be called *active coping*, or *problem-focused stress management*, for they all have certain features in common.

Basics of Active Coping Approaches

How does a person solve a problem in everyday life? Let us begin by considering the story of a student with a car problem:

> For a month my car has been acting up. Twice a week, it simply wouldn't start, and I would have to take public transportation, something I did not relish. It seemed the car just wouldn't work on colder days. After procrastinating and hoping that things would improve on their own, I finally called the mechanic. She took note that the car wouldn't start on cold days and checked the battery. It was dead and needed to be replaced. It didn't take much time for me to decide to buy the new battery. Not having a reliable car was getting to be a real nuisance; every day without my car was a real punishment for procrastinating. So I took action and that was a big relief. I signed a contract with the garage; for $100 I would get a new battery and a working car. Once it was fixed, I carefully checked how it started every day, especially on the cold days, to see if the garage had done the job.

Notice that in this story, initial data were collected about a concrete and specific problem. The student avoided abstract, vague, and overemotional generalities such as "getting around is always crazy," or "when things don't go right, I'm up in the air." Specifically, the student noted that the car didn't always start. Such record taking is an important part of stress management that establishes the baseline of the problem.

In stress management programs, the process of compiling a baseline record involves keeping daily charts and diaries. In the case of the student, an important piece of information concerned external stimuli that seemed to be associated with the problem: cold mornings when the car wouldn't start. Similarly, most forms of stress management incorporate an assessment of early warning signs and critical moments, stimuli that indicate that a problem is emerging and that it is time to take action. In addition, often controlling environmental stimuli (in the student's case, storing the car in a warm garage) is enough to reduce stress. For example, moving from a noisy room, increasing lighting, changing jobs, and spending more time with friends are all ways of changing a person's interpersonal and environmental world.

Our story of the student also illustrates the importance of *reinforcement*. The general principles are that behavior followed by an aversive stimulus (procrastinating followed by having to take public transportation) tends to cease. Behavior followed by relief from punishment, or *negative reinforcement* (calling a mechanic followed by no longer having to take public transportation), is strengthened. Similarly, behavior followed by rewards, or *positive reinforcement* (calling a mechanic followed by having one's car back), is also strengthened.

The entire process of actively coping is formalized through a *contract* that is *monitored* for success. In our example, the contract was a simple business transaction. Monitoring involved examining the car's starting performance against the baseline to see if it had been fixed. In most forms of stress management, a contract clearly identifies what is to be done, when it is to be done, the specific rewards for accomplishing the targeted goal (and the punishments for not accomplishing it), how the behavior change will be monitored, and when the reward (or punishment) will be given. In a sense, a stress management contract summarizes all major features of a stress problem. This can be seen in the following example of a student who is having difficulty studying on Monday night:

> I have an important class on Tuesday and should study on Monday night. But I have a problem. If I had put an *X* on my calendar for every Monday night I actually studied, I would have only one *X* this month [*monitoring*]. I hereby contract to study from eight to ten on Monday night, starting this week [*specified behavior and time*]. If I do this, I will reward myself by going out for ice cream later that night; if I do not do this, I will punish myself by not watching my favorite Monday evening TV show. If I study four Monday nights in a row, I will go out for a movie. I will record my progress by putting an *X* on my calendar for each Monday night I study, plus an indication of how many minutes I study.

In addition to the process described, stress management involves many other factors, such as the general characteristics of a therapist as well as techniques by which a therapist may present skills (instruction, modeling, etc.). We shall address four major approaches to active coping—*problem-solving, assertiveness training, negotiation training*, and *time management*—that focus primarily on changing behaviors and that involve a set of specific coping skills.

Problem-Solving

Problem-solving is both a general characteristic of all active approaches to stress management and a specific approach on its own. In this technique, a problem is defined as a situation in which "no effective response alternative is immediately available" (D'Zurilla & Goldfried, 1971, p. 108). Problem-solving makes available a variety of potentially effective response alternatives and increases the probability of selecting the most effective response.

Steps in Problem-Solving

Problem-solving stress management is based on social problem-solving theory (D'Zurilla, 1986), which involves five general stages:

1. *Problem orientation.* A person develops a constructive "set," or problem-solving frame of mind. Such a set involves learning how to identify problems, view them as concrete and specific challenges, respond with positive emotions (such as hope and eagerness), and actively approach a problem and handle it with dispatch.
2. *Problem definition and formulation.* Avoiding vague, imprecise definitions of the problem, a person gathers relevant data and facts, breaks down the problem into realistic and solvable units, and identifies realistic goals.
3. *Generation of alternatives.* In the brainstorming stage, a person initially defers judgment and tries to think of numerous possible solutions. An attempt is made to generate strategies, or general directions that might be taken, and then tactics to implement the strategies. The tactics are evaluated in terms of their appropriateness to the strategies.
4. *Decision-making.* A person estimates the potential costs and benefits, both long-term and short-term, for various likely solutions and then chooses among them.
5. *Solution implementation and verification.* One puts the selected solution into action and observes and evaluates the results. If it is not successful, a person returns to problem definition and formulation.

Scientific Support for Problem-Solving

The D'Zurilla problem-solving system of stress management has invited a number of criticisms. Kanfer and Busemeyer (1982) have commented that the complete model is most useful when only one decision has to be made. Examples of such static decision-making situations include whether to go to college, marry a particular individual, obtain a loan, and go through surgery. However, many stressful situations are dynamic, and have goals and alternatives that change and evolve over time. Evaluation takes place not only when a solution is attempted but at every stage of the problem-solving process. This interactive quality of problem solving can be seen in the following example of searching for a job:

My goal is to find a job. My first alternative solution was to call relatives for job leads. I called Uncle Joe and Aunt Bea. They argued strongly that I would have a hard time finding a job since I did not finish high school. After careful consideration, I decided that my first priority should be to get my high school diploma by taking the equivalency exam. I generated a number of solutions on how to prepare for this exam, and decided the best was to enroll in a special preparatory course. However, to pay for the course, I had to earn some money. Once again, I generated alternatives, and decided upon taking a part-time job as a phone operator. I kept this job until I got my diploma. However, the experience of school taught me something I hadn't known: I have no problem getting good grades. Perhaps I should go on to college. Once again I generated and evaluated alternatives. I decided to take another part-time job and go to a local community college.

Notice how in this example the initial goal, finding a job, changed. This is often the case in stress management.

However, if not viewed as a rigid sequence, the problem-solving approach has considerable applicability. A person can flexibly apply just about any stage in stress management, often automatically. It is a technique that can fit with just about any problem-focused or emotion-focused approach to coping. At best, it is a way of fostering an optimistic, "can do" attitude toward stressful situations.

Considerable research has shown the effectiveness of problem-solving approaches for both hospitalized psychiatric patients as well as normal individuals. Researchers have found that the process has led to improvements in alcoholic behavior, cigarette smoking, depression, academic underachievement, vocational indecision, marital and family conflict, obesity, blood pressure, aggression, community group problem-solving effectiveness, and a wide range of other stress-related problems (D'Zurilla, 1986).

Negotiation Training

Negotiation is a problem-solving skill that has shown considerable promise in interpersonal conflict situations (Goldstein & Keller, 1987). Although a variety of approaches are available, Goldstein and Keller's negotiation training includes many ideas frequently suggested. In their model, the parties in a conflict choose goals that they consider to be fair, and then select a calm and neutral time and place where face-to-face talks can proceed.

Steps in Negotiation

The five steps Goldstein and Keller (1987) suggest can be outlined as follows:

1. *Each party states their position.* Each party makes an opening statement that is reasonable and moderate.
2. *Each party states their understanding of the other's position.* Listen to what the other person is saying. Perhaps try to "get into the other person's shoes" before communicating what you understand that party's position to be.

People from quite different perspectives can often negotiate a resolution to
conflict.   *(Photo by Joel Gordon.)*

3. *Each party makes sure they agree with the other's understanding of their position.* In
   other words, check out the accuracy of one another's understanding. Before suggesting a compromise, it is essential to know what the other person is proposing.
4. *Listen openly to the response.* Being a good listener means not judging, interrupting,
   or tuning out what the other person is saying.
5. *Propose a compromise.* When both parties feel they have clearly stated their position and understands each other, it is time to work for a compromise. Com-
   promises, like contracts, should be direct, specific, explained, and indicative of
   true priorities.

   Finally, as with problem-solving, negotiation training may be most useful not in
offering the specific steps shown but in fostering a practical, give-and-take attitude of
mutual concern and respect.

Assertiveness Training

Assertiveness training is perhaps the most popular interpersonal approach to stress
management. Most people define *assertiveness* as the honest and straightforward
expression of thoughts and feelings in a socially appropriate manner that considers
the feelings and welfare of others (Masters, Burish, Hollon, & Rimm, 1987).
Assertiveness is typically differentiated from aggressiveness and passivity. In most
general terms, aggression involves expressing or acting on one's desires without sufficient concern for others, whereas passivity involves simply not expressing one's
wants and feelings, even when appropriate.

Assertiveness trainers often differentiate assertive goals, roles, and nonverbal behavior. As mentioned, the assertive goal is to express oneself. This can involve sharing feelings and attempting to solve a problem, but often it is not possible to achieve both. For example, a person may assertively object to the failure to receive a raise and still not get the raise. In considering the assertive option, it is important to recognize when sharing feelings, or "getting them off your chest," is acceptable as a goal.

In contrast, the nonassertive goal is to keep feelings withdrawn and "not make waves." The aim is to protect oneself, win the approval of others, avoid conflict, and so on. Assertive and aggressive goals are often confused. Both involve expressing oneself. However, the aggressive person does so at the expense of others, by hurting or putting people down.

A more general way of looking at assertiveness is in terms of the role a person plays. The assertive role is that of a mature adult, an equal, a peer. One relates to others in a calm, responsible fashion. The nonassertive role is something of a child or an inferior. Others are placed in a superior, dominating position. And the aggressive role is that of someone who is superior or dominating.

Finally, assertive behavior goes beyond what a person says to others to include an immense world of nonverbal behavior. Assertive nonverbal behavior includes appropriately looking the other person in the eye (rather than looking aside or hostilely staring), facing the other person at an appropriate distance (rather than turning aside, or standing too close or far away), assuming an assertive posture (sitting or standing up straight, rather than slumping or bowing over), using gestures and facial expressions that are consistent with the point one is making (such as not smiling while making an angry point), and speaking with an appropriate tone, inflection, and volume (such as not yelling when making a minor point, or not mumbling when expressing anger).

Types of Assertiveness Problems

Interpersonal stressful situations are problems to be solved. One of the first steps of effective problem-solving is to define the problem concretely and specifically. Statements like, "I wish I could say what's on my mind," or "Too many people take advantage of me," are vague and not particularly useful. It is better to take a *situational* approach and identify when, where, and with whom a person is not assertive. Christoff and Kelly (1985) have distinguished three types of such behavior: (1) refusal assertiveness (saying no to requests, not acquiescing to the pressure of others, standing up for one's rights when challenged); (2) commendatory assertiveness (expressing positive feelings); and (3) request assertiveness (making requests from others). One may well be assertive in one situation and not in another.

The DESC Script

Bower and Bower (1976) have developed a very useful system for managing many stressful situations. They call it the *DESC script*, which stands for *describe, express, specify, consequences*:

- *Describe* the other person's behavior that is a concern for you.
- *Express* what you feel and think about this behavior.
- *Specify* explicitly what changes you would like in this behavior.
- Spell out the *consequences* to both of you if your concern is or is not resolved.

The usefulness of the DESC script can be seen by looking at the following problem situation:

> Matt and David work together in a local paint shop. Over the last few weeks, Matt has taken several days off to visit his sister. David has had to do Matt's work to ensure that customers would not leave dissatisfied. During lunch one day, Matt turns to his partner and unexpectedly asks, "Dave, would you mind taking over for the rest of the day? I have to go." David has had enough. He feels that Matt has taken advantage of him and isn't doing his share of the work. He responds, "Matt, you just aren't carrying your weight around here. I've just about had it. I would really appreciate it if you would be a bit more responsible."

If you look carefully at what Matt said, you can see they do not follow good problem-defining rules. The problem, as well as David's emotional response and request, is vague and imprecise. Here is Dave's answer to Matt rewritten to be more effective:

> Matt, last Tuesday, Thursday, and Friday you did not show up for work. I had to complete your painting contracts for you. And now you are asking me to do this again. This is beginning to irritate me. I feel it is unfair that you ask favors for nothing in return. Please, the next time you can't do your work, please give me at least a week's notice, and make arrangements to do some of my work in exchange. If we can work this out, I'll feel more comfortable working with you and helping you out.

Notice how this response is specific and concrete. It gets to the point, and is not distracted by needless emotionality or pointless personal attacks. It focuses specifically on the problem behavior and makes a specific request.

Assertive Rights

Most books on assertiveness emphasize the importance of assertive rights. An assertive right is a course of action a person may reasonably and realistically follow. Jakubowski and Lange (1978) have identified eleven such rights:

1. The right to act in ways that promote your dignity and self-respect as long as others' rights are not violated in the process.
2. The right to be treated with respect.
3. The right to say no and not feel guilty.
4. The right to experience and express your feelings.
5. The right to take time to slow down and think.
6. The right to change your mind.
7. The right to ask for what you want.
8. The right to do less than you are humanly capable of doing.

In this argument between two boys, we can clearly see who is passive and who is aggressive.   *(Photo by Patsy Davidson,* The Image Works.*)*

9. The right to ask for information.
10. The right to make mistakes.
11. The right to feel good about yourself. (pp. 80–81)

These rights might seem perfectly obvious. However, when people hesitate expressing their thoughts, feelings, and wants, it is often because they feel they do not have the right to be assertive. They may think:

- "I can't say no when a friend asks to borrow my car. She would think I'm selfish."
- "I can't let my wife know how depressed I am. She just wouldn't understand."
- "They want me to tell them right away what I think of their plan. I can't tell them that I want time to think. They'll think I'm indecisive."
- "I can't change my mind after I told them what I think."
- "I can't let myself make a mistake on this project. I would feel just terrible."

Each assertive right is actually a response to an irrational belief or expectation. To believe that a person should never promote self-respect, say no, express his feelings, take time to think, change his mind, and so on is simply unreasonable. One of the first steps in learning to be more assertive is identifying and challenging such irrational denials of "perfect rights," and affirming which rights a person can reasonably claim. It is thinking:

- "I can't say no . . . now, wait a minute. I have my needs and rights. I don't *have* to go along with what others want, just as they don't *have* to go along with what I want."
- "I can't let my wife know how depressed I am . . . now, wait a minute. I'm only human. Everyone has feelings, both good and bad. After all, she's my wife. She deserves to know how I feel."

- "I can't tell them that I want time to think . . . hey, I have the right to take my time."
- "I can't let myself make a mistake . . . but no one's perfect."
- "I can't change my mind . . . hey, no one's perfect. I have good reasons for changing my opinion, and I want to be honest."

Scientific Support for Assertiveness Training

Assertiveness training has become something of a stress management fad. This is particularly apparent in popularized presentations of assertive rights. I remember a talk I had with a good friend, who is a librarian. He was joking about all the books on assertiveness. The one point that seemed to stick in his mind was that "these books seem to say I have the right to say or do anything. It's almost as if my reaction to any problem or frustration should be a firm declaration, 'I have the right to. . . .' " Therapists (Masters et al., 1987) often caution that affirming a person's rights is not the same as assuming a self-righteous attitude. Others have rights too. The assertive response is often one of honest negotiation and compromise among people with equally legitimate concerns. In addition, if a person embraces her own wishes with a sense of self-righteousness, the failure to achieve those wishes can be even more disheartening and self-defeating. Finally, by overemphasizing assertive rights, one might forget that assertiveness is, as stated in the title of one popular book, an *option* (Jakubowski & Lange, 1978). There is a time and place for both aggressiveness and nonassertiveness.

Studies on adults and children have looked primarily at changes in nonassertive and aggressive behavior and beliefs. However, as people become more assertive, other problems often diminish. Researchers have looked at the positive effects of assertiveness on anxiety, hypertension, Type A behavior, the ability of the physically disabled to accept their disabilities, and athletic performance (Masters et al., 1987).

Researchers have also made an attempt to identify which features of assertiveness training are most important. First, they found that training in groups is often as effective as one-on-one training. This is an important finding, since group training can be considerably less expensive than individual training. In addition, researchers have examined the effects of two types of assertiveness: overt and covert. Overt practice involves rehearsing assertive skills in actual life, while covert practice involves a person imagining he is rehearsing his skills. Both appear to improve assertiveness, although the superiority of one over another is still being debated (Masters et al., 1987).

Time Management

For clients suffering from overload (see Chapter 11), time management can be an appropriate approach to stress management. Most time management strategies have been developed in business, and begin by identifying and ranking priorities. The client is asked to review life tasks, roles, and responsibilities. Lakein (1973) suggests grouping activities into three categories: *A* (high priority), *B* (moderate priority), and *C* (low priority). High priority activities should be addressed before those of lower priority.

Another feature of many time management programs is developing specific tactics for efficiently completing high priority tasks, and limiting distraction and procrastination. Taylor (1981) has identified fifty-six "time wasters" that can be addressed by such strategies, including poor control of meetings, telephone interruptions, and so on. Time management experts also focus on specific tactics for coping with specific stressful situations, including the following:

1. Assertively saying no to those who introduce unnecessary, time-wasting demands.
2. Setting limits on how long one will be involved with people or activities that interrupt scheduled tasks.
3. Planning for situations that may interrupt a task.
4. Delegating authority for completing parts of a task to others.
5. Seeing a task through from beginning to end, rather than "nibbling away" at it in piecemeal fashion.
6. Building "safety zones" into schedules, periods of time that can be devoted to priority activities that take longer than expected.
7. Pacing oneself, and alternating between strenuous and relaxing activities.

Scientific Support for Time Management

Of the many approaches to stress management now available, time management has received the least research attention. Perhaps this is due to the common-sense nature of many of its procedures. In addition, time management often includes other, well validated approaches to stress management (such as cognitive restructuring), and is a part of larger, validated programs (such as job stress management).

Although not yet demonstrated in the research, there may be a risk to some time management. It is important to remember that the goal is not to become a well-organized robot or the classic "Type A" individual. At its best, time management reminds us to take stock of what we are doing with the days of our lives, and to organize the tasks of living in a way that fits our real beliefs, values, and commitments.

When Active Coping Fails

Active coping techniques, like relaxation techniques, are rarely used by themselves in stress clinics. Although for minor stress problems, it is often enough simply to plan carefully, be assertive, or manage one's time, many stress problems call for more complex solutions. To these we shall turn in our next and final chapter.

APPLICATION BOX 14.1

Assertive Coping and You

Select a stressful situation that involves other people. Can you identify examples of aggressive, assertive, and passive behavior? What are the costs and advantages of each?

References

BOWER, S. A., & BOWER, G. H. (1976). *Asserting yourself*. Menlo Park, CA: Addison-Wesley.

CHRISTOFF, K. A., & KELLY, J. A. (1985). A behavioral approach to social skills training. In L. L'Abate & M. A. Milan (Eds.), *Handbook of social skills training and research* (pp. 361–387). New York: Wiley.

D'ZURILLA, T. J. (1986). *Problem-solving therapy: A social competence approach to clinical intervention*. New York: Springer.

D'ZURILLA, T. J., & GOLDFRIED, M. R. (1971). Problem solving and behavior modification. *Journal of Abnormal Psychology, 78*, 107–126.

GOLDSTEIN, A. P., & KELLER, H. (1987). *Aggressive behavior: Assessment and intervention*. New York: Pergamon Press.

JAKUBOWSKI, P., & LANGE, A. J. (1978). *The assertive option*. Champaign, IL: Research Press.

KANFER, J. H., & BUSEMEYER, J. R. (1982). The use of problem solving and decision making in behavior therapy. *Clinical Psychology Review, 2*, 239–266.

LAKEIN, A. (1973). *How to get control of your time and your life*. New York: Signet.

MASTERS, J. C., BURISH, T. G., HOLLON, S. D., & RIMM, D. C. (1987). *Behavior therapy*. New York: Harcourt, Brace, Jovanovich.

TAYLOR, H. L. (1981). *Making time work for you*. Don Mills, Ontario: General.

CHAPTER 15

Active Coping: Cognitive and Combination Approaches

Throughout this book we have frequently encountered the notion that thoughts influence emotions and behavior. Indeed, cognitive appraisal is central to the transactional perspective on stress and coping. In this chapter we shall return to cognitions, and examine cognitive and combination approaches to stress management that often incorporate cognitive coping strategies.

Cognitive Approaches

Rational Restructuring

Ellis's (1962) rational emotive therapy (RET) was one of the first cognitive approaches to stress management. As we saw in Chapter 4, Ellis's *ABC* model of stress specifies activating events (*A*), intervening beliefs (*B*) about these events, and negative consequences (*C*) resulting from irrational beliefs.

Rational emotive therapy is a very active and directive form of treatment. Its goals are to identify the irrational beliefs that underlie a client's problems, help the client dispute and change these beliefs, and train the client to generalize belief-disputing skills outside of treatment. In most general terms, the client is encouraged to develop a philosophy of life that is more rational, realistic, and fulfilling.

TECHNIQUES.   Generally, the procedures of RET involve direct instruction, persuasion, and logical analysis and challenge. Specific techniques can involve first questioning the empirical support for particular beliefs. For example, a therapist might help a client question the assumption "I must do extremely well and win approval," by asking, "Let's look at this rationally. Can you think of any situations where you might not win approval, and yet rate as an OK person?"

At times there may well be some evidence for a client's negative appraisal. A client may well feel frustrated or disappointed when things do not go a certain way. Here, the goal is not to dispute disappointment but to "decatastrophize" it. One strategy for doing this is to explore the worst case scenario, and to assess

254

AIDS counseling is one form of crisis intervention often done at urban community centers.   *(Photo by Rhoda Sidney,* The Image Works.*)*

how catastrophic it would really be. At times this can be accomplished through homework assignments in which a client actually confronts a situation felt to be stressful.

SCIENTIFIC SUPPORT.   Rational approaches may work well for test anxiety and social anxiety, and possibly assertiveness problems (although no more than the behavioral approaches considered in Chapter 14). Research shows that RET offers promising results for depression and social phobia, but is an inferior technique for agoraphobia (Haaga & Davison, 1991). Finally, there is little research identifying which techniques of RET work, for example, disputing irrational beliefs, homework assignments, and so forth. Some of this difficulty stems from a confusion as to what actually constitutes RET. Ellis (1980) emphatically distinguishes between "pure," and "preferential," RET and "general" RET. The pure variants strictly adhere to the goal of fostering a rational philosophy of life by learning to dispute irrationality, whereas the general approaches focus more on pragmatically changing symptoms. The empirical approaches we shall consider next are examples of pragmatic general approaches.

Empirical Approaches

Whereas RET emphasizes logically disputing irrational assumptions, *cognitive therapy approaches* to stress management focus more on empirical validation. The client and therapist seek evidence that either supports or disputes maladaptive cognitive structures or schema that underlie a client's problems. Beck's (1976) cognitive therapy (CT) is an empirical approach that was developed for depression but has been expanded for use with many other stress-related problems.

TECHNIQUES.   Most clients are initially unaware of the negative, automatic thoughts that underlie their problem. A variety of techniques are often employed to sensitize clients to these thoughts. Clients may be asked to stop whatever they are doing and state "what is going through your mind right now." Client and therapist may also act out stressful situations through role-playing and then examine the underlying thinking.

Several strategies are often used for probing basic beliefs. Burns (1980) suggests applying the *downward arrow method*. This simply involves identifying a stressful thought, and asking again and again, "What would be upsetting to you about that?" A client might think, "I would be upset if my girlfriend didn't call me tonight." The first answer to the question might be, "That would be upsetting because I want her to call." In response to the next question, "What would be upsetting if your desire to have her call is frustrated?" The answer might be, "I always want to get what I desire." This identifies an underlying belief that is easy to explore.

Once identified, automatic thoughts can then be modified. The therapist does not actively challenge a thought, but asks for the evidence for that belief. In addition, a therapist may ask if there is any other way of looking at or testing for evidence that may appear to support biased, negative assumptions. Clients might also consider if a belief's consequences are as bad as initially feared, or if a belief, even if partly true, is functional. Once again, the emphasis is on designing and testing hypotheses. When considering alternative beliefs, a client need not make a complete change all at once. A belief can be "tried on for size," and the client may simply express a willingness to consider and experiment with it. Finally, CT places considerable emphasis on generating data that can be used to assess stressful beliefs. Personal experiments can involve role-playing stressful situations with a therapist.

SCIENTIFIC SUPPORT.   A good deal of research has supported the value of cognitive therapy for depression. Indeed, it appears that CT has a greater impact on short-term symptom reduction than no therapy, pharmacotherapies, other behavioral treatments, or a heterogeneous set of other psychotherapies (Dobson, 1989). The approach may work better for those scoring high on learned resourcefulness (Rosenbaum, 1980), presumably because they are more comfortable with the self-control rationale of CT. Modifications of CT have been successfully applied to problems other than depression, including panic, anxiety, impulsiveness, phobias, obsessive-compulsive disorders, lack of assertiveness, anger, Type A behavior, marital distress, obesity, stuttering, and eating disorders (Hollon & Beck, 1986).

Repetition Approaches

Meichenbaum's (1977) self-instructional training focuses on negative or maladaptive thoughts or self-statements rather than underlying beliefs and assumptions. The idea is that if more appropriate self-statements are repeated or rehearsed, they can eventually replace the negative thoughts.

TECHNIQUES.   Although self-instructional training can incorporate features of both RET and CT, it emphasizes five steps:

1. The therapist models a task by verbalizing the steps involved in acquiring the task.
2. The client completes the task while the therapist verbalizes the steps.
3. The client repeats the task while saying the steps aloud.
4. The client completes the task again while silently mouthing the steps.
5. The client completes the task while thinking the task through silently.

In addition, each time a client attempts to complete a task, she finishes with self-reinforcement ("good job"), and a self-evaluation of the strengths and errors of performance.

As an illustration, to teach someone to start an automobile, an instructor would first explain the steps, such as placing the key in the ignition, putting the car in neutral, stepping on the accelerator, and turning the key. The student would then complete each step as it is described. Next, the student speaks and finally thinks through each step while completing it.

These same steps can be applied to stress management. For example, to rehearse an assertive encounter, the therapist would explain the sequence of walking up to someone and assertively asking for directions. The client practices doing this while first verbalizing and eventually thinking through the steps.

SCIENTIFIC SUPPORT.   Self-instructional training has been successfully applied to problems with assertiveness, anger, and aggression. It is often combined with stress inoculation training, a combination approach, which we shall consider below, that has attracted considerable research.

Cognitive Approaches and Emotion

In more general terms, some people have criticized cognitive approaches for overemphasizing the control rather than the experience of emotions (Mahoney, 1980). It is indeed true that many people are under stress partly because they ignore their feelings. However, it is an overstatement to say that cognitive approaches are "overcontrolling." Ellis would consider the overcontrol of emotions to be irrational. It is the rare person who does not have some thoughts and beliefs about his feelings. And such cognitions can do much to contribute to stress.

Cognitive therapies are now paying more attention to the role of feeling (Haaga & Davison, 1991). Greenberg and Safran (1989) describe the place of emotions in cognitive therapy: "The goal of therapy is not to get rid of feelings but to help clients become aware of their meaning and to become more responsive to the action tendencies toward which feelings prompt them" (p. 21). They go on to note that what becomes problematical is "blocking or avoidance of potentially adaptive emotions and the information associated with them" (p. 23). This new emphasis moves cognitive therapy closer to a relatively unresearched approach to treatment: focusing.

Focusing

Gendlin's (1978) *focusing* is an approach to therapy and "self-treatment" that rightly belongs among the cognitive-affective approaches to stress management. Focusing theory explores the relationship between emotion and cognition. Some emotions are global summaries of complex emotions and cognitions that have yet to be articulated. A client may begin therapy by saying, "I feel down in the dumps." This feeling, which is quite real to the client, may summarize a variety of underlying hidden thoughts, for example, "I feel rejected," "I don't know what to do with my life," or "I'm lonely." Focusing aids in uncovering hidden thoughts.

TECHNIQUES.   In attempting to focus, the client first "clears a space" by putting aside deliberate and analytic thought, and simply attending to the global feeling of distress he might have at the time. He might, for example, attend to "feeling in the dumps." The client then asks, "What is the gist or crux of this feeling?" and waits for answers to come on their own. Once again, by avoiding deliberate thought and analysis, a variety of associations and images may emerge. For example, he may think about dinner, an upcoming exam, and a television show. However, an association may emerge that seems to express the essence of his feeling. At this point, a subjective shift or movement occurs, and he has a deeper and clearer appreciation of his felt problem. "Feeling in the dumps" may now be experienced as "feeling sad because I have no one important in my life."

There is much more to focusing than can be described here. It is essentially a process of uncovering hidden meanings to an experienced source of distress. It is both affective, in that a person starts by attending to both an initial "felt sense" of distress and how this feeling evolves. It is cognitive in that each uncovered feeling has a meaning; a person then explores these meanings by performing the paradoxical cognitive act of setting aside deliberate thought, and appraising the "goodness of fit" of meanings that arise as associations in focusing.

SCIENTIFIC SUPPORT.   Unfortunately, little research has examined the value of focusing in stress management. Clients who have the ability to focus do better in psychotherapy (and presumably stress management), and this ability apparently can be taught (Gendlin, 1986). As a brief exercise, focusing has been used as a preparation for therapy, creativity enhancement, and dream interpretation. It has also been used to help patients deal with illness. Numerous modifications and applications have been attempted, most without empirical validation.

But focusing skills, perhaps not as a specific exercise but as a general ability to get in touch with cognitions and affect, may play an important part in many active and cognitive approaches to stress management. For example, clients in RET can identify superficial beliefs that, although irrational, in fact are not the actual source of distress. Focusing could help identify the irrational beliefs that are more closely linked to distressing affect. Similarly, clients in assertiveness training can readily identify superficial interpersonal issues; focusing might be useful as a strategy to identify assertiveness skill weaknesses that truly cause problems.

Combination Approaches

Crisis Intervention

Crisis intervention strategies have attracted considerable research and theory. Crisis theory (see Chapter 9) begins by outlining the psychological costs of a catastrophic precipitating event. A person experiences initial disorganization and disequilibrium, vulnerability and reduced defensiveness, and often a breakdown in coping resourcefulness and efficacy (Slaikeu, 1990). However, a crisis is a time-limited state (lasting no more than six months) during which a problem can be successfully worked through or rigid defenses established. Because of the potential for maladaptive readjustment, early intervention is emphasized.

TECHNIQUES. Slaikeu (1990) has identified two levels of crisis intervention: first-order intervention, or psychological first aid, and second-order intervention, or crisis therapy. First-order intervention clearly merits classification as an approach to stress management that begins with an initial focus and ventilation of feelings, and proceeds to directed problem-solving (Chapter 14). Second-order intervention is not so much stress management as psychotherapy. Its goal is to help the client rebuild a life damaged by crisis. Specifically, techniques are used to help a client identify and express feelings in a socially appropriate manner, develop more appropriate cognitive appraisals of a crisis, and master new interpersonal skills.

SCIENTIFIC SUPPORT.   Crisis intervention has been effectively taught to paraprofessionals (nonprofessionals who are taught basic helping skills under the supervision of a qualified health professional). It has been applied by teachers, lawyers, emergency room personnel, police, and clergy as well as health professionals.

Desensitization

Desensitization was formally introduced by Wolpe in 1958. Initially, it was designed as a treatment for phobias, or serious and often incapacitating fears that have no basis in reality. Common phobias include fears of crowds, heights, open places, strangers, taking tests, and going to the doctor. It should be noted that a true phobia is truly irrational; that is, the feared object is not really dangerous and the phobic person actually has the skills to cope but is too anxious to use them.

TECHNIQUES.   The desensitization procedure is fairly simple. First, a client masters an approach to relaxation. Then a phobic stimulus is named, and a hierarchy of increasingly fearful versions is identified. For example, a hierarchy of ten stimuli relating to a fear of driving might include the following:

1. Driving a car through heavy business district traffic in a large city with people honking their horns at you (most anxiety-arousing);
2. driving a car through heavy business district traffic in a large city;
3. driving a car through heavy traffic on an eight-lane freeway;
4. driving a car through moderate traffic on a four-lane freeway;
5. driving a car through a small town;
6. driving a car alone on an empty country road;
7. driving a car on an empty road with a driving instructor sitting next to you;
8. driving down a driveway to a street with a driving instructor sitting next to you;
9. starting a car; and
10. walking up to a car and opening the door (least-anxiety arousing).

Then desensitization begins. A client relaxes and starts imagining the least anxiety-arousing situation on the hierarchy (walking up to a car). He continues imagining this situation until the first signs of anxiety are experienced. At this point, the imagined exposure stops, and the client starts practicing relaxation again. When calm, the imagined exposure begins again. Once a client can imagine the complete situation without feeling anxious, he graduates to the next least anxiety-arousing situation (starting a car) and repeats the imagination-relaxation process. Eventually every situation on the hierarchy is covered.

A number of variations of desensitization have evolved over the years. *In vivo desensitization* (Kipper, 1980) involves confronting hierarchy items in real life rather than in one's imagination (that is, actually walking out and starting a car). In *contact desensitization* (Bandura, 1969) the therapist actually models the behavior (gets into the car) and provides tactile support (holding the client's hand as they approach the car).

With desensitization, anxiety is replaced by relaxation. How does this happen? Because relaxation is consistently paired with fear, stimuli that evoke fear eventually evoke its opposite, relaxation. This is called *counterconditioning*. Second, by gently confronting a fearful stimulus, the client learns that it is not as dangerous as originally seemed. Fear thus decays or *extinguishes*.

Stress Inoculation Training

Stress inoculation training (Meichenbaum, 1985) is very similar to desensitization. However, greater emphasis is placed on modifying cognitions and self-instruction. Like desensitization, stress inoculation training incorporates relaxation and graduated exposure.

TECHNIQUES.   Stress inoculation training proceeds in three general phases: conceptualization, skill acquisition, and application and follow-through. In the *conceptualization phase*, the counselor gets to know the client and helps the client understand her problem in terms of stress management terms. The role of cognitions and emotions in stress is discussed. Finally, both the client and counselor identify specific treatment goals. In the *skill acquisition phase*, specific skills are mastered. These can include assertiveness, relaxation, negotiation, problem-solving, and so on. Particular emphasis is placed on cognitive restructuring and self-instruction. One of Meichenbaum's innovations was to break a stressful situation into four components: (1) preparing for the stressor; (2) confronting and handling the stressor; (3) coping with feelings of being overwhelmed; and (4) evaluating efforts and providing self-rewards. Each phase can call for its own self-instructional skills and self-statements. Here is an example of driving a car as a stressful situation:

1. *Preparing for the stressor.* Walking up to the car.
   PURPOSE:
      Focus on preparing for driving and combat destructive thinking.
   EXAMPLES:
      In a second I will be in the car.
      I can manage this.
      Worrying won't help.
      Feeling tense is normal and will help me stay alert.
      Just keep busy with each step.
2. *Confronting and handling the stressor.* Starting the car.
   PURPOSE:
      To manage anxiety that may emerge.
      To reinterpret anxiety in more positive terms.
   EXAMPLES:
      I know what to do.
      Breathe deeply and start the car.
      Put the key in the ignition and turn.
      It will be over in a few minutes.
3. *Coping with feelings of being overwhelmed.* The car is running, and I am starting to feel anxious. I wonder if I can deal with this. Am I failing?
   PURPOSE:
      To establish backup plans to deal with possible setback.
      To maintain some control even when things go wrong. To keep on going.

EXAMPLES:

Take a deep breath.

Just get back to the task. Start the car. Put the gear in drive. Push the accelerator. One step at a time.

4. *Evaluating coping efforts and providing self-rewards.* The situation is over. I did well.

PURPOSE:

To evaluate what I've done.

To praise myself for trying.

To recognize my strengths and weaknesses.

To recognize even small gains.

EXAMPLES:

Great, it wasn't so bad.

At least I put up with it.

I got upset, but I knew how to manage it.

I handled this fairly well.

I'll know how to do even better next time.

Stress inoculation training actually *inoculates* a client for stress by enabling the person to prepare for possible setback. By learning how to manage a small setback before it occurs, a client is prepared for larger problems that may arise. This is an especially creative feature of stress inoculation training, since it turns possible failure into success.

The third and final step of stress inoculation training is *application and follow-through.* Here, the client rehearses the skills just acquired. She might practice being assertive in certain situations, relaxing, or replacing negative self-statements with coping self-statements. As in desensitization, the client and counselor construct a hierarchy of increasingly stressful situations, which are then rehearsed while the client is taught to relax. Once again, possible setback situations are built into the process so that the client can learn to manage a wide range of problems.

SCIENTIFIC SUPPORT.   Desensitization and stress inoculation training have been the most rigorously researched approaches to stress management, and have been successfully applied to a wide array of problems and situations, including abusive parents; athletic performance; hypertension; medical outpatients; military trainees; pain management; parachuting; phobias; police officer confrontations; preparation for open heart surgery; cardiac catheterization, and dental procedures and surgery; public speaking anxiety; rape victims; scuba divers; teaching frustrations; terrorist attack victims; Type A behavior; and writing block (Masters, Burish, Hollon, & Rimm, 1987; Meichenbaum, 1985).

Although there is little debate as to whether these combination approaches work, debates continue over the most important components. Is relaxation necessary? Must clients undergo a careful graduated exposure, or is an intensive exposure to serious stressors equally effective? Concerning such controversies, it does appear that real-life (or *in vivo*) rehearsal is more effective than mental imagery alone. At the very least, careful and structured exposure to a stressor under the guidance of a health professional appears to be a crucial factor in effectiveness.

We conclude our discussion of stress inoculation training with a slightly different type of program. The approaches we have considered all involve teaching subjects to manage or prevent stress. However, another goal can be to teach subjects to perform under highly stressful situations. Here, it is assumed that even when stress is more or less unavoidable, it is possible for people to learn to work effectively under such conditions. It is easy to think of people for whom this might be appropriate, including air traffic controllers, professional athletes, and debaters. One promising approach, *phased training* (Kienan, Friedland, & Sarig-Naor, 1990), involves three steps. In *task acquisition*, one masters a task under stress-free conditions. In the next step, *stress exposure*, one is simply exposed to a stressful stimulus. Finally, in *practice under stress*, one rehearses the designated task while exposed to various degrees of stress.

Combination Approaches to Life-Style Management

A broader understanding of stress management must eventually consider all behaviors that contribute to and aggravate stress. In Chapter 8 we saw how life-style risk behaviors, including lack of exercise, poor nutrition and overeating, cigarette smoking, alcohol abuse, and substance abuse, can be related to stress. It is far beyond the scope of this book to review all approaches to life-style management; however, we can sample a few approaches that illustrate the application of many of the strategies we have considered.

EXERCISE.   Most experts agree that an exercise program should involve from fifteen to sixty minutes of fairly intense, continuous aerobic exercise three to five times a week. Good activities include jogging, swimming, aerobic dancing, jumping rope, continuous bicycling, vigorous tennis, cross-country skiing, and racket ball. Weight lifting, golf, baseball, and chess are not aerobic exercises. However, most people who start an exercise program either quit or practice too little to benefit (Genest & Genest, 1987).

A number of factors appear to increase the likelihood of maintaining an exercise program (Oldridge, 1984). Observable signs of improvement (in weight, number of exercises done, heart rate, and blood pressure) should be monitored daily. Contracts are useful for specifying exercise times, rewards for practice, and punishments for not practicing. It can also be helpful to identify and eliminate environmental stimuli that might interrupt an exercise routine (such as television and the presence of food). Finally, exercising with others can provide social support for continuing the program.

NUTRITION.   We have seen that good nutrition is important to maintaining health and can moderate stress. Most nutritional advice emphasizes the importance of eating a balanced and varied diet; maintaining ideal body weight; and avoiding fats, processed food, sugar, and salt.

Obesity is the most pervasive eating disorder. Generally, there are five approaches to weight loss (Straw, 1983). *Dieting* involves dietary education and moderation. It is relatively harmless but often ineffective. *Fasting* involves severely restricting food intake over several days. Although this approach can quickly produce dramatic weight losses, it can be dangerous. *Appetite-suppression drugs* can contribute to quick initial weight loss, but they have side effects and cannot be taken for a long period. *Surgical intervention* to by-pass part of the small intestine or reduce the size of the stomach has been used to reduce caloric intake. Results are promising, but the medical risks can be severe.

One of the most promising approaches to modifying weight (Brownell, 1982; Stunkard, 1979) combines *behavior modification* with dieting, exercise, and possibly fasting. Such combination approaches include eliminating environmental stimuli that suggest eating, confining eating to certain times and places, controlling the process of eating (by chewing slowly, etc.), keeping records of diet, rewarding success, countering irrational and self-defeating thoughts that can interfere with a weight loss program, introducing booster sessions to deal with special problems, and involving others in the process for social support.

SMOKING.   Cigarette smoking is the largest preventable cause of death in the United States. However, it is difficult to stop smoking. Treatment approaches include *aversion therapy*, in which smoking is paired with an unpleasant stimulus, such as an electric shock or imagined aversive scene; *stimulus control strategies*, in which environmental stimuli that suggest smoking (such as smoking with friends or leaving cigarettes around the house) are eliminated; *response substitution*, in which smoking is replaced with an incompatible behavior such as sucking candy; *contracts*, in which precise smoking-reduction goals, timetables, and rewards are identified; *fading*, in which cigarette brands are gradually changed to those that contain less and less tar and nicotine; and *pharmacological approaches*, in which nicotine gum is chewed to break the dependency on cigarettes for nicotine. Most programs include follow-up to enhance the long-term cessation of smoking. These include buddy systems and calls from friends to monitor progress. Even admonitions from a physician can be a useful form of follow-up.

Most treatments are initially quite successful but have high dropout rates after six months to a year (Benfari, Ockene, & McIntyre, 1982; Leventhal & Cleary, 1980). Virtually all approaches are about equally effective, although combination approaches appear to have somewhat greater impact. It may well be that those who quit successfully do so after several attempts, each one adding new skills. Eventually, the smoker may acquire sufficient motivation and skill to stop forever (Schachter, 1982). Such attempts are even more successful if used with comprehensive smoking control programs at work. Here peer support, financial incentives, and a sense of healthy competition combine to enhance attempts to quit (Stachnik & Stoffelmayr, 1983).

ALCOHOL ABUSE.   The most effective long-term treatment of alcohol abuse involves multiple strategies. Disulfiram (Antabuse), a drug that makes drinking highly unpleasant, can be used initially to help break a drinking cycle in preparation for treatment. Then a wide range of behavioral approaches can be introduced, including implementing stimulus control (removing temptations to drink), engaging in behaviors incompatible with drinking alcohol (such as drinking coffee), contacting for change, monitoring drinking, and rewarding abstinence. Group therapy can help alcoholics face their problems and their avoidance strategies while learning coping options. Alcoholics Anonymous (AA) is a popular nonprofessional self-help treatment. Its basic philosophy is that alcoholics are "alcoholics for life," even if they never drink again. Taking just one drink is believed to be enough to trigger complete relapse. The AA philosophy has nonsectarian spiritual roots; one of its twelve steps to recovery states that alcoholics must "admit to God, to ourselves, and to another human being the exact nature of our wrongs." However, it is difficult to find empirical evidence of the success of AA since members must maintain anonymity. It is known that many drop out of the program. In addition, some studies show AA to be somewhat less effective than professional approaches (Brandsma, Maultsby, & Welsh, 1980).

SUBSTANCE ABUSE.   Apart from alcohol, the most widely abused drugs in America are *narcotics* (opium, codeine, and heroin), *sedatives* (barbiturates), *stimulants* (cocaine and amphetamines), *anti-anxiety drugs* (meprobamates and minor tranquilizers), and *hallucinogens* (marijuana, LSD, mescaline, and PCP). Addictions are very difficult to treat, but the little research that has been conducted shows that, once again, after detoxification, a combination of behavioral and cognitive approaches may be useful. In addition, for narcotic addiction, drugs such as methadone appear to be a useful part of treatment (Callahan, 1980; Rounsaville, Kosten, Weissman, & Kleber, 1986).

The Coping Philosophy

This brief survey of stress management approaches completes our explorations of stress. However, we are left with certain questions: Why do we attempt to manage stress? Why do we continue to do so in the face of failure and relapse? At one level, to answer such questions has been the goal of this book. Stress is real, but it has preventable and manageable costs. Managing stress can contribute to a healthier and more productive life. But this is only a partial answer. Why be healthy? Why be productive?

Any serious consideration of stress management quickly touches philosophical questions of life, questions about basic beliefs, values, and commitments. Throughout my writings, I have suggested that central to effective stress management is a *coping philosophy* (Smith, 1987, 1989, 1990, 1991, 1992, 1993). Such a philosophy has three elements: *enduring beliefs* about what is real and factual, *enduring values* about what is important, and *enduring commitments* to specific choices of action.

There is no one right and true coping philosophy for everyone. In fact, the varieties are endless. For one person, a coping philosophy may emphasize achieving potential, as illustrated below:

I believe I have untapped abilities that, if unleashed, will lead to my personal fulfill-ment. I value reaching my potential, even if this involves sacrificing short-term comfort for long-term growth.

A coping philosophy can involve caring for and sharing with others:

I believe love and sharing keeps us together. Through love and sharing, I touch what is true in others, and let others encounter the real me. Love for myself and love for others gives me the energy to go on.

Such a philosophy can, of course, be religious. It can also be unconnected with any religion, as illustrated here:

The past is history, and the future is simply a wish. What is really true is the present. My current feelings and thoughts are important. When I am upset, I do something rather than just wait for things to change. When I am relaxed, I fully enjoy the feeling. All of this means living one day at a time, living in the present, and putting aside various wor-ries about the past and future.

Whatever form one's coping philosophy may assume, it does several things (Smith, 1991):

In most general terms, a coping philosophy helps us attend to and confront problems we might be tempted to avoid. It helps us let go of that which cannot be changed. And, most important, it can give us the courage to take risks, to experiment even when the results are uncertain or hard to predict. These are three philosophical dimensions of all coping—confronting, letting go, and risking. (p. 130)

And just why do we do these things? Let me close with another thought (Smith, 1991):

The promise of relaxation, and of coping, is always there, silently waiting to be discov-ered. When tension is calmed, often something of lesser importance is set aside. A source of noise is stilled. And we can see with clearer perspective and act with greater honesty and freedom. By letting go of what is truly expendable, it is easier to find what really matters. (p. 130)

APPLICATION BOX 15.1

Your Coping Philosophy

What is your personal coping philosophy? First describe those coping tech-niques that you have found most useful. Then describe your philosophy of coping and living.

References

BANDURA, A. (1969). *Principles of behavior modification.* New York: Holt, Rinehart & Winston.

BECK, A. T. (1976). *Cognitive therapy and the emotional disorders.* New York: International Universities Press.

BENFARI, R. C., OCKENE, J. K., & McINTYRE, K. M. (1982). Control of cigarette smoking from a psychological perspective. *Annual Review of Public Health, 3,* 101–128.

BRANDSMA, J. M., MAULTSBY, M. C., & WELSH, R. J. (1980). *Outpatient treatment of alcoholism: A review and comparative study.* Baltimore: University Park Press.

BROWNELL, K. D. (1982). Obesity: Understanding and treating a serious, prevalent, and refractory disorder. *Journal of Consulting and Clinical Psychology, 50,* 820–840.

BURNS, D. D. (1980). *Feeling good: The new mood therapy.* New York: William Morrow.

CALLAHAN, E. J. (1980). Alternative strategies in the treatment of narcotic addiction: A review. In W. R. Miller (Ed.), *The addictive behaviors: Treatment of alcoholism, drug abuse, smoking, and obesity* (pp. 143–167). New York: Pergamon.

DOBSON, K. S. (1989). A meta-analysis of the efficacy of cognitive therapy for depression. *Journal of Consulting and Clinical Psychology, 57,* 414–419.

ELLIS, A. (1962). *Reason and emotion in psychotherapy.* New York: Lyle Stuart.

ELLIS, A. (1980). Rational-emotive therapy and cognitive behavior therapy: similarities and differences. *Cognitive Therapy and Research, 4,* 325–340.

ELLIS, A., & BERNARD, M. E. (1985). What is rational-emotive therapy (RET)? In A. Ellis & M. E. Bernard (Eds.), *Clinical applications of rational-emotive therapy* (pp. 1–30). New York: Plenum Press.

GENDLIN, E. T. (1978). *Focusing.* New York: Everest House.

GENDLIN, E. T. (1986). What comes after traditional psychotherapy research? *American Psychologist, 41,* 131–136.

GENEST, M., & GENEST, S. (1987). *Psychology and health.* Champaign, IL: Research Press.

GREENBERG, L. S., & SAFRAN, J. D. (1989). Emotion in psychotherapy. *American Psychologist, 44,* 19–29.

HAAGA, D. A. F., & DAVISON, G. C. (1991). Cognitive change methods. In F. H. Kanfer & A. P. Goldstein (Eds.), *Helping people change* (pp. 248–304). New York: Pergamon.

HOLLON, S., & BECK, A. T. (1986). Research on cognitive therapies. In S. L. Garfield & A. E. Bergin (Eds.), *Handbook of psychotherapy and behavior change* (pp. 443–482). New York: John Wiley & Sons.

KIENAN, G., FRIEDLAND, N., & SARIG-NAOR, V. (1990). Training for task performance under stress: The effectiveness of phased training methods. *Journal of Applied Social Psychology, 20,* 1514–1529.

KIPPER, D. A. (1980). In vivo desensitization of nyctophobia: Two case reports. *Psychotherapy: Theory, Research, and Practice, 17,* 24–29.

LEVENTHAL, H., & CLEARY, P. D. (1980). The smoking problem: A review of the research and theory in behavioral risk modification. *Psychological Bulletin, 88,* 370–405.

MAHONEY, M. J. (1980). *Psychotherapy process: Current issues and future directions* (pp. 157–180). New York: Plenum Press.

MASTERS, J. C., BURISH, T. G., HOLLON, S. D., & RIMM, D. C. (1987). *Behavior therapy.* New York: Harcourt Brace Jovanovich.

MEICHENBAUM, D. (1977). *Cognitive-behavior modification.* New York: Plenum.

MEICHENBAUM, D. (1985). *Stress inoculation training.* New York: Pergamon.

OLDRIDGE, N. B. (1984). Adherence to adult exercise fitness programs. In J. D. Matarazzo, S. M. Weiss, J. A. Herd, N. E. Miller, & S. M. Weiss (Eds.), *Behavioral health: A handbook on health enhancement and disease prevention* (pp. 467–487). New York: Wiley.

ROSENBAUM, M. (1980). A schedule for assessing self-control behaviors: Preliminary findings. *Behavior Therapy, 11*, 109–121.

ROUNSAVILLE, B. J., KOSTEN, T. R., WEISSMAN, M. M., & KLEBER, H. D. (1986). A 2.5 year follow-up of short-term interpersonal psychotherapy in methadone-maintained opiate addicts. *Comprehensive Psychiatry, 27*, 201–210.

SCHACHTER, S. (1982). Recidivism and self-cure of smoking and obesity. *American Psychologist, 37*, 436–444.

SLAIKEU, K. S. (1990). *Crisis intervention.* Boston: Allyn and Bacon.

SMITH, J. C. (1987). *Meditation: A sensible guide to a timeless discipline.* Champaign, IL: Research Press.

SMITH, J. C. (1989). *Relaxation dynamics: A cognitive-behavioral approach to relaxation.* Champaign, IL: Research Press.

SMITH, J. C. (1990). *Cognitive-behavioral relaxation training: A new system of strategies for treatment and assessment.* New York: Springer.

SMITH, J. C. (1991). *Stress scripting: A guide to stress management.* New York: Plenum.

SMITH, J. C. (1992). *Spiritual living for a skeptical age: A psychological approach to meditative practice.* New York: Insight/Plenum.

STACHNIK, T. J., & STOFFELMAYR, B. E. (1983). Worksite smoking cessation programs: A potential for national impact. *American Journal of Public Health, 73*, 1395–1396.

STRAW, M. K. (1983). Coping with obesity. In T. G. Burish & L. A. Bradley (Eds.), *Coping with chronic disease: Research and applications* (pp. 219–258). New York: Academic Press.

WOLPE, J. (1958). *Psychotherapy by reciprocal inhibition.* Palo Alto, CA: Stanford University Press.

Name Index

Subject Index